Health and Elite Sport

Health and Elite Sport is the first book to critically examine the relationship between participation in high performance sport and health outcomes. Drawing on theory and empirical data from a wide range of disciplines, including sociology, developmental psychology, epidemiology and physical education, the book explores the benefits and detriments of participation in elite sport for both individuals (athletes, coaches, spectators) and communities.

Written by a team of leading international sport researchers, the book examines key issues including:

- Talent identification and young athletes
- Abuse in sport
- Positive youth development through sport
- Athlete psychological and mental health in periods of transition
- Health, sport and the family
- Health in professional sport
- The Olympics, Paralympics and public health
- Long-term effects of participation in elite sport
- Injury risk in sport
- Sport's role in aging and longevity

Highlighting the connections and contradictions between high performance sport and health, the book also discusses the clear and important implications for our socio-cultural, political and developmental understanding of sport. *Health and Elite Sport* is fascinating and important reading for all students and researchers with an interest in youth sport, sports development, sport policy, sports coaching, exercise and health, physical education, the sociology of sport or the sociology of health.

Joseph Baker is an Associate Professor and head of the Lifespan Health and Performance Laboratory in the School of Kinesiology and Health Science, at York University, Canada. He has also held visiting researcher/professor positions in the United Kingdom, Australia and Germany. His research considers the varying influences on optimal human development, ranging from issues affecting athlete development and skill acquisition to barriers and facilitators of successful aging. Joe is author/editor of six other books including the forthcoming

Routledge Handbook of Sport Expertise (with Damian Farrow). He has authored more than 150 peer reviewed articles and book chapters.

Parissa Safai is an Associate Professor in the School of Kinesiology and Health Science in the Faculty of Health at York University. Her research interests focus on the critical study of sport at the intersection of risk, health and healthcare. This includes research on sports' 'culture of risk', the development and social organization of sport and exercise medicine, as well as the social determinants of athletes' health. Her work has been published in such journals as the *Sociology of Sport Journal*, the *International Review for the Sociology of Sport*, *Sport History Review* and the *Canadian Bulletin of Medical History/Bulletin canadien d'histoire de la medicine*.

Jessica Fraser-Thomas is an Assistant Professor in the School of Kinesiology and Health Science at York University in Toronto, Canada. Her research focuses on children and youths' development through sport, with a particular interest in positive youth development, psychosocial influences (i.e., coaches, family, peers) and withdrawal. Currently she is working on three key projects exploring children's earliest introductions to organized sport, the characteristics of sport programs that facilitate optimal youth development, and how youth sport models may inform Masters athletes' development; all projects are supported by the Social Sciences and Humanities Research Council of Canada (SSHRC) and Sport Canada's Research Initiative (SCRI).

Routledge Research in Sport, Culture and Society

Health and Elite Sport

Is high performance sport a healthy pursuit?

Edited by
Joseph Baker, Parissa Safai and
Jessica Fraser-Thomas

Routledge
Taylor & Francis Group

LONDON AND NEW YORK

First published 2015
by Routledge
2 Park Square, Milton Park, Abingdon, Oxon OX14 4RN

and by Routledge
711 Third Avenue, New York, NY 10017

Routledge is an imprint of the Taylor & Francis Group, an informa business

British Library Cataloguing-in-Publication Data
A catalogue record for this book is available from the British Library

Library of Congress Cataloging-in-Publication Data
Health and elite sport : is high performance sport a healthy pursuit? /
edited by Joe Baker, Parissa Safai and Jessica Fraser-Thomas.
p. ; cm. — (Routledge research in sport, culture and society ; 38)
Includes bibliographical references and index.
I. Baker, Joe, 1969– editor. II. Safai, Parissa, editor. III. Fraser-Thomas,
Jessica, editor. IV. Series: Routledge research in sport, culture and society ; 38.
[DNLM: 1. Athletes. 2. Health Status. 3. Athletic Performance—physiology.
4. Risk Factors. 5. Sports—physiology. 6. Sports—psychology. QT 260]
RC1235
612'.044—dc23
2014016389

ISBN: 978-0-415-70866-1 (hbk)
ISBN: 978-1-315-88591-9 (ebk)

Typeset in Times New Roman
by FiSH Books Ltd, Enfield

Contents

Figures and tables

Figures

Tables

Acronyms and abbreviations

ACL	anterior cruciate ligament
AMA	American Medical Association
APA	adapted physical activity
BCHLA	British Columbia Healthy Living Alliance
BMI	body mass index
CBC	Canadian Broadcasting Corporation
CCHS	Canadian Community Health Survey
CIHA	Canadian Institute for Health Information
CP-ISRA	Cerebral Palsy – International Sport and Recreation Association
CTE	chronic traumatic encephalopathy
CVD	cardiovascular disease
DMSP	developmental model for sport participation
DPA	daily physical activity
FASD	fetal alcohol spectrum disorder
FIFA	Fédération Internationale de Football Association
FIMS	Fédération Internationale de Médécine du Sport
FMS	fundamental movement skills
GDP	gross domestic product
IBSA	International Blind Sports Federation
ICICS	inner-city inclusivity commitment statement
IIRPP	International Injury Register for Potential Paralympians
IOC	International Olympic Committee
IOSD	International Organisation for Sport for the Disabled
ISF	International Skiing Federation
ISMWSF	International Stoke Mandeville Wheelchair Sports Federation
ISOD	International Sports Organisation for the Disabled
IYSPE	international year of sport and physical education
LDI	life development intervention
LOCOG	London Organizing Committee of the Olympic and Paralympic Games
MLB	Major League Baseball
MRI	magnetic resonance imaging
NCCSIR	National Center for Catastrophic Sports Injury Research

NFL	National Football League
NHS	National Health Service
NOC	National Olympic Committee
OA	osteoarthritis
PYD	positive youth development
RIO	high school reporting information online
SDT	self-determination theory
SER-Q	sport emotional response questionnaire
SES	social economic status
TID	talent identification and development
TIDS	talent identification and development systems
TOYA	training of young athletes
USOC	United States Olympic Committee

Foreword

The struggle to make sports safe and health enhancing is both personal and political, involving not only the participant's private choices but the social construction of the conditions, rules and expectations of training and competition. The penny began to drop for me years ago when, as a long-distance runner coming off still another injury, a close friend who happened to be an orthopaedic surgeon suggested that I give up my ambition to make another Olympic team and concentrate instead on running for health. "If you step up your mileage in the way you want, you'll continue to experience injuries and in a few years you won't be able to run at all," he advised. "But if you scale down to five miles a day, you'll be in great health for the rest of your life." At the time, the idea was incomprehensible to me and everyone else I knew in Canadian sport and I rejected it. But as the injuries took their toll and it did become too painful to run, I've revisited that conversation over and over again. I still believe that we should continue to strive to push the boundaries and that exceptional performance is possible without crippling injury, but now I wonder about whether there's another way.

The struggle for humane high performance sport has a long and complicated history, and has touched upon every sport we play, not only the combat and collision sports like boxing, hockey and football where other forms of injury have long provoked debate. Today, it is as urgent and important a necessity as the other great struggle to realize the liberal, humanitarian rhetoric of modern sports – the campaign for full equity and inclusion. Fortunately, three scholars who have struggled with these issues both as athletes and investigators – Joe Baker, Jessica Fraser-Thomas and Parissa Safai – have assembled a multi-disciplinary team of experts to examine and illuminate it. The result is a wide-ranging discussion of the benefits and inherent risks of high performance sport, along with many insightful suggestions and policy recommendations for improved practice and policy reform. It's an invaluable contribution.

Bruce Kidd

Bruce Kidd, OC is Professor of Kinesiology and Physical Education at the University of Toronto. He was twice selected Canada's Male Athlete of the Year and competed in the 1964 Olympics. He was awarded the Order of Canada in 2004 for his tireless contributions to the elimination of discrimination in sport nationally and internationally.

1 Sport and health of the high performance athlete

An introduction to the text

Parissa Safai, Jessica Fraser-Thomas and Joseph Baker

In the lead up to the 2014 Winter Olympic Games in Sochi, Russia, the Canadian Broadcasting Corporation (CBC) – the host television broadcaster for the Games in Canada – began unfurling a whole series of Olympic-related programming including promotional commercials, news coverage, journalistic-style mini-documentaries and a documentary called *Road to the Olympics* geared towards "showcasing a collection of Canada's athletes heading to the Winter Olympic Games in Sochi, Russia" (retrieved from www.cbc.ca/player/Sports/ID/2427918370/). While some of this pre-Olympic coverage examined the social and political issues surrounding the Games, including criticisms of the exorbitant US$50 billion price-tag for the Games and protests of Russia's discriminatory anti-gay laws, much of the content of this pre-Olympic programming was geared towards introducing the public to Olympic athletes preparing for the Sochi Games, with particularly heavy emphasis on past and potential medal winners.

As social scientists who study health and sport, we were struck by the paradox of experiences that made up these Olympians' journeys. We recognized their incredible physical capabilities of fitness, strength and skill, their psychological motivation, determination and focus, coupled with their widespread appeal as models of health, work ethic, sportspersonship and character. But we were also struck by the notable and consistent attention paid to pain and injury as part of each athlete's personal story. Each segment of *Road to the Olympics* highlighted an individual athlete's journey to the Sochi Games, offering viewers numerous examples of the joys of sport – the confidence that arose from being masterful in their discipline, the feelings of connection, belonging and camaraderie that developed from being a member of the Canadian Olympic team, or the pleasures associated with travelling around the world and having new experiences. The program was inspiring as a function of the very inspirational character of each athlete profiled. This should be of little surprise given the empirical evidence supporting high performance athletes' embodiment of strong personal, psychological and social characteristics; research among top-ranking Olympic and international-level athletes highlights their sense of confidence in their capabilities, their unfaltering motivation and their tremendous work ethic, coupled with their strong sense of self-awareness and ability to remain optimistic and effectively use coping skills in the face of adversity (Durand-Bush and Salmela, 2002;

Gould *et al.*, 2002). These athletes have also been found to have an eagerness to learn, be creative and intelligent in the learning process, and show strong values and morals in their approach to elite sport.

However, in the *Road to the Olympics*, each athlete profile also included some mention of that athlete's struggle with sport-related injury and ill health; in fact, the return to international sport after injury became a central narrative for the athletes profiled in the documentary. We, as viewers, were led through how that athlete became injured in sport, how they received medical care (most often surgery), how they engaged in long hours of intensive physical therapy to regain function and mobility, and then how they overcame their doubts or fears of re-injury or lessened ability as they re-entered high-level competition. Dramatic music, somber narration and stark images of the athletes on the surgical table or in the rehab clinic framed this sequence and provided a sense of gravitas for this narrative arc. Everything about the *Road to the Olympics* production made it easy to get swept up into the documentary's celebration of these athletes' perseverance through and recovery from pain and injuries in the pursuit of sporting success for themselves and for their nation at the 2014 Games. Simply put, there was no critical evaluation or discussion of the health and well-being of these athletes, specifically, or the healthfulness of the high performance sport endeavour more broadly; this in spite of our growing understanding of athletes' immersion in sport's "culture of risk" (Nixon, 1992) – a culture that sees the unquestioned acceptance, production and reproduction of health-compromising norms and practices (e.g., pain/injury tolerance) (see also Safai, 2013).

As editors in the last stages of drawing together a collection of essays on the relationship between health and high performance sport, athletes showcased in *Road to the Olympics* did not register as simply entertaining television but, rather, as a visual example of the very question this edited volume is attempting to unpack: is high performance sport a healthy pursuit? On the one hand, we witnessed stories of individuals who were confident, motivated, focused, persistent and resilient in spite of their pain and injuries; their injuries were seen as part of the sport process, which included adversity, that they were required to overcome in order to achieve their goals. On the other hand, we witnessed a complete absence of critical discussion of the tolerance of pain and injury by athletes and other sport participants (e.g., coaches, administrators, etc.) as part-and-parcel of the high performance sport experience; or the long-term consequences of multiple surgeries on knees and hips worn down by training regimes and competition schedules that may be more suitable for robots than for human beings; or the stress (and its toll on health) experienced by athletes and their loved ones (parents, spouses, families, friends) as they dedicate their bodies and minds to the pursuit of medal-winning performances. These stories provided another, very timely, reminder of the routine normalization and romanticizing of the pain and injury involved in the high performance sport process, yet it did so with no critical insight into the complex relationships between elite sport, health and healthcare.

Sport and our commonplace assumptions about health

This lack of critical discussion is not particularly surprising given other health-related messages we routinely hear in connection with such sporting mega-events as the Olympics or the FIFA (Fédération Internationale de Football Association) World Cup. A popular assumption among the public, reinforced by politicians and policy makers alike, is that high performance sport positively and enduringly influences sport and health for all. In fact, countries aspiring to host the Games must now include legacy plans as part of their bid submissions to the International Olympic Committee (IOC) – plans that outline how their hosting of the Games will provide long-term benefits to their community/region/country in such areas as "economic and infrastructural development, new housing, new sports facilities, and a more active and healthy population who would have been inspired to get out of their La-Z-Boys by the performances of top athletes from their country" (Donnelly, 2012). The IOC mandated the inclusion of a legacy plan in bid documents as of 2002 in recognition that the high costs of hosting the Games must be justified through such 'social goods'. During the bid for the 2012 Games, promotional materials for London routinely touted that the Games would boost grassroots sport in the UK and make the nation "fitter and healthier" (Coalter, 2004: 91), and then Prime Minister Tony Blair went so far as to suggest that the 2012 Games would encourage a 10 per cent increase in sports participation across the UK.

This concept, commonly referred to as the 'trickle down effect' – the belief that hosting or winning medals at a major games or mega-event positively trickles down to non-elite athletes and non-athletes and promotes participation and health for all – is grounded in theories of message framing in physical activity promotion that suggest positively framed messages delivered through optimal models of fitness (i.e., Olympic sport) are more effective (Berry and Spence, 2009; Latimer *et al.*, 2008). While the trickle-down rhetoric is exceptionally popular, particularly in the lead-up to and during an Olympic year, research into this theory is relatively absent and empirical support for the theory is tenuous at best. In large systematic reviews of research and databases, Mahtani and colleagues (2013) conclude that there is little evidence to suggest increased participation in sport or health benefits following an Olympic Games. They note that such claims cannot be made or upheld without thorough evidence-based evaluation before, during and after such mega-events. McCartney *et al.* (2010) go further to suggest that until such evidence is procured and until long-term evidence-based evaluations are integrated into the design and delivery of major games, the costs of such events cannot be justified in terms of benefits to host communities.

Two major criticisms can be levelled at the trickle-down theory. The first is its lack of attention to the wide variety of social, cultural and structural factors necessary for full and equitable sport participation among participants. Trickle-down rhetoric assumes that all individuals will be in a position to and will want to increase their participation in sport following exposure to a major games (i.e., after being inspired), yet there is considerable evidence of the barriers for some individuals and communities around sport access and opportunity (Donnelly and Coakley, 2004; Donnelly and Harvey, 1996). Donnelly *et al.* (2010) have comprehensively examined the trickle-down effect theory and concluded that, despite the widespread assumption of a trickle-down effect, the effect is often in the form of increased interest (i.e., phone calls, email inquiries) in sport programs, while anecdotal accounts are often stories of already successful athletes being inspired by previous Olympians. In other words, the Games themselves are insufficient to lead to population level behavior change in the area of sport involvement.

The second major criticism rests in the intertwining assumptions that sport participation is a healthy pursuit for all people all the time and that high performance sport is the ideal of healthful sport participation. Both assumptions are problematic. With regards to the latter, we have already noted how elite athletes' endurance of injuries, including long and difficult recoveries from injury, takes centre stage in mediated narratives. A critical assessment of these narratives highlights the reality that individuals who routinely push their bodies to the limit (and, oftentimes, beyond the limit) in training and competition experience tremendous bodily wear-and-tear as they pursue excellence; they are caught in a 'sporting paradox' where they are breaking down their bodies as they move up the competitive sporting ladder (Safai, 2004). In recent years, there has been growing public, research, media and government attention paid to sport-related injury and its prevention that is poking holes at the assumption that sport participation is healthy for all people all the time. In fact, several conditions are now considered 'public health issues' rather than taken-for-granted or inevitable features of sport participation, including (but not limited to): sport's "culture of risk" (Nixon, 1992); injuries arising from bodychecking in youth hockey (Warsh *et al.*, 2009); the increased rates of anterior cruciate ligament knee injuries among female athletes (Sokolove, 2008); and the short- and long-term consequences of concussion and other head injuries (Stern *et al.*, 2011). Compared to previous generations, there is more active discussion and debate (although rarely heard during the bid process for or in the lead-up to an Olympic Games) among athletes, coaches, parents, healthcare professionals, sport governing bodies, researchers (from a wide variety of disciplines) and policy makers about the healthfulness of organized sport.

This should not be surprising given the rates of injury as a result of sports participation documented by researchers in various countries around the world. In Canada, drawing on 2009–2010 Canadian Community Health Survey (CCHS) data, Billette and Janz (2011) highlight that an estimated 4.27 million Canadians aged 12 or older suffered an injury severe enough to limit their usual activities and that 35 per cent of those injuries occurred during participation in some type of sports or exercise. Furthermore, they note that two thirds (66 per cent) of injuries among young people (aged 12 to 19) were related to sports; more than twice as high as working-age adults (29 per cent) and about seven times higher than seniors (9 per cent). A more recent Canadian Institute for Health Information (CIHI) (CIHI, 2012) study suggests that, in 2010–2011, more than 5600 Canadians of all ages were hospitalized (for at least one night) with serious injuries related to winter sports such as skiing, snowboarding, hockey and ice skating. The report highlights that, in the province of Ontario alone (where complete data were available), there were over 45,000 visits to emergency departments as a result of winter activities; an average of 285 emergency department visits a day. These figures do not include visits to a doctor's office or deaths at the scene, and therefore the report's authors emphasize that the total number of injuries is likely much higher (CIHI, 2012). The consequences of such injury rates are significant for the Canadian healthcare system in a variety of ways, including access to and usage of acute and long-term healthcare facilities, services and healthcare providers (including specialists). The economic burden associated with sport-related injury is notable as well; Smartrisk (2009) estimates that direct costs (healthcare costs arising from injury) and indirect costs (costs related to reduced productivity from hospitalization, disability and premature death) associated with sport-related injury in Canada in 2004 was approximately CAN$188 million. Again, this is a conservative estimate given the fact that, as noted above, not all sport-related injuries are treated by clinicians or within the healthcare system and therefore not all sport-related injuries are captured statistically through visits to clinicians or treatment facilities.

Given such significant figures, why then the widespread assumption that all levels of sport are good for health? One answer to this question rests in the commonplace conflation of sport with physical activity, exercise, fitness and play. An example of this is seen with the United Nations' declaration of 2005 as the International Year of Sport and Physical Education (IYSPE):

> Sport and play improve health and well-being, extend life expectancy and reduce the likelihood of several non-communicable diseases including heart disease. Regular physical activity and play are essential for physical, mental, psychological and social development. Good habits start early: the important role of physical education is demonstrated by the fact that children who exercise are more likely to stay physically active as adults. Sport also plays a major positive role in one's emotional health, and allows... valuable social connections, often offering opportunities for play and self-expression.
>
> (UN, 2005: 7)

In the above passage, 'sport', 'physical activity', 'physical education', 'exercise' and 'play' are used almost interchangeably in spite of the fact that these terms refer to different forms of movement. As Safai (2007: 156) writes: "sport is a physical activity; sport is often used in physical education curricula; it incorporates exercise; it may even involve an element of play. However, this does not mean that sport is the same as physical education, exercise or play". While the intent behind the IYSPE is positive, collapsing these terms together conceals critical differences between organized, competitive sport, at one end of the continuum, and spontaneous, free-form play, at the other end. As Waddington (2000: 20) notes:

In short, to suggest that a 30-minute gentle swim three times a week is good for one's health does not mean that running 70 miles a week as a means of preparing for running marathons is good for one's health in an equally simple or unproblematic way.

The enduring 'goodness' of sport

In unpacking the language we use with sport (i.e., in resisting the blending together of sport with exercise, play and physical education), we move towards a more sensitive understanding of, and appreciation for, the positives *and* negatives associated with sport participation. Much of the discussion so far in this introductory chapter has focused on some of the negative features of participation in sport, particularly within elite sport, but we must acknowledge that there is compelling evidence that supports the health benefits of regular, mild to moderate-level participation for all people of all ages (see Alwan, 2011; Lee *et al.*, 2012). The consistent message from international physical activity epidemiology studies is that physical activity and exercise effect human health in a dose-response fashion, with the greatest benefits coming from vigorous forms of involvement that, on the surface, seem to mirror the intensity inherent in the training of high performance athletes (e.g., Samitz *et al.*, 2011; Sattelmair *et al.*, 2011).

Furthermore, there is persuasive data that supports the social, economic and health benefits of sport specifically (as compared to physical activity broadly). Almost 90 per cent of those canvassed in a national survey of households in Canada in 2004 believed that sport had a positive impact on their personal skills, and survey respondents identified a number of benefits through sport participation including health and physical fitness, fun and relaxation, a stronger sense of accomplishment, and greater opportunities to socialize and connect with others (Bloom *et al.*, 2005). Economically, Bloom *et al.* (2005) identify that sport spending in 2004 constituted 1.2 per cent of Canada's gross domestic product (GDP), a significant impact on the national economy. Furthermore, it is important to acknowledge that volunteerism rates are routinely higher in sport than other areas of social life – adding to the importance of sport as a driver for increased social capital (Harvey *et al.*, 2007). In synthesizing data on the socio-economic benefits of sport, Bloom *et al.* (2005) do acknowledge that sport is not a panacea for all social problems nor is it without negative features that take away from its benefits. However, they do stress that sport – when organized and delivered in thoughtful and accessible ways – can be a positive transformative activity for all. Perhaps this can be no better seen than in the role of sport in fostering positive youth development and enhancing quality of life for older individuals.

The value of the sporting experience for developing youth has been highlighted via the burgeoning field of 'positive youth development', which focuses on an 'asset building' approach to youth development (i.e., compared to the traditional 'deficit reduction' approach; see Benson, 1997). From this perspective, extra-curricular activities provide avenues for youth to develop outcomes that have social value (e.g., compassion, integrity, initiative). Fraser-Thomas *et al.* (2005) argue that sport, with its increased opportunity for growth experiences, the necessity of developing emotional regulation, the diversity of peer relationships, etc. has the potential to offer *the optimal environment* for youth development. Emerging evidence from several researchers around the world (e.g., Fraser-Thomas and Côté, 2009; Gould *et al.*, 2007; Jones *et al.*, 2011; Zarrett *et al.*, 2008) has supported this conclusion.

Similar positive outcomes have been highlighted through older adults' participation in Masters sport (see Baker *et al.*, 2010b). Recent work suggests that Masters athletes – those who participate in competitive sport beyond the age of peak performance – have greater maintenance of physical and cognitive functioning compared to their age-matched counterparts from the general population. Moreover, in societies that highlight, both implicitly and explicitly, the disadvantages of growing older, Masters athletes challenge our preconceived notions of what older adults are capable of and provide important role models for the next generation of older adults (Baker *et al.*, 2010b). Baker *et al.* (2010a) argue that the competition inherent in Masters sport participation provides something above and beyond the physical stimulus older athletes get while participating in a physiologically demanding task. Put more simply, they postulate that 'sport is more than just exercise', providing opportunities for greater social engagement, increased challenge as well as regular evaluations (i.e., through competition) of current levels of physical and cognitive functioning.

The positive and negative dimensions of sport participation noted so far reinforce the notion that sport has great potential for good or ill and, importantly, that we have an inadequate understanding of the most appropriate delivery systems, modes and intensities to maximize performance while not compromising the health of individuals, families and communities. The gaps in our understandings of the complex inter-relationships between health and sport are amplified at the highest levels of sport participation – elite or high performance sport – and by the lack of consistent and critical public and scholarly attention. This edited collection attempts to address these deficits in our understanding through a multi-disciplinary examination of the question: is high performance a healthy pursuit?

The relationships between health and elite sport

Despite the large range and volume of scientific research focused on elite sport, a critical and balanced consideration of the relationships between participation in high performance sport and health outcomes has been largely missing, despite the clear social, cultural and developmental implications. Organized into three sections, this edited collection addresses this gap by providing the reader a focused and multi-faceted overview of research that examines the benefits and detriments of participation in elite sport for individuals and communities. Our objective with this text was to provide a 'state of the science' synopsis of the positive and negative health consequences of participation in high performance sport as identified by emerging and established researchers from a range of social scientific disciplines. Each contributor was invited to define health and the sport–health relationship from their disciplinary perspective, which promoted a more nuanced and comprehensive exploration of the connections and contradictions between high performance sport and health.

Section One, *Health and the Developing Elite Athlete*, examines the health of the athlete during their formative years. In the first chapter, authors Jessica Fraser-Thomas and Leisha Strachan explore positive youth development (PYD) in elite youth sport contexts, employing Ecological Systems Theory as a lens through which to understand if and how elite youth sport can serve to develop and foster healthy psychosocial attributes such as character, leadership and initiative among youth. The following two chapters focus on specific systems within which athletes are immersed and which influence, and are influenced by, the developing athletes' health. In Chapter 3, Fieke Rongen, Stephen Cobley, Jim McKenna and Kevin Till, explore the health impact of talent identification and development systems (TIDS) on youth athletes. The authors note that sporting nations have increasingly turned to early talent identification and development strategies to improve podium performance but that these processes lead to an early focus on specialized training in childhood and youth. The chapter reviews, from a social-psychological perspective, the consequences of early talent identification and development approaches specifically as they impact health and development. This is paralleled in Chapter 4 by Edward Cope, Stephen Hardy and David Kirk's examination of another system with profound influence on developing elite athletes: the family. Recognizing that the family unit is the main social, emotional and financial support structure for youth athletes, the authors explore the extent to which this key support structure can provide a healthy environment for young athletes, given the often-conflicting demands of elite youth sport. The final chapter of this section, by Tanis Hastmann-Walch and Dennis Caine, offers a comprehensive review of the epidemiological data on the incidence of injury in and the long-term health consequences of participation in elite youth sport.

The second section of the book, *Elite Sport Participation Over the Lifecourse*, shifts our attention towards issues that impact upon and frame elite sport participation past youthhood. In Chapter 6, Ashley Stirling and Gretchen Kerr delve into the issue of emotional abuse in the coach–athlete relationship, noting that such maltreatment is sadly all too common a feature of 'win-at-all-costs' elite sport cultures. After providing a thorough review of the extant research on athletes' experiences with, and health consequences of, emotional abuse in the coach–athlete relationship, the authors raise provocative questions of whether personal growth may be derived from these experiences. The next chapter in this section (Chapter 7) by Paul Wylleman, Nathalie Rosier and Paul De Knop focuses on transitions throughout elite athletes' careers, including retirement from sport, and how potential transitional challenges may influence athletes' mental health, while offering practical recommendations to facilitate this process. In Chapter 8, Joseph Baker, Nick Wattie and Srdjan Lemez focus their attention on the impact of high performance sport participation on lifespan length and, in so doing, they offer a summary of the limited research done to date on high performance sport's impact on mortality. In Chapter 9, James Gillett, Alison Ross and Amanda Switzer expand upon the complex relationships between elite sport participation and chronological age by exploring two counterposing narratives. The first narrative establishes elite sport as degenerative and as an activity that prompts premature aging, specifically as a result of sport-related injury. The second narrative examined by the authors focuses on sport as regenerative, as an activity that staves off death and that improves quality of life for chronologically older athletes.

The final section of the book, *From Self to Society: Select Topics on the Elite Sport–Health Question*, is comprised of four chapters that examine a range of topics in attempts to expand discussions regarding relationships between health and elite sport. Martin Roderick and Ben Gibbons kick things off with an exploration of mental illness among high performance athletes, squarely situating issues of mental health and illness among high-level athletes as conditioned by and features of intensive, high-pressure sport workplaces. In Chapter 11, P. David Howe questions the healthfulness of Paralympic sport. Drawing on his years of experience as Paralympian, coach as well as researcher, Howe argues that the very ways in which competition is organized within the Paralympic Games foster health-compromising behaviors and practices among athletes. Shifting our attention to the health of communities, in Chapter 12 Amanda De Lisio, Inge Derom and Robert VanWynsberghe investigate the concept of health legacies, an increasingly prevalent feature of sporting mega-events, as noted earlier in this introduction. Using the 2010 Vancouver Winter Olympic/Paralympic Games as a case study, the authors outline the ways in which 'health' becomes a powerful branding tool for communities hosting sporting mega-events and the consequences of such branding on the (re)construction of local identities. The final chapter of the book continues the focus on Olympic sport and offers a synthesis of many of the major themes raised throughout the book. Louise Mansfield and Dominic Malcolm concentrate their attention to, what they term, the sport–health ideological nexus in the context of the Olympic Movement. In so doing, they probe into such areas as the conflation of physical activity and sport, the links between medical science and elite sport, and the tensions between sport at elite and mass/community levels.

We do not see this text as a definitive guide to relationships between high performance sport and health. Rather, we hope it serves as the catalyst to a much-needed discussion exploring the varying ways elite athletes may positively and/or negatively experience high performance sport in relation to their health. In particular, we anticipate this work will initiate a more critical reflection of how the broader support systems of elite athletes, from coaches, administrators, parents and community members, to communities, organizations and sport systems as a whole, may be contributing directly or indirectly to elite athletes' positive and negative health outcomes. We began this chapter by discussing the journeys of Olympians, profiled by CBC's documentary, *Road to the Olympics*, as paradoxical – as courageous, challenging and inspiring, and also as injury laden and (potentially) health compromising. In light of our compilation of essays, the irony of the Canadian Olympic Committee's core value of human development positing, "that the short and long term physical, social, mental and spiritual well-being of all should be enhanced" is not lost on us (Canadian Olympic Committee, 2013). Understanding the risks and benefits of elite sport participation is critical not only for the countless individuals – from youth and adolescent athletes to masters athletes – aspiring to athletic greatness, but for all of us, from sport practitioners, professionals, researchers and policy makers, who play diverse roles in their journeys. We are optimistic that our collection sheds some initial light on underlying processes of health among elite athletes.

References

Alwan, A. (2011) *Global Status Report on Noncommunicable Diseases 2010*, World Health Organization. Online at: http://whqlibdoc.who.int/publications/2011/9789240686458_eng.pdf?ua=1 (accessed 13 February 2014).

Baker, J., Fraser-Thomas, J., Horton, S. and Dionigi, R. (2010) 'Sport participation and positive development in older persons', *European Review of Aging and Physical Activity*, 7: 3–12.

Baker, J., Horton, S. and Weir, P.L. (2010) *The Masters Athlete: Understanding the role of sport and exercise in optimizing aging*, London: Routledge.

Benson, P. L. (1997) *All Kids Are Our Kids: What communities must do to raise caring and responsible children and adolescents*, San Francisco: Jossey-Bass.

Berry, T. and Spence, J.C. (2009) 'Automatic activation of exercise and sedentary stereotypes', *Research Quarterly for Exercise and Sport*, 80: 633–40.

Billette, J.-M. and Janz, T. (2011) 'Injuries in Canada: Insights from the Canadian Community House Survey. Health at a Glance (June 2011), Catalogue no. 82-624-X', Ottawa, ON: Statistics Canada. Online at: www.statcan.gc.ca/pub/82-624-x/2011001/article/11506-eng.htm (accessed 8 February 2014).

Bloom, M., Grant, M. and Watt, D. (2005) *Strengthening Canada: The Socio-economic Benefits of Sport Participation in Canada*, Ottawa: Author.

Canadian Olympic Committee (2013) 'Values'. Online at: http://olympic.ca/canadian-olympic-committee/values/ (accessed 10 March 2014).

CIHI (Canadian Institute for Health Information) (2012) 'More than 5,600 Canadians seriously injured every year from winter activities'. Online at: www.cihi.ca/CIHI-ext-portal/internet/en/document/types+of+care/specialized+services/trauma+and+injuries/release_17jan12?WT.ac=home_banner_20120117_e (accessed 8 February 2014).

Coalter, F. (2004) 'Stuck in the blocks: A sustainable sporting legacy', in A. Vigor, M. Mean and C. Tim (eds) *After the Goldrush: A sustainable Olympics for London*, London: ippr and Demos, 91–108.

Donnelly, P. (2012) 'Turning Canada's Olympic success into increased participation in Sports', *The Toronto Star* (July 23). Online at: www.thestar.com/opinion/editorial opinion/2012/07/23/turning_canadas_olympic_success_into_increased_participation_in_sports.html (accessed 19 February 2014).

Donnelly, P. and Coakley, J. (2004) 'Recreation and youth development: What we know', in B. Kidd and J. Phillips (eds) *From Enforcement and Prevention to Civic Engagement: Research on community safety*, Toronto: Centre of Criminology, University of Toronto, 156–67.

Donnelly, P. and Harvey, J. (1996) *Overcoming Systemic Barriers to Access in Active Living*, Ottawa: Fitness Branch, Health Canada and Active Living Canada.

Donnelly, P., Nakamura, Y., Kidd, B., MacNeill, M., Harvey, J., Houlihan, B., Toohey, K. and Kim, K. (2010) 'Sport participation in Canada: Evaluating measurements and testing determinants of increased participation', Report of findings of SSHRC Standard Research Grant No: 410 2006 2405, Toronto: Centre for Sport Policy Studies.

Durand-Bush, N. and Salmela, J. (2002) 'The development and maintenance of expert athletic performance: Perceptions of world and Olympic champions', *Journal of Applied Sport Psychology*, 14: 154–71.

Fraser-Thomas, J. and Côté, J. (2009) 'Understanding adolescents' positive and negative developmental experiences in sport', *The Sport Psychologist*, 23: 3–23.

Fraser-Thomas, J., Côté, J. and Deakin, J. (2005) 'Youth sport programs: an avenue to foster positive youth development', *Physical Education and Sport Pedagogy*, 10: 19–40.

Gould, D., Dieffenbach, K. and Moffett, A. (2002) 'Psychological characteristics in the development of Olympic champions', *Journal of Applied Sport Psychology*, 14: 172–204.

Gould, D., Collins, K., Lauer, L. and Chung, Y. (2007) 'Coaching life skills through football: A study of award winning high school coaches', *Journal of Applied Sport Psychology*, 19: 16–37.

Harvey, J., Lévesque, M. and Donnelly, P. (2007) 'Sport volunteerism and social capital', *Sociology of Sport Journal*, 24(2): 206–23.

Jones, M.I., Dunn, J.G.H., Holt, N.L., Sullivan, P.J. and Bloom, G.A (2011) 'Exploring the 5C's of positive youth development', *Journal of Sport Behavior*, 34: 250–66.

Latimer, A.E., Rench, T.A., Rivers, S.E., Katulak, N.A., Materese, S.A. and Cadmus, L. (2008) 'Promoting participation in physical activity using framed messages: An application of prospect theory', *British Journal of Health Psychology*, 13: 659–81.

Lee, I.M., Shiroma, E.J., Lobelo, F., Puska, P., Blair, S.N. and Katzmarzyk, P.T. (2012) 'Effectof physical inactivity on major non-communicable diseases worldwide: An analysis of burden of disease and life expectancy', *The Lancet*, 380(9838): 219–29.

Mahtani, K.R., Protheroe, J., Slight, S.P., Demarzo, M.M.P., Blakeman, T., Barton, C.A., Brijnath, B. and Roberts, N. (2013) 'Can the London 2012 Olympics "inspire a generation" to do more physical or sporting activities? An overview of systematic reviews', *British Medical Journal open*, 3(1), doi: 10.1136/bmjopen-2012-002058.

McCartney, G., Thomas, S., Thomson, H., Scott, J., Hamilton, V., Hanlon, R., Morrison, D.S. and Bond, L. (2010) 'The health and socioeconomic impacts of major multi-sport events: Systematic review (1978–2008)', *British Medical Journal*, 340: c2369.

Nixon, H. (1992) 'A social network analysis of influences on athletes to play with pain and injuries', *Journal of Sport and Social Issues*, 16(2): 127–35.

Safai, P. (2004) 'Negotiating with risk: Exploring the role of the sports medicine clinician', in K. Young (ed.) *Sporting Bodies, Damaged Selves: Sociological Studies of Sports Related Injury*, Oxford: Elsevier, 269–86.

Safai, P. (2007) 'Sport and Health', in B. Houlihan (ed.) *Sport and Society: A Student Introduction*, 2nd edn, London: Sage, 155–73.

Safai, P.(2013) 'Sports medicine, the state and the politics of risk', in D.L. Andrews and B. Carrington (eds) *A Companion to Sport*, Malden, MA: Wiley-Blackwell, 112–28.

Samitz, G., Egger, M. and Zwahlen, M. (2011) 'Domains of physical activity and all-cause mortality: Systematic review and dose–response meta-analysis of cohort studies', *International Journal of Epidemiology*, 40: 1382–400.

Sattelmair, J., Pertman, J., Ding, E.L., Kohl, H.W., Haskell, W. and Lee, I.M. (2011) 'Dose response between physical activity and risk of coronary heart disease', *Circulation*, 124: 789–95.

Smartrisk (2009) *The Economic Burden of Injury in Canada*, Toronto, ON: Smartrisk.

Sokolove, M. (2008) *Warrior Girls: Protecting Our Daughters Against the Injury Epidemic in Women's Sports*, New York, NY: Simon and Schuster.

Stern, R.A., Riley, D.O., Daneshvar, D.H., Nowinski, C.J., Cantu, R.C. and McKee, A.C. (2011) 'Long-term consequences of repetitive brain trauma: chronic traumatic encephalopathy', *Physical Medicine and Rehabilitation*, 3(10): S460–S467.

UN (United Nations) (2005) 'International Year of Sport and Physical Education (IYSPE)'. Online at: www.un.org/sport2005/resources/concept.pdf (accessed 12 February 2014).

Waddington, I. (2000) *Sport, Health and Drugs: A Critical Sociological Perspective*, London and New York: E. & F.N. Spon.

Warsh J., Constantin S.A., Howard A.W. and Macpherson A.K. (2009) 'A systematic review of the association between bodychecking and injury in youth ice hockey', *Clinical Journal of Sport Medicine*, 19(2): 134–45.

Zarrett, N., Lerner, R.M., Carrrano, J., Fay, K., Peltz, J.S. and Li, Y. (2008) 'Variations in adolescent engagement in sports and its influence on positive youth development', in N.L. Holt (ed.) *Positive Youth Development through Sport*, New York: Routledge, 9–23.

Section 1

Health and the developing elite athlete

2 Personal development and performance?

Exploring positive youth development in elite sport contexts

Jessica Fraser-Thomas and Leisha Strachan

As the most popular form of structured leisure among children and youth worldwide (Larson and Verma, 1999), it has been suggested youth sport has three main objectives: 1) to provide opportunities for youth to be physically active and healthy, 2) to develop motor skills to serve as a foundation for recreational or performance-based sport participation, and 3) to facilitate youths' psychosocial development, providing opportunities to learn important life skills such as discipline, commitment, and teamwork (Fraser-Thomas and Côté, 2011). However, these objectives may sometimes be in conflict. For example, a program focused primarily on the development of sport skills (e.g., an elite training academy) may come at the cost of children's optimal physical and psychosocial health (e.g., injuries, lack of enjoyment), raising a commonly asked but rarely addressed critical question: Is the development of children and adolescents' optimal physical, psychological, and social development (i.e., the 'whole person') in conflict with the pursuit of victory, talent development, and performance (i.e., the best athlete)?

High-level sport is commonly associated with a performance-oriented climate, focused on winning, social comparison, and public recognition (Duda and Nicholls, 1992). However, in youth contexts, researchers have highlighted that coaches who place too much emphasis on winning may be hindering youths' overall development by failing to advance their personal and social progression (e.g., Gould *et al.*, 2007; Smoll and Smith, 2002). A more mastery-oriented climate focused on effort, self-improvements, and intrinsic motivation has been associated with numerous positive experiences for youth athletes (Duda and Nicholls, 1992), and it has been argued that sport programs should assure all youth have positive experiences to facilitate their optimal developmental outcomes (Fraser-Thomas *et al.*, 2005). While the age-old slogan, "sport builds character" has become ubiquitous with the importance of enrolling young children in sport, high dropout rates (Gould, 1987) suggest many youth do not successfully navigate through the sport system. These apparent dichotomies raise questions regarding the sport environments that facilitate youths' optimal personal and social development, and how these contexts are best facilitated.

This chapter addresses these questions through the lens of positive youth development (PYD). We begin by outlining our definition of health within the framework of the 5Cs of PYD (Lerner *et al.*, 2005). We then focus on

Bronfenbrenner's (1995, 1999) Ecological Systems Theory to structure our discussion of work examining elite athletes' PYD, using the nested levels of microsystem, mesosystem, exosystem, macrosystem, and chronosystems. Finally, we outline areas for future research to advance understanding of PYD in elite youth sport contexts.

Health: 3Cs of positive youth development

In this chapter, we draw upon the World Health Organization's (1948) definition of health – "a state of complete physical, mental and social well-being and not merely the absence of disease or infirmity" – with a particular focus on psychosocial health, and the the the facilitation of individuals' positive attributes, within the broader framework of PYD. With its roots in developmental psychology, the tenants of the field of PYD are that young people are resources to be developed through a strength-based or asset-building approach (Lerner *et al.*, 2005; Roth *et al.*, 1998); this conceptualization of youth is in direct contrast to the traditional deficit-reduction approach, where youth are viewed as problems to be solved (i.e., their problem behaviors such as delinquency or gang involvement need to be eliminated) (Lerner *et al.*, 2005). While there is no singular definition, PYD represents a societal vision for adolescents' optimal development (Holt, 2008), with the overall aim of youths' "engagement in pro-social behaviors and avoidance of health compromising behaviors and future jeopardizing behaviors" (Roth *et al.*, 1998: 426). PYD has gained increasing attention within the current social climate, marked by social media, difficult economic times, and a disappearing job market among young people. As such, academics and practitioners alike have highlighted the importance of challenging youth to take charge of their lives (Larson, 2000) and being responsive to the needs of others (Hellison *et al.*, 2008).

Lerner *et al.*'s (2005) conceptualization of the 5Cs is among the most popular PYD frameworks, proposing five desired outcomes for young people: competence, confidence, connections, character, and caring/compassion. Fraser-Thomas *et al.* (2005) proposed the 5Cs within an applied sport-programing model of PYD, a functional framework for promoting and researching PYD in sport. More recently, it was proposed that, in sport, the 5Cs were best represented as 4Cs, with the collapsing of caring/compassion with character (Côté *et al.*, 2010; Vierimaa *et al.*, 2012). Further, Vierimaa *et al.* (2012) also argued that in sport, competence is conceptualized as achievement, ability, or performance in technical, tactical, and physical skills. Given our primary emphasis in this chapter on psychosocial rather than physical development within the framework of PYD, our focus is primarily on 3Cs: confidence, connection, and character. According to Lerner *et al.* (2005), confidence is represented by youth's internal sense of overall positive self-worth, self-efficacy, and global self-regard. Connection relates to youths' positive relationships with people, institutions, and broader society. Character reflects an individual's respect for societal and cultural rules, and in sport (Vierimaa *et al.*, 2012) has been conceptualized as sportspersonship, moral development, engagement in prosocial behaviors, and avoidance of antisocial behaviors.

Consistent with past researchers (De Knop *et al.*, 1996), we define youth as children and adolescents up to 18 years of age. We were unable to identify a consistent definition of "elite" within the youth sport literature. As such, in addition to examining studies of "elite" youth athletes, we also focus on studies identifying athletes as "high performance", "high investing", "select", "early specializing", and "talented". Given changing social structures and increased interest in emerging adulthood (from ages 18–25 years; Arnett, 2000), coupled with a growing trend toward prolonged careers among elite athletes through to middle and later adulthood (Allemang, 2012), our definitions may be considered somewhat narrow; however, they highlight a need to explore the complexities of optimal psychosocial development in high-level sport beyond childhood and adolescence.

Bronfenbrenner's Ecological Systems Theory

Bronfenbrenner's (1995, 1999) Ecological Systems Theory is among the most widely used and interpreted theories in developmental psychology, providing an appropriate structure to guide our discussion of PYD in elite youth sport. The theory proposes that human development and human behavior are the materialization of person-context interactions (Bronfenbrenner, 1995); from this perspective, the study of an individual separate from his/her environment does not provide a clear picture of human development. Ecological theory is centered on two propositions (Bronfenbrenner, 1999). Proposition 1 stipulates that human development, particularly in its early phases, occurs through processes of complex, reciprocal interactions between an active human organism and persons, objects, and symbols in its immediate environment. These interactions, or "proximal processes" (e.g., play, learning new skills, athletic activities), must occur on a regular basis and over a long period of time. Proposition 2 expands upon the nature of the proximal processes and states that the form, power, content, and direction of the proximal processes affecting development vary systematically as a joint function of: 1) the characteristics of the developing person, 2) the environment in which the processes are happening, 3) the developmental outcomes under consideration, and 4) the changes occurring over the time period in which the processes are taking place.

Further, development through proximal processes may be explained through five nested systems of the Ecological Systems Theory (Bronfenbrenner, 1977, 1999). First, the most inner level, the microsystem, involves engagement by the developing person in a pattern of activities, roles, and interactions. The mesosystem is the second nested level, and involves interrelationships between two or more of the developing person's microsystems (e.g., athlete and coach). The exosystem is the third nested level, involving interrelationships between other microsystems not containing the person but that may have an indirect influence on the developing person (e.g., coach mentoring). The macrosystem is the fourth nested level and includes cultural and social forces that impact human development. Finally, the chronosystem involves changes or consistencies over time to personal characteristics and/or the environment. Previous research has drawn upon the Ecological Systems Theory, examining its propositions in youth sport settings within the context of PYD (Côté *et al.*, 2008; García Bengoechea and Johnson, 2001). In the sections that follow, we discuss health in elite youth sport, as defined within the context of PYD, using the nested systems of the Ecological Systems Theory to structure our discussion.

Chronosystem

We focus first on the chronosystem, as the element of time reflects a key consideration cutting across all other nested systems. One of the defining features of elite youth sport is the amount of time required in the activity in order to reach elite levels. Ericsson, Krampe, and Tesch-Roemer (1993) proposed that an extensive commitment to deliberate practice is required to reach expertise in any domain including sport (see Chapter 3: Talent identification and development). In developmental psychology, time invested has increasingly become a variable of interest in examining PYD outcomes. Time spent in a particular activity each week (i.e., intensity) and stability or duration over time (i.e., continuity) are positively associated with developmental outcomes such as academic achievement, prosocial behavior, civic engagement, initiative, identity formation, emotional regulation, and positive interpersonal and social relationships (Hanson and Larson, 2007; Simpkins *et al.*, 2005; Zaff *et al.*, 2003).

Youth sport researchers have subsequently asked: Does high time investment in a sport lead to more positive developmental outcomes? In a large longitudinal study of 1122 American students tracked from 5th through to 7th grades, Zarrett and colleagues (Zarrett *et al.*, 2008) found that time invested in sport per year and years of involvement were associated with higher PYD scores measured through the 5Cs (competence, confidence, character, connection, and caring), higher contribution scores (i.e., contribution to family and community), as well as decreased depression. Further, Wilkes and Côté (2010) found female youth basketball players involved in programs that required a greater amount of time (i.e., community competitive and intra-scholastic), had more positive developmental experiences in the areas of identity, initiative, and time management, than youth involved in programs that required a lesser time commitment (i.e., community recreational). Similarly, Strachan *et al.* (2009) investigated sport experiences and personal development in a sample of 74 young (aged 12–16) Canadian "specializing" athletes (i.e., who invested a mean of 19 hours per week in one primary sport) and "sampling" athletes (i.e., who invested approximately 14 hours per week in multiple diverse sports). They found specializers experienced more positive developmental experiences in domains relating to positive relationships, adult networks and social capital, and diverse peer relationships. Collectively, these findings align with Larson's (2000) work on initiative; he proposes initiative is critical to youths' healthy development, and structured activities such as sports offer an optimal context for initiative development, as they require concerted engagement, and effort directed towards a goal over time.

Others have suggested more time in sport may offer more opportunities to teach problem-solving competencies and comprehensive knowledge and foster intimate relationships (Petitpas *et al.*, 2005; Strachan *et al.*, 2009), while also demanding a strong work ethic and requiring commitment, discipline, and perseverance (Fraser-Thomas and Côté, 2009).

Despite this, the developmental psychology literature suggests extensive time in any one activity can be associated with increased risk behaviors (Busseri *et al.*, 2006), raising concerns for youth highly engaged in sport. For example, Strachan *et al.* (2009) found that specializers experienced more physical and emotional exhaustion, and less family integration and links to community than samplers. It has been suggested that elite youth athletes may perceive their entire identity and sense of self-worth within their sport, resulting in a unidimensional self-concept (Gould, 1993; Tofler *et al.*, 1996). Athletes may also experience a sense of social isolation, given unique training, living, and travelling demands that often result from heavy time investments in sport (Gould, 1993; Tofler *et al.*, 1996). Rebecca Marino, a Canadian professional tennis player recently spoke publicly about both these issues when she announced her retirement at age 22 due to clinical depression, citing the need to "put the person before the athlete" (Brady, 2013) (see Chapter 10: 'To thine own self be true': Sports work, mental illness and the problem of authenticity). Greater time investment has also been associated with increased stress, particularly as related to juggling sport, academic, and family commitments (Kirk *et al.*, 1997; Wilkes and Côté, 2010). As an Australian junior netball participant highlighted, "I like to get good marks and do the best I can, I just get stressed . . . everything will worry me if I haven't got enough time, I just go 'ohhh, and just get all stressed out'" (Kirk *et al.*, 1997: 61). Thus, while the continuity and intensity of elite youth sport have been associated with healthy outcomes related to confidence, connections, and character, our review also highlights the potential for compromised health in these areas. These contradictions are discussed further throughout the chapter.

Macrosystem and exosystem

Next, we review the nested systems of the macrosystem and exosystem, which do not directly involve the developing child but indirectly influence his or her development. The macrosystem includes the cultural and social structures related to sport (e.g., sport ethics), while the exosystem involves the broader institutional and organizational structures within an elite youth sport context (e.g., sport policy). Many researchers have suggested sport's structure and, in particular, the element of competition is a key contributor to youths' developmental experiences and outcomes associated with sport. Competitive sport contains clear rules, goals, and incentives, offering a forum for personal challenge and requiring youth to take risks in order to develop skills (Larson, 2000). Further, competitive sport offers a context where youth must learn to give and receive feedback, overcome setbacks and obstacles, appropriately respond to wins and losses, and persevere in the face of adversity (e.g., Larson, 2000; Petitpas *et al.*, 2005). These claims align with Hansen *et al.*'s

(2003) findings of higher emotional regulation among youth involved in sport than youth in other activities. Yet little work has investigated youths' development through competition at the elite level. Do healthy learning and growing experiences remain, or are they lost within the "win at all costs" mentality?

Some emerging evidence suggests that elements of the elite competitive environment facilitate youths' learning of life skills. For example, a recent case study of an elite tennis player in the UK found she learned life skills such as work ethic, communication, and self-awareness because the situation (i.e., elite competitive sport) required them (Jones and Lavallee, 2009). Similarly, elite rugby coaches in the UK identified several essential practice behaviors for the development of high-level youth athletes including: professionalism (e.g., arriving prepared, being punctual, being honest, showing respect), commitment and effort (e.g., dedication, work ethic), concentration (e.g., staying focused, following instructions), and information seeking (e.g., seeking feedback, providing feedback, self-evaluating) (Oliver *et al.*, 2010). However, a growing body of work is drawing attention to youths' negative experiences and potential unhealthy development in elite sport contexts. High expectations, feelings of entrapment, fear of failure, and fear of injury have been found to be sources of stress for youth in competitive sport (Scanlan *et al.*, 2005). Further, elite youth athletes report negative experiences, often resulting in isolation, withdrawal, emotional disruption, identity fragility, decreased confidence in one's ability, dropout, and burnout (Fraser-Thomas and Côté, 2009; Gould *et al.*, 1996; Tamminen *et al.*, 2013).

While the competitive stress of sport may initially be interpreted as a negative experience, it has been suggested that athletes who learn to confront their emotions in these challenging situations, engage in reflective practice, and work through this state, in turn develop optimal emotional regulation skills such as focus and problem solving (Connaughton *et al.*, 2010; Fraser-Thomas and Côté, 2009; Scanlan *et al.*, 2005). Past work supports this contention as Anshel and Porter (1996) found that elite competitive swimmers showed more advanced emotional regulation than non-elite swimmers, as they were better able to identify problems and execute performance strategies. Additional studies of international level youth athletes highlight coping and resiliency as critical psychosocial competencies for success, detailing the importance of being able to remain positive following adversity, overcome potential personal and contextual obstacles, use positive coping responses through failure and success, and remain confident and mentally strong in order to manage the demands (e.g., Holt and Dunn, 2004). Most recently, Tamminen *et al.* (2013) examined perceptions of growth in international athletes who had experienced substantive adversity; athletes suggested adversity allowed them to find their strengths, gain perspective, attach meaning to their sport involvement, while also fostering in them a desire to help others. Collectively, these studies suggest that the adversity and conflict of elite competitive sport environments may indirectly facilitate youths' healthy psychosocial development; however, this proposal must be considered carefully in light of past work highlighting concerns for the welfare of elite child athletes, within sport systems with "win at all costs" cultures (Donnelly, 1993).

Mesosystem and microsystem

The most inner level of the Ecological Systems Theory, the microsystem, focuses on the developing athlete's dyadic relationships (e.g., coach–athlete), while the mesosystem links two or more microsystems of the developing athlete (e.g., relationships between the athlete's coach(es), parent(s), sibling(s), and/or broader communities). A commonly considered mesosystem is the 'athletic triangle' representing the coach–parent–athlete triad (Smoll *et al.*, 2011); however, little research has focused on the influence of parent–coach relationships on the developing athlete, highlighting a need for more innovative methodologies in examining the interacting influences of significant others. Rather, the athlete–coach and athlete–parent dyads (i.e., microsystems) have garnered a great deal of attention in youth sport literature.

One of the most consistent findings in the PYD sport literature is that coaches and quality coach–athlete relationships play a critical role in assuring healthy developmental outcomes (Fraser-Thomas *et al.*, 2005; Petitpas *et al.*, 2005). Recent studies suggest this also holds true in elite sport contexts, where coaches have been found to be key delivery agents (Fraser-Thomas and Côté, 2009; Gould *et al.*, 2007; Hassell *et al.*, 2010; Strachan *et al.*, 2011; Woodcock *et al.*, 2011); findings suggest many coaches in elite sport recognize their responsibility in promoting positive learning and growth through teaching and modeling life skills such as goal setting, communication, responsibility, self-awareness, mental toughness and respect. The findings further suggest that this can be achieved through well-developed coaching philosophies based on core values, and well thought out coach strategies to teach life skills.

Despite this, elite sport contexts present a challenge for some coaches whose ultimate objective is performance, irrespective of personal development. Gervis and Dunn (2004) highlight disturbing examples of coaches emotionally abusing elite child athletes in the form of belittling, humiliating, shouting, scapegoating, rejecting, isolating, threatening, and ignoring, with all participants reporting increased abuse as they progressed through the elite sporting ranks (see also Chapter 6: In the name of performance: Threats, belittlement, and degradation). Similarly, Fraser-Thomas and Côté's (2009) study found highly invested adolescent athletes experienced negative coach experiences in the form of favoritism and ignoring, intimidation, and inappropriate behaviors, particularly related to weight loss and body image among young girls. These works are in line with a large body of psychological, sociological, and popular literature highlighting concerns regarding harassment and abuse in elite sport contexts (Donnelly, 1993; Fasting *et al.*, 2004; International Olympic Committee, 2014). As such, more research is needed to better understand the circumstances, processes, and mechanisms of how coaches successfully negotiate conditions for youths' optimal performance, while avoiding compromising youths' health, and also optimizing their personal development. Gould and colleagues' (2007) work with award-winning football coaches is among the first studies offering insight into programs with an integrated approach whereby coaching strategies for winning, personal development of players, and performance enhancement are simultaneously prioritized and can lead to optimal athlete health alongside optimal performance.

The parent–child dyad has also typically been investigated within the microsystem. Parents often have special relationships with their elite child athletes (Fraser-Thomas and Côté, 2009). Recent work by Lauer *et al.* (2010) involving retrospective interviews with world-ranked professional tennis players sheds light on parents' positive behaviors across development; these included modeling and engaging in effective communication with their child (e.g., emotionally intelligent discussions, offering advice, helping make important decisions), and fostering appropriate psychosocial development (e.g., teaching life skills, instilling work ethic and values, stressing appropriate court conduct, modeling emotional control). Parents' roles have also been found to include helping young athletes take criticism, develop honest self-appraisal, foster confidence and self-efficacy, and remain determined under pressure (Woodcock *et al.*, 2011). Despite this, the media regularly profiles examples of inappropriate parental involvement and behaviors in youth sport. Examples of parents' negative behaviors include ineffective communication, overemphasizing winning, breeding dependence (e.g., doing too much for the child, controlling the child) and poorly fostering psychosocial development (e.g., emotional and embarrassing reactions to performance) (Lauer *et al.*, 2010).

Given past work suggesting parents' criticisms, high expectations, and pressures to perform and persist in sport have been associated with both dropout and burnout (Fraser-Thomas and Côté, 2009; Fraser-Thomas *et al.*, 2008, Gould *et al.*, 1996), these findings raise concern surrounding parents' facilitation of elite youth athletes' healthy development. It appears parents need guidance and knowledge regarding how to best facilitate their child's healthy psychosocial development in elite sport; however, researchers are cognizant that parent–child dyads do not exist in a bubble but, rather, must interact harmoniously with other dyads within the mesosystem. Future work should focus not only on parent–athlete dyads but, specifically, on how parents influence the athlete-coach relationship. Smoll and colleagues (2011) suggest specific guidelines should be in place to help navigate relationships within the coach–athlete–parent triad, including acknowledging parents' challenges, clarifying parents' responsibilities, facilitating proper two-way communication, and detailing how to run effective coach–parent meetings; however, more research is necessary to follow-up on the operationalization and effectiveness of these idealistic positive interactions, given the complexities of the elite youth sport context, and the overarching prioritization of performance.

Other mesosystem interactions within the family unit have been minimally investigated in the youth sport literature (e.g., parent–sibling, sibling–sibling), but are of significant interest in the healthy development of elite athletes. Seminal works on the role of families in developing talented athletes suggest siblings often perceive unequal distribution of resources, and experience feelings of jealousy, rivalry, and isolation (Bloom, 1985; Côté, 1999). Kirk and colleagues (1997) also found stress within the family unit as a result of junior athletes' sport involvement, often leading to little flexibility and spontaneity in the family lifestyle, an inability to treat all children within the family equally in terms of attention and time, and consequently, breakdowns in family communication. In their recent review of family influences in sport development, Fraser-Thomas *et al.* (2013) proposed differences according to developmental trajectory and phase, submitting that strained sibling relationships may be most enduring among early specializing athletes, given the substantive investment over time, while sibling relationships may be marked by more support, encouragement, and shared work ethic throughout more progressive athlete development paths (see Chapter 4: Health and the athletic family). These findings highlight the complexities within these mesosystemic interactions, suggesting a whole-family perspective may be crucial to assuring the optimal family connections of elite youth athletes.

A final mesosystem for consideration links the athlete with his/her broader communities. The National Research Council Institute of Medicine (2002) identified the integration of family, school, and community as a crucial setting feature for PYD. In non-elite sport contexts, this integration appears strong, as participation in high-school sport has been positively linked to school grades, school attendance, time spent on homework, educational aspirations, and college attendance (Eccles *et al.*, 2003; Larson and Verma, 1999; Marsh and Kleitman, 2003). However, recent research found coaches of elite youth athletes did not always prioritize connections with school and community (Strachan *et al.*, 2011). Strachan and colleagues (2009) suggested youth involved primarily in one sport (i.e., specializers) may not have the same opportunities to be involved in school and community undertakings as youth participating in many different sports (i.e., samplers), perhaps leading them to feel less connected. However, evidence demonstrates elite athletes experience other important connections as a result of their intensive involvement in their sport. For example, elite athletes may have close and unique friendships with a diverse group of peers, in addition to strong connections with families of other youth within their sporting communities (Fraser-Thomas and Côté, 2009; Hassell *et al.*, 2010; Wilkes and Côté, 2010). It has been suggested higher level sport may bring together individuals from different programs, while more cumulative periods of time with teammates may lead to richer relationships (Wilkes and Côté, 2010). Further, elite sport also offers a context for special relationships with different aged peers, fostering opportunities for leadership and role modeling (Fraser-Thomas and Côté, 2009). In their study of adolescent basketball teams, Wilkes and Côté (2010) found the majority of higher level competitive teams deliberately facilitated leadership opportunities for athletes to coach or referee, while only half of recreational programs offered similar opportunities. Collectively, these findings align with past suggestions for all youth sport programs to facilitate PYD by offering athletes planned opportunities for cross-aged teaching, leading, and modeling, which in turn facilitate increased confidence, self-efficacy, responsibility, and sense of belonging within a community (Hellison *et al.*, 2008; Petitpas *et al.*, 2005).

Future directions

We began the chapter by outlining the objectives of youth sport programs (i.e., health, motor skills for recreational or performance-based sport, and psychosocial development), and asking whether these objectives may be in conflict. Our review suggests that in some cases they are not in conflict, as elite athletes' involvement is often viewed as healthy, fostering psychosocial development and life skills. Yet we also presented evidence to suggest elite athletes experience unhealthy psychosocial development. This is consistent with past work in non-elite contexts suggesting both positive and negative experiences and outcomes are associated with youth sport participation (Fraser-Thomas *et al.*, 2005; Fraser-Thomas and Côté, 2009). This review continues to emphasize the importance of asking the questions: 1) Under what *conditions* is elite youth sport a healthy pursuit?; and 2) What processes and mechanisms may be used to assure PYD? As stated by Tofler and colleagues with regards to elite youth gymnastics:

> At its best, elite gymnastics can provide a profoundly meaningful experience for the athletes, promoting their self-esteem and self-discipline and contributing to their development into productive and successful adults. At its worst, the sport can result in serious, life-endangering physical and psychological disabilities... We need to remember that the development of health, and well-being of these gifted children must be assigned the highest priority.
>
> (Tofler *et al.* 1996: 282)

In the final section, we highlight a few areas that we see as priorities for future investigation.

Unpacking the "black box" of sport programs

In the developmental psychology literature, sport has been treated as a "black box" (Larson, 2000). Over the past decade, researchers have consistently emphasized the importance of examining differences that may exist in youths' development according to program type, structure, context, environment, and delivery (Fraser-Thomas *et al.*, 2005; Holt and Sehn, 2008), but only a handful of studies have begun to tap into this black box, and fewer still have focused specifically on elite youth sport contexts. Our review highlights that although there is tremendous diversity between programs, there are also similarities that require additional attention. For example, Strachan *et al.* (2009) found specializers' and samplers' sport environments were more similar than different. Further research is necessary to better understand what is contributing to these similar and different healthy and unhealthy developmental outcomes in elite and non-elite youth sport contexts, and how best to harness optimal outcomes across all contexts.

Understanding negative experiences and growth

We feel one of the most unexplored but intriguing areas requiring further research relates to the role of elite youth athletes' negative experiences in contributing to their healthy development. While this may initially appear a paradox and is in direct contradiction to past claims that youth need to have positive experiences in sport to assure their positive developmental outcomes (e.g., Fraser-Thomas *et al.*, 2005), our review suggests that the challenges, stress, and adversity of elite youth sport may in fact be a key contributing component to the facilitation of developmental attributes such as resiliency among some youth athletes. As such, policies aimed at assuring positive developmental experiences for all in less competitive programs such as equal playing time, shuffling of teams to keep game scores close, and not keeping score may indirectly be depriving some youth of optimal experiences for growth (Wilkes and Côté, 2010). Similarly, Collins and MacNamara (2012) recently argued "talent needs trauma"; that developmental benefits emerge only through discomfort and lessons learned, with coaches playing a key role in debriefing challenges on an individual level. However, further consideration and understanding of the boundaries of youths' negative sport experiences is of particular importance, given past work highlighting the elite youth sport system as a context for unhealthy relationships, harassment, abuse, and victimization (Donnelly, 1993).

Social influences in elite athletes' health

Coaches, families, parents, teams, and peers play significant roles in elite athletes' healthy development. While coaches' roles have been among the most largely investigated in the PYD literature, there is much that remains to be explored. In particular, findings highlight coaches play very dichotomous roles in the development of elite youth athletes, from deliberately facilitating opportunities for the development of confidence, connections, and character, to emotionally abusing child athletes (see Chapter 6: In the name of performance: Threats, belittlement, and degradation). More research is necessary to understand the circumstances surrounding particular coaching approaches in elite youth sport, and clarify links between coaching behaviors and specific healthy and unhealthy psychosocial outcomes. Researchers should also aim to expand upon Gould and colleagues' (2007) work with award-winning football coaches to gain a better understanding of how coaches can simultaneously promote winning and athlete development. While practical strategies for coaches aiming to facilitate PYD have recently been proposed (e.g., Camiré *et al.*, 2011), further work is required to examine the effectiveness of these strategies specifically in elite youth sport contexts.

Findings on parents' behaviors in elite youth sport raise questions regarding similar dichotomies, highlighting a need for further study surrounding the concept of "positive push" by parents and its correlation to psychosocial development (Fraser-Thomas *et al.*, 2013). Siblings are also very poorly understood in elite youth sport contexts, given minimal research and associated complexities surrounding siblings' birth order, sex/gender, socialization processes, and sport involvement. In particular, more research is necessary to investigate whether siblings of child athletes following the increasingly popular early specialization path experience more psychosocial difficulties and distresses.

Additional social influences commonly associated with youths' healthy development include teams, teammates, and other sport-related peers. Much research has attempted to identify and understand the developmental attributes associated with team dynamics of sport, by examining differences between team and individual sports (e.g., Fraser-Thomas et al., 2012; Martens et al., 2006); however, Bruner et al. (2011) found interdependence (i.e., the structure of interactions among participants in a setting; Rusbult and Van Lange, 2003) had a stronger relationship than sport type with athletes' developmental experiences. Such findings raise important questions about how youth in elite sport contexts may interact, and how this may contribute to their developmental outcomes. For example, how do the unique conditions surrounding elite athletes' high amounts of time training and travelling with teammates, intense competition with teammates for positions on the team, and constant flux in teammates, influence developmental experiences and outcomes such as communication skills and sense of belonging?

Longitudinal, process, and evaluation research

Longitudinal, process, and evaluation research is needed to improve understanding of PYD in real life elite youth contexts. Investment should be made in prospectively tracing the development of youth athletes throughout their athletic careers and following retirement – not only for their athletic performances, but also their psychosocial health. To fully comprehend how optimal PYD outcomes emerge in elite youth athletes, it is essential not only to understand the early childhood sport socialization processes of successful cases (i.e., healthy elite youth athletes), but also to examine those of less successful cases (unhealthy, non-elite or dropout youth athletes). Process focused questions should explore how sport experiences may have differed for these groups. For example, were life skills intentionally taught, demonstrated, modeled, and practiced by early coaches?

Evaluation research is also sorely lacking in the field of PYD in sport, to identify best practices and enhance service delivery (Hellison et al., 2008; Petitpas et al., 2005). McCallister et al.'s (2000) study of American youth baseball programs found coaches' value-driven well-intentioned philosophies often did not align with their actual behaviors. While the field of PYD in sport is growing rapidly, most intervention research is being conducted in recreational not elite sport contexts. Recent research presents a strong case for the benefits of coach training on how to incorporate personal and social development into one's program (Conroy and Coatsworth, 2006; MacDonald et al., 2010); however, much more work is needed to delineate the processes and mechanisms by which confidence, connections, and character are most effectively integrated into elite youth sport programs.

Revisiting PYD and the bi-directional influences within ecological systems

In conclusion, we revisit the definition of PYD and Bronfenbrenner's (1995, 1999) Ecological Systems Theory. While the most widely accepted definitions of PYD reflect societal visions (e.g., youths' "engagement in pro-social behaviors and avoidance of health compromising behaviors and future jeopardizing behaviors"; Roth *et al.*, 1998: 426), such conceptualizations represent the ideals of outsiders to the PYD experience, and further work may be warranted to explore visions of PYD through insiders' perspectives – the lens of youth. Also requiring further consideration is Bronfenbrenner's (1995, 1999) proposition of human development as the materialization of reciprocal person–context interactions that occur between individuals and other persons, objects, and symbols in their immediate environment. To date, the majority of PYD sport research has been done through a one-directional lens focusing on how the outer levels of the Ecological Systems Theory can facilitate optimal development of the individual, at the inner most level of the system. Within the context of the current chapter, elite athletes' confidence, connections, and character have been viewed primarily as a product of their microsystem, mesosystem, exosystem, macrosystem, and chronosystem. Much less work has focused on interactions in the opposite direction: how individuals, or specifically elite athletes, may be facilitating contributions at community or societal levels (Holt and Sehn, 2008; Lerner *et al.*, 2005). But as Bailey (2008) points out, we have recently seen an increasing interest in how all levels of sport can facilitate broader societal improvement. At a grassroots level, the United Nations declared 2005 as the International Year of Sport and Physical Education, so that sport could be used to promote "education, health, development, and peace," so as to "bridge social, religious, racial, and gender divides" (United Nations, 2005: 1). At the elite level, we continue to see examples of the belief in this possibility, as evidenced in John Furlong's (CEO, Vancouver Organizing Committee) speech at the closing ceremonies of the 2010 Olympic Games:

> Athletes of the world ... you have injected hope into the lives of youth everywhere ... youth that will rise tomorrow ready to emulate you. Boys and girls you will never meet now know that it is possible to achieve greatness through the power of a dream. You have set the course for the next generation of great champions. You return to your homes as the best ambassadors we have for a better world. You are the future. The youth of the world await your leadership and your example.
>
> (cited in Furlong, 2010)

While uplifting, empirical investigation of visionary claims such as these remain limited, highlighting the need for more research focused on examination of individuals' influences on society. Innovative methodologies are also necessary to expand understanding of the reciprocal interactions between nested levels of the

Ecological Systems Theory to in turn more fully comprehend the processes of development. It is our belief that with continued research advancement, particularly in the areas described above, we will begin to see more opportunities for elite athletes' healthy development, while society will simultaneously experience the reciprocal benefits of elite athletes' confidence, connections, and character.

References

Allemang, J. (2012) 'The Olympic Games aren't just for the young', *Globe and Mail*. Online at: www.theglobeandmail.com/sports/olympics/the-olympic-games-arent-just-for-the-young/article4431776/?page=all (accessed 21 July 2012).

Anshel, M.H. and Porter, A. (1996) 'Self-regulatory characteristics of competitive swimmers as a function of skill level and gender', *Journal of Sport Behavior*, 19: 91–110.

Arnett, J. (2000) 'Emerging adulthood: A theory of development from the late teens through the twenties', *American Psychologist*, 55: 469–80.

Bailey, R. (2008) 'Youth sport and social inclusion', in N.L. Holt (ed.) *Positive Youth Development through Sport*, New York, Routledge, 85–96.

Bloom, B.S. (1985) *Developing Talent in Young People*, New York: Ballantine.

Brady, R. (2013) 'Rebecca Marino and learning to put the person before the athlete', *Globe and Mail*. Online. Online at: www.theglobeandmail.com/sports/more-sports/rebecca-marino-and-learning-to-put-the-person-before-the-athlete/article9003243/ (accessed 23 February 2013).

Bronfenbrenner, U. (1977) 'Toward an experimental ecology of human development', *American Psychologist*, 32: 513–31.

Bronfenbrenner, U. (1995) 'Developmental ecology through space and time: A future Perspective', in P. Moen, G.H. Elder, Jr., and K. Lüscher (eds) *Examining Lives in Context: Perspectives on the ecology of human development*, Washington, DC: American Psychological Association.

Bronfenbrenner, U. (1999) 'Environments in developmental perspective: Theoretical and operational models', in S.L. Friedman and T.D. Wachs (eds) *Measuring Environment Across the Life Span*, Washington, DC: American Psychological Association, 3–28.

Bruner, M.W., Hall, J., and Côté, J. (2011) 'The influence of sport type and interdependence on the developmental experiences of young athletes;, *European Journal of Sport Science*, 11: 131–42.

Busseri, M.A., Rose-Krasnor, L., Willoughby, T., and Chalmers, H. (2006) 'A longitudinal examination of breadth and intensity of youth activity involvement and successful development', *Developmental Psychology*, 42: 1313–26.

Camiré, M., Forneris, T., Trudel, P., and Bernard, D. (2011) 'Strategies for helping coaches facilitate positive youth development though sport', *Journal of Sport Psychology in Action*, 2: 92–9.

Collins, D. and McNamara, A. (2012) 'The rocky road to the top. Why talent needs trauma', *Sports Medicine*, 42: 907–14.

Connaughton, D., Hanton, S., and Jones, G. (2010) 'The development and maintenance of mental toughness in the world's best performers', *The Sport Psychologist*, 24: 168–93.

Conroy, D.E. and Coatsworth, J.D. (2006) 'Coach training as a strategy for promoting youth social development', *The Sport Psychologist*, 20: 128–44.

Côté, J. (1999) 'The influence of the family in the development of talent in sports', *The Sport Psychologist*, 13: 395–417.

Côté, J. and Fraser-Thomas, J. (2011) 'Youth involvement and positive development in sport', in P.R.E. Crocker (ed.) *Sport Psychology: A Canadian perspective*, 2nd edn, Toronto: Pearson Prentice Hall, 226–55.

Côté, J., Strachan, L., and Fraser-Thomas, J. (2008) 'Participation, personal development, and performance through youth sport', in N.L. Holt (ed.) *Positive Youth Development through Sport*, New York: Routledge, 34–45.

Côté, J., Bruner, M., Erickson, K., Strachan, L., and Fraser-Thomas, J. (2010) 'Athlete development and coaching', in J. Lyle and C. Cushion (eds) *Sport Coaching: Professionalism and practice*, Oxford: Elsevier, 63–79.

De Knop, P., Engström, L.M., and Skirstad, B. (1996) 'Worldwide trends in youth sport', in P. De Knop, L.-M. Engström, B. Skirstad and M. Weiss (eds) *Worldwide Trends in Youth Sport*, Champaign, IL: Human Kinetics, 276–81.

Donnelly, P. (1993) 'Problems associated with youth involvement in high-performance sport', in B.R. Cahill and A.J. Pearl (eds) *Intensive Participation in Children's Sport*, Champaign, IL: Human Kinetics, 95–126.

Duda, J. and Nicholls, J. (1992) 'Dimensions of achievement motivation in schoolwork and sport', *Journal of Educational Psychology*, 84: 290–9.

Eccles, J.S., Barber, B.L., Stone, M., and Hunt, J. (2003) 'Extracurricular activities and adolescent development', *Journal of Social Issues*, 59: 865–89.

Ericsson, K.A., Krampe, R., and Tesch-Roemer, C. (1993) 'The role of deliberate practice in the acquisition of expert performance', *Psychological Review*, 100: 363–406.

Fasting, K., Brackenridge, C., and Sundgot-Borgen, J. (2004) 'Prevalence of sexual harassment among Norwegian female elite Athletes in relation to sport type', *International Review for the Sociology of Sport*, 39: 373–86.

Fraser-Thomas, J. and Côté, J. (2009) 'Understanding adolescents' positive and negative developmental experiences in sport', *The Sport Psychologist*, 23: 3–23.

Fraser-Thomas, J., Côté, J., and Deakin, J. (2005) 'Youth sport programs: An avenue to foster positive youth development', *Physical Education and Sport Pedagogy*, 10: 19–40.

Fraser-Thomas, J., Côté, J., and Deakin, J. (2008) 'Understanding dropout and prolonged engagement in adolescent competitive sport', *Psychology of Sport and Exercise*, 9: 645–62.

Fraser-Thomas, J., Strachan, L., and Jeffery-Tosoni, S. (2013) 'Family influence on children's involvement in sport', in J. Côté and R. Lidor (eds) *Conditions of Children's Talent Development in Sport*, Morgantown: Fitness Information Technology, 179–96.

Furlong, J. (2010) *Vanoc Closing Ceremony Speech*. Online at: www.theepochtimes.com/ n2/canada/vanoc-ceo-john-furlongs-closing-ceremony-speech-30576.html (accessed 19 March 2014).

García Bengoechea, E. and Johnson, G.M. (2001) 'Ecological systems theory and children's development in sport: Toward a process-person-context-time research Paradigm', *Avante*, 7: 20–31.

Gervis, M. and Dunn, N. (2004) 'The emotional abuse of elite child athletes by their coaches', *Child Abuse Review*, 13: 215–23.

Gould D. (1987) 'Attrition in children's sports', in D. Gould and M.R. Weiss (eds) *Advances in Pediatric Sport Sciences: Behavioral Issues*, Champaign, IL: Human Kinetics, 61–85.

Gould, D. (1993) 'Intensive sport participation and the prepubescent athlete: Competitive stress and burnout', in B.R. Cahill and A.J. Pearl (eds) *Intensive Participation in Children's Sports*, Champaign, IL: Human Kinetics, 19–38.

Gould, D., Udry, E., Tuffey, S., and Loehr, J. (1996) 'Burnout in competitive tennis players: I. A quantitative psychological assessment', *The Sport Psychologist*, 10: 322–40.

Gould, D., Collins, K., Lauer, L., and Chung, Y. (2007) 'Coaching life skills through football: A study of award winning high school coaches', *Journal of Applied Sport Psychology*, 19: 16–37.

Hansen, D.M. and Larson, R.W. (2007) 'Amplifiers of developmental and negative experiences in organized activities: Dosage, motivation, lead roles, and adult-youth ratios', *Journal of Applied Developmental Psychology*, 28: 360–74.

Hansen, D.M., Larson, R.W., and Dworkin, J.B. (2003) 'What adolescents learn in organized youth activities: A survey of self-reported developmental experiences', *Journal of Research on Adolescence*, 13: 25–55.

Hassell, K., Sabiston, C.M., and Bloom, G. (2010) 'Exploring the multiple dimensions of social support among elite female adolescent swimmers', *International Journal of Sport Psychology*, 41: 340–59.

Hellison, D., Martinek, T., and Walmsh, D. (2008) 'Sport and responsible leadership among youth', in N. Holt (ed.) *Positive Youth Development through Sport*, Routledge: New York, 49–60.

Holt, N.L. and Dunn, J.G.H. (2004) 'Toward a grounded theory of the psychosocial competencies and environmental conditions associated with soccer success', *Journal of Applied Sport Psychology*, 16: 199–219.

Holt, N.L. and Sehn, Z.L. (2008) 'Process associated with positive youth development and participation in competitive youth sport', in N.L. Holt (ed.) *Positive Youth Development through Sport*, Routledge: New York, 24–33.

Jones, M.I. and Lavallee, D. (2009) 'Exploring perceived life skills development and participation in sport', *Qualitative Research in Sport and Exercise*, 1: 36–50.

Kirk, D., O'Connor, A., Carlson, T., Burke, T., Davis, K., and Glover, S. (1997) 'Time commitments in junior sport: Social consequences for participants and their families', *European Journal of Physical Education*, 2: 51–73.

Larson, R. (2000) 'Towards a psychology of positive youth development', *American Psychologist*, 55: 170–83.

Larson, R.W. and Verma, S. (1999) 'How children and adolescents spend time across the world: Work, play, and developmental opportunities', *Psychological Bulletin*, 125(6): 701–36.

Lauer, L., Gould, D., Roman, N., and Pierce, M. (2010) 'Parental behaviors that affect junior tennis player development', *Psychology of Sport and Exercise*, 11: 487–96.

Lerner, R.M., Lerner, J.V., Almerigi, J. Theokas, C., Phelps, E., Naudeau, S., *et al.* (2005) 'Positive youth development, participation in community youth development programs, and community contributions of fifth grade adolescents: Findings from the first wave of the 4-H study of Positive Youth Development', *Journal of Early Adolescence*, 25: 17–71.

MacDonald, D.J., Côté, J., and Deakin, J. (2010) 'The impact of informal coach training on the personal development of youth sport athletes', *International Journal of Sport Science and Coaching*, 5: 363–72.

Marsh, H.W. and Kleitman, S. (2003) 'School athletic participation: Mostly gain with little pain', *Journal of Sport and Exercise Psychology*, 25: 205–28.

Martens, M.P., Watson, J.C., and Beck N.C. (2006) 'Sport-type differences in alcohol use among intercollegiate athletes', *Journal of Applied Sport Psychology*, 18: 136–50.

McCallister, S.G., Blinde, E.M., and Weiss, W.M. (2000) 'Teaching values and implementing philosophies: Dilemmas of the youth sport coach', *The Physical Educator*, 57: 35–45.

National Research Council and Institute of Medicine (2002) *Community Programs to Promote Youth Development*, Washington, DC: National Academy Press.

Oliver, E.J., Hardy, J., and Markland, D. (2010) 'Identifying important practice behaviors for the development of high-level youth athletes: Exploring the perspectives of elite coaches', *Psychology of Sport and Exercise*, 11: 433–43.

International Olympic Committee (2014) *Sexual Harassment and Abuse in Sport*. Online at: www.olympic.org/sha (accessed 19 March 2014).

Petitpas, A.J., Cornelius, A.E., Van Raalte, J.L., and Jones, T. (2005) 'A framework for planning youth sport programs that foster psychosocial development', *The Sport Psychologist*, 19: 63–80.

Roth, J., Brooks-Gunn, J., Murray, L., and Foster, W. (1998) 'Promoting health adolescents: Synthesis of youth development program evaluations', *Journal of Research on Adolescence*, 8: 423–59.

Rusbult, C.E. and Van Lange, P.A.M. (2003) 'Interdependence, interaction, and relationships', *Annual Review of Psychology*, 54: 351–75.

Scanlan, T.K., Babkes, M.L., and Scanlan, L.A. (2005) 'Participation in sport: A developmental glimpse at emotion', in J.L. Mahoney, R.W. Larson, and J.S. Eccles (eds) *Organized Activities as Contexts of Development*, Mahwah, NJ: Lawrence Erlbaum, 275–310.

Simpkins, S.D., Ripke, M., Huston, A., and Eccles, J.S. (2005) 'Predicting participation and outcomes in out-of-school activities: Similarities and differences across social ecologies', *New Directions for Youth Development*, 105: 51–69.

Smoll, F.L. and Smith, R.E. (2002) 'Coaching behavior research and intervention in youth sports', in F.L. Smoll and R.E. Smith (eds) *Children and Youth in Sport: A biopsychosocial perspective*, 2nd edn, Dubuque, IA: Kendall Hunt, 211–31.

Smoll, F.L., Cumming, S.P., and Smith, R.E. (2011) 'Enhancing coach-parent relationships in youth sports: Increasing harmony and minimizing hassle', *International Journal of Sport Science and Coaching*, 6: 13–26.

Stirling, A.E. and Kerr, G.A. (2008) 'Defining and categorizing emotional abuse in sport', *European Journal of Sport Science*, 8: 173–81.

Strachan, L., Côté, J., and Deakin, J. (2009) '"Specializers" versus "samplers" in youth sport: Comparing experiences and outcomes', *The Sport Psychologist*, 23: 77–92.

Strachan, L., Côté, J., and Deakin, J. (2011) 'A new view: Exploring positive youth development in elite sport contexts', *Qualitative Research in Sport, Exercise and Health*, 3: 9–32.

Tamminen, K.A., Holt, N.L., and Neely, K.C. (2013) 'Exploring adversity and the potential for growth among elite female athletes', *Psychology of Sport and Exercise*, 14: 28–36.

Tofler, I.R., Stryer, B.K., Micheli, L.J., and Herman, L.R. (1996) 'Physical and emotional problems of elite female gymnasts', *New England Journal of Medicine*, 335: 281–3.

United Nations (2005) *Sport to Promote Education, Health, Development and Peace*, Vienna: United Nations Information Service.

Vierimaa, M., Erickson, K., Côté, J., and Gilbert, W. (2012) 'Positive youth development: A measurement framework for sport', *International Journal of Sport Science and Coaching*, 7: 601–14.

Wilkes, S. and Côté, J. (2010) 'The developmental experiences of adolescent females in structured basketball programs', *PHENex Journal*, 2(2). Online at: http://ojs.acadiau.ca/index.php/phenex/article/view/6/1162 (accessed 19 March 2014).

Woodcock, C., Holland, M.J.G., Duda, J.L., and Cumming, J. (2011) 'Psychological qualities of elite adolescent rugby players: Parents, coaches, and sport administration staff perceptions and supporting roles', *The Sport Psychologist*, 25: 411–40.

World Health Organization (1948) 'Preamble to the Constitution of the World Health Organization as adopted by the International Health Conference', New York, 19–22 June, 1946; signed on 22 July 1946 by the representatives of 61 States (Official Records of the World Health Organization, no. 2, p. 100) and entered into force on 7 April 1948.

Zaff, J.F., Moore, K.A., Papillo, A.R., and Williams, S. (2003) 'Implications of extracurricular activity participation during adolescence on positive outcomes', *Journal of Adolescent Research*, 18: 599–630.

Zarrett, N., Lerner, R.M., Carrrano, J., Fay, K., Peltz, J.S., and Li, Y. (2008) 'Variations in adolescent engagement in sports and its influence on positive youth development', in N.L. Holt (ed.) *Positive Youth Development through Sport*, Routledge: New York, 9–23.

3 Talent identification and development

The impact on athlete health?

Fieke Rongen, Stephen Cobley, Jim McKenna and Kevin Till

Within the last 15 to 20 years, there has been substantial growth in the global deployment of sporting talent identification and development systems (TIDS), both across and within sports (e.g., sport governing bodies), and at more localized levels (e.g., soccer and rugby league/union clubs). Yet, irrespective of their broader function (e.g., political or economic) or their structure, their fundamental purpose remains consistent: 1) identify talented young athletes early in their lives, and then 2) provide a more optimal environment for athletes to accelerate their development (Williams and Reilly, 2000).

The popularity of TIDS is based on the assumption that youth athletes selected into TIDS will be exposed to better quality learning experiences compared to what is accessible for non-selected athletes. Additionally, TIDS are believed to increase the likelihood of long-term athletic success without compromising the well-being of the selected athletes. Yet, this notion has been questioned as concerns have been raised in regards to TIDS involvement having the potential to cause harm to youth athlete health and well-being (Baxter-Jones and Helms, 1996; Lang, 2010). Therefore, closer attention to the validity of these themes is warranted, especially when considering that few athletes eventually 'make it' into adult professional sport despite making similar personal investments, costs and sacrifices as those who do.

In this chapter, we address the question: 'How healthy is TIDS involvement?'. To answer, we first provide an outline of what TIDS entail and outline experiences of involvement. Second, we articulate our conceptualization of health within the scope of this chapter before using the available and relevant research to address both the positive and negative health impacts linked to TIDS involvement. We set out to reflect 'both sides of the fence', acknowledging the tension between optimizing positive developments while minimizing negative effects. We foresee that TIDS have the potential to be (un)healthy and (in)humane depending on how well practitioners working within them can get this balance right. Lastly, we offer some evidence-based recommendations to help practitioners achieve this balance.

TIDS

What do TIDS look like?

Figure 3.1 summarizes the components and stages of a TIDS, and how they typically operate. Beginning with identification, youth with potential are selected from the broader participating population, allowing access to the talent identification and development (TID) environment. TIDS typically offer specific training facilities, coaching knowledge and expertise, equipment and extensive support services, although the nature of these services varies considerably from one system to another. These support services may include strength and conditioning, injury management and prevention (e.g., physiotherapists and sport scientists), as well as sport psychology and lifestyle support (Baker *et al.*, 2012; Güllich and Emrich, 2012b). Youth may be selected into these systems on the basis of formal subjective performance assessments by coaches or scouts in competition or trials, as well as informal recommendations (e.g., physical education teachers), or by physical or performance testing. Selection age varies according to sport context. For example, gymnasts and swimmers commonly begin to identify and differentiate between 6 and 8 years of age (Lang, 2010), whereas for rugby players, using annual-age groupings, this does not occur until 13–15 years of age (e.g., Till *et al.*, 2012). However, many TIDS are being implemented at earlier ages: for example, 8 years of age in UK professional football academies, even though peak adult performance occurs at 24–30 years of age (Green, 2009; Premier League, 2011).

Within potential age-group bands, selected youth then compete for selection into various tiers of representation, according to performance level. This is often repeated across age-group bands through to senior adult ages. With every representation stage, the pool of athletes decreases (see left–right in Figure 3.1), thereby creating a 'pyramid structure' of participation (Güllich and Emrich, 2012b). When athletes either hit a ceiling stage or are deselected, they transfer to lower levels or withdraw from the TIDS.

What is it like in a TIDS?

Intensified and highly structured training

Compared to recreational sport participation, involvement in a TIDS is characterized by training and competition spread over much of the year (Baxter-Jones and Helms, 1996; Lang, 2010). This feature represents a marked increase in training, travel and competition (Beckmann *et al.*, 2006), mandating youth athletes to make substantial time commitments. Intensification of involvement also occurs across the stages of development (see Figure 3.1). For example, weekly training hours for talented young soccer players increased from 2.8 hours at age 11, to 12 hours a week at age 17 (Baxter-Jones and Helms, 1996). In swimmers, weekly training kilometres increased from 24 to 65 between ages 9 and 14 (Lang, 2010).

Although intensification seems beneficial, research suggests that early sport 'sampling' is likely to have featured in the early careers of many high

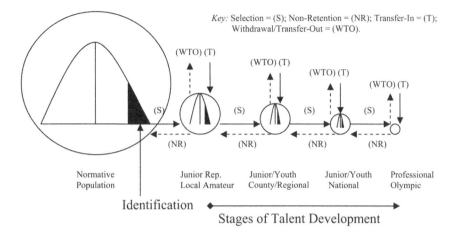

Figure 3.1 Conceptual diagram highlighting general components and stages within TIDS
Source: Cobley *et al.*, 2012, with permission

performance athletes, suggesting diversification is more conducive to long-term (performance) development and eventual sport success (e.g., Côté and Hay, 2002; Côté *et al.*, 2009; Güllich and Emrich, 2012a). Yet, many TIDS still aim to 'catch them young', which is associated with early specialization and valuing increased specific training loadings at a young age (Gonçalves *et al.*, 2012; Malina, 2010a). Youth TIDS have been linked with having to prioritize one sport over other activities, structured time schedules, and extensive adult supervision (Diehl *et al.*, 2012; Hendriksen, 2010). For instance, some UK football academies require 'signed' youth to no longer participate in other high-injury risk sports like rugby (Green, 2009). These features are critiqued for being prescriptive and restrictive, controlling the daily life choices of youth athletes (Beckmann *et al.*, 2006).

Abiding the performance narrative

In some sport contexts, TIDS create social conditions and values representing distinctive cultures of 'eliteness'. These conditions are united by endorsing and embodying the 'performance narrative'. Typically, this narrative rewards and reinforces behaviors and stories based on athletes who offer unwavering dedication toward winning, or contribution toward achieving performance outcomes (Christensen and Sorensen, 2009; Douglas and Carless, 2006; McGillivray *et al.*, 2005). The narrative and the reality is captured in the phrase 'sport is life and life is sport' (Dacyshyn 1999: 217), with life revolving around an athlete being fully committed to the social context (e.g., team or club). Since this all-encompassing narrative is reinforced by stakeholders, including coaches, selectors, governing bodies, peers, and media, it spans the 'entire fabric of elite sports' (Carless and Douglas, 2009: 64).

TIDS that explicitly, or even implicitly, promote the performance narrative can create an over challenging psychological and social climate for youth (Carless and Douglas, 2013; Coakley, 1992; Gould, 1993). TIDS may represent a competitive, pressurized, stressful, ego-based social climate, where demonstration of progression and continuous delivery of 'up to scratch' performances is mandated and continually put to the test. Deselection may be the threat or the result for those not conforming and/or performing. In fact, deselection is a permanent feature of TIDS. Exposing youth athletes to such conditions intensively over time may not only result in the aspired performance outcomes but unintended health and developmental impacts may also occur (such as overtraining or burnout). As epidemiologists remind us, 'There ain't no effects without side effects'. Of course, not all TIDS promote such performance narratives or expose youth to these features, but close consideration of how the climate builds facilitative and/or dysfunctional adaptations is required. This will then help to establish a balanced understanding of TID and its relationship with health and well-being.

TIDS and health

Defining health

In speaking about health, often an individual is considered 'healthy' when they are regarded as being free from disease or infirmity. However, the 1946 charter of the World Health Organization's definition emphasizes a wider stance: 'Health is a state of complete positive physical, mental and social well-being and not merely the absence of disease or infirmity'. More recent developments have built on the prominence of humanistic psychology, endorsing the notion of 'positive health' (Seligman, 2008), consisting of scoring high on three health elements: subjective, (e.g., 'feeling great'), biological, (e.g., having excellent physiological capacities) and functional (i.e., functioning well and/or being productive in daily life activities). In this view, not only is health multidimensional, consisting of subjective, biological and functional aspects, it can also be placed on a continuum reflecting individual to societal health. Within the remainder of this chapter we consider TIDS against this newer widened health template as offered by Seligman (2008). Doing so allows us to evaluate not only the extent to which TIDS might cause harm, but also consider opportunities for positive development.

Existing concerns regarding the 'healthiness' of TIDS practices

Research and sporting communities expressing health related concerns related to youth engagement in TIDS is certainly not new. Previously these have included evidence of physical and psychological exploitation or abuse (e.g., Brackenridge and Fasting, 2002; David, 2005), violence (e.g., Tenenbaum *et al.*, 1997), labor exploitation (e.g., Donnelly, 1997) and doping (e.g., Laure and Binsinger, 2005;

Ungerleider, 2001), as well as unforeseen inequalities (Cobley *et al.*, 2013). These worrying features have led to suggestions that intensified youth sport involvement is nothing more than a 'modern form of child abuse' (Lang 2010: 1). Precise rates of such prevalence are not available and while we are cognisant that events like abuse are clearly unhealthy and unacceptable, we are hopeful that these experiences are not reflective of the more general and normative daily life in TIDS (see also Chapter 6). Indeed, given contemporary definitions for health, TIDS could generate considerable opportunities for growth and well-being as well as harm.

Taking this perspective, TID athletes have the potential to develop in positive and/or negative directions in terms of subjective, biological and functional health capacities. The challenge is to identify and respond to what is consistently regarded as positive or negative development, and then attempt to achieve this whilst making sure athletes within the system are not becoming overwhelmed by the demands of that developmental process. Additionally, as early developmental experiences 'sow the seeds' of later life success (or problems), it is necessary to refine TID impact as comprising both immediate and longer-term health issues. Research designs aimed at determining long-term developmental trajectories, often drawn from life-course epidemiology (Elder, 1998), help demonstrate how the consequences of early experiences only become apparent in later life.

Presenting the evidence

This section focuses on health outcomes, positive and negative, that can be *logically associated* with TIDS involvement. We use the term *logically associated* as there is limited research addressing the issue of health in relation to specific TID samples and settings. Therefore we present evidence from studies that have explored health impacts in relation to: 1) established TID practices (i.e. early selection, specialisation and training intensification), or 2) features of the social context and culture in which young athletes are immersed.

Physical/physiological: risks and potential negatives

Overtraining

Representing an unintended decrement in performance capacity resulting from a failure to recover from the accumulation of training and non-training stress (Budgett, 1998), overtraining is an ever-present concern in TIDS. If not properly balanced, the helpful features of 'over-reaching' tip into unwanted harm from over-burden. Elite youth athletes have been suggested to often push themselves too far or hard, experience extreme tiredness on a regular basis, and never reach their potential due to excessive training and inadequate recovery (Gould and Dieffenbach, 2002; Meeusen *et al.*, 2006). In a review on trainability and over-training in youth athletes, Matos and Winsley (2007) estimated a 30 per cent prevalence of overtraining, attributed to a combination of heavy training loads, insufficient recovery and restrained social support networks brought on by early specialization and intensification. Overtraining is signalled by general apathy, loss of appetite, disturbed sleep, irritability and vulnerability (Uusitalo, 2001), as well as mood disturbances (Meeusen *et al.*, 2006; Tobar, 2012), indicating compromised physical health and psychological well-being.

Injury

Injury is the most concerning factor associated with short and longer term increases in volume and intensity of training (Myklebust and Bahr, 2005). Sport is the leading cause of injury in youth populations in many countries (Emery *et al.*, 2006; Emery and Tyreman, 2009) and early specialization has been linked to increased risk of injury (Kaleth and Mikesky, 2010). A recent review (Steffen and Engebretsen, 2010) explored injury risk across 13 studies including youth soccer, rowing, field hockey, badminton and gymnastics. Alongside consideration of other factors, explanations for the occasionally high levels of injury were related to mismatches between competition and training/recovery (Söderman *et al.*, 2002), inappropriate transitions from low to high intensive training, resulting in tensile loading and stresses on the musculoskeletal system (Yung *et al.*, 2007) as well as the possibility of mismatches in biological maturity of competitors.

Yet, contrasting evidence suggests that injury is not a (big) problem for talented young athletes. The Training of Young Athletes (TOYA) study, which sampled elite UK youth athletes (age upon entry ranging from 8–16 years) from TIDS in gymnastics, swimming, soccer and tennis, identified low injury rates in each sport (i.e., less than one injury per 1000 training hours) (Baxter-Jones *et al.*, 1993; Baxter-Jones and Helms, 1996). Nonetheless, many of the youth athletes incurred an injury of some sort; the greatest injury incidence was identified in soccer (67 per cent) and the lowest in swimming (37 per cent) with the majority of acute injuries occurring in the limbs. Overuse injuries often required longer periods of rest (20 days) than acute injuries (13 days). Likewise short-term injuries were predominantly minor and did not constitute health challenges.

More disturbing though were findings from the TOYA ten-year follow-up study, which tracked injury from adolescence to young adulthood (Maffulli *et al.*, 2005). Data revealed that 16 per cent of participants had withdrawn due to sport related injuries; and 45.8 per cent had suffered a sports-related injury (soccer 63 per cent; gymnastics 51.9 per cent; tennis 50 per cent; swimming 28.1 per cent). Level of sport involvement was related to injury risk, with 88 per cent of international athletes suffering an injury compared to fewer than 50 per cent in recreationalists. These findings suggest that most elite youth athletes who progressively train will almost certainly experience musculoskeletal injuries.

Injury data are highly relevant to longer term individual and public health. Compared to age-matched control populations, early life athletic injuries occurring within long-term, high-skill level, intensive training and competition have been associated with an increasing prevalence of knee and hip osteoarthritis (OA) and arthroplasty (Caine and Golightly, 2011; Turner *et al.*, 2000; Tveit *et al.*,

2012). Athletes from contact sports showed a higher risk for both hip and knee OA with the latter being associated with previous injury; whereas the prolonged sport engagement of non-contact athletes (e.g., runners) left them three times more likely than non-athlete controls to get knee OA (Tveit *et al.*, 2012). It should also be noted that these long-term outcomes are sometimes accompanied by psychological and lifestyle problems such as pain, disability and depression (Turner *et al.*, 2000), resulting in an accumulative negative impact on the biological, subjective and functional features that combine to create an individual's conception of 'health' (for more on injury risk in youth sport see Chapter 5).

Concussion and chronic traumatic encephalopathy (CTE)

Recently, concussion and CTE have been highlighted as an immediate long-term sporting injury health concern. Annually, in the US alone, there are an estimated 1.6–3.8 million sports-related concussions (Harmon *et al.*, 2013). However, where concussions are repeated and/or sufficiently severe, as can occur in intensive sport competition over years, case studies of former athletes suggest this can lead to CTE (Bailes and Cantu, 2001; Greenwald *et al.*, 2008; Miller, 1966; Stern *et al.*, 2011). CTE is a form of accelerated brain neuro-degeneration (i.e., neural atrophy and cell death), which subsequently leads to dementia. CTE is accompanied by a host of cognitive and physical functional losses over time with social implications (e.g., Corsellis *et al.*, 1973; Gavett *et al.*, 2011) as well as the likelihood of a shortened lifespan (including higher risk of suicide; Omalu *et al.*, 2010).

Previously CTE was only associated with boxing (i.e., 'dimentia pugilista'; Martland, 1928), but it is now being investigated in athletes who have experienced repeated concussions in sports like American football, codes of rugby, Australian rules football, ice-hockey and soccer. The potential link between CTE and early athletic specialization is highlighted by McKee *et al.* (2009) who reviewed 46 confirmed CTE cases. All were former athletes (i.e., 39 boxers, five American footballers, a wrestler and soccer player) and reported repeated or severe concussions during participation. Cases began their participation in youth (i.e., 11–19 yrs; M = 15.4 yrs), which would be considered a very late start today in most sports, and had careers exceeding 14 years at amateur or professional levels. One third reported CTE symptoms upon retirement, while half reported symptoms as appearing within four years. Noting this sample's late start, children today might be at an even increased risk as they are commonly starting sports, and subsequently potentially having first concussions, earlier than 11–19 years. While such data do not directly link early participation in collision sports with CTE occurrence in later-life, or a growing prevalence, it is a plausible explanation because the maturing brain may be particularly vulnerable (Field *et al.*, 2003). Without comparisons of concussion and CTE occurrence in the normative population, and tracked over time, it remains difficult to link these conditions to high-level or early sporting performance. Nonetheless, it is worth noting that the National Football League (NFL) recently announced a US$50 million investment to investigate such concerns in ex-professionals. Additionally, concussion is increasingly highlighted as a serious concern in relation to youth sport, both in terms of short- and long-term consequences (e.g., Gourley *et al.*, 2010) (see Chapter 8 for more discussion).

Physical/physiological: from 'no harm' to positives

On the positive side, there is no doubt that TIDS create increased and regular opportunities for physical activity, the development of physiological capacities and a range of other health benefits. A recent review (Malina, 2010b), addressing physical activity and youth health, identified these benefits as including lower body fat percentage and body mass index (BMI), a more favorable metabolic profile, heightened bone health (e.g., greater bone mineral content; Bailey *et al.*, 1999), enhanced muscular strength and power (Baxter-Jones and Helms, 1996) as well as higher levels of aerobic fitness resulting in advanced cardiovascular health compared to less active youth. Recently, involvement in vigorous activity during youth ages has been highlighted to result in higher bone mineral density being maintained up to 30 years into retirement, as well as having a lower risk of fractures in older age (Tveit *et al.*, 2013a; Tveit *et al.*, 2013b).

Additionally, while initially intensive training and competition was suggested to have a detrimental effect on physical size and rate of growth in youth athletes (Maffulli and Helms, 1988), both cross-sectional and longitudinal studies have subsequently identified that this is not the case (Baxter-Jones and Maffulli, 2002; Malina, 1994; Morris *et al.*, 1997). Any observed differences in size and maturation of athletes across sports have since been attributed to either self or coach selection processes within those contexts (Baxter-Jones and Helms, 1996).

Although the development of fundamental movement skills (FMS) in childhood is not specific to TID, but a consequence of general sport participation, the high-quality TID environment is expected to promote continued development of FMS and sport-specific skills and has been linked to favourable motor skills development in the associated sport context (Malina, 2010b). However, specialization in a single sport, in some cases a key characteristic of TID, might provide a potential pitfall. Specialization is proposed to inhibit broader balanced FMS development (Branta, 2010; Côté *et al.*, 2009), and to have a detrimental impact on long-term sport participation (Gould *et al.*, 1996; Russell and Limle, 2013; Wall and Côté, 2007). Collectively, this limits opportunities for optimizing well-being and fitness for life (National Association for Sport and Physical Education, 2010). In terms of promoting long-term engagement in health behaviors, the importance of TIDS getting the balance right between offering quality skill-learning opportunities without becoming overly focused on sport-specific skills is highlighted.

Psycho-social: isolation, pressure, burnout?

Youth sport participation in general is praised for offering opportunities for social interaction, relationship building as well as developing and practicing pro-social behaviors (e.g., Fraser-Thomas *et al.*, 2005). However, the intensified engagement associated with TIDS has been critiqued for having important potential negative psychosocial health impacts. Researchers have highlighted the risk of social isolation, and feelings of alienation that result from spending substantial amounts of time away from family and inevitably having fewer opportunities to make and retain friendships outside sport (e.g, Coakley, 1992; Wiersma, 2000). Additionally, being identified as talented can also change the nature of peer relationships (Malina, 2010a). However, the TOYA study showed no systematic link between athletes' ability to make or retain friendships and engagement in intensive training at a young age (Baxter-Jones and Helms, 1996). Furthermore, involvement in intensive training offered a protective effect from adopting unhealthy and risky behaviors. Compared to other children in the UK, youth athletes reported watching less TV, experimenting with smoking less often and a reduced alcohol intake at younger ages. Yet, these findings might not apply to every intensive youth sport context. Whereas a recent systematic literature review showed high-involved adolescent athletes to be less likely to smoke or use recreational drugs, they were more likely to use alcohol, steroids and smokeless tobacco (Diehl *et al.*, 2012).

Another concern is that an overriding focus on performance can result in high levels of perceived pressure, feelings of low self-esteem and confidence (Fraser-Thomas *et al.*, 2005) as well as a fear of failure associated with the risk of being evaluated negatively and letting down significant others (Sagar *et al.*, 2007). These significant others, which include parents, coaches and peers, have also been highlighted as important participants in TIDS for different reasons. Both parents and coaches have been accused of advocating the 'winning at all cost' mentality, or deploying specific behaviors in reaction to failure and in pursuit of better results, such as urging athletes to 'push harder', belittling, shouting, rejecting, humiliating – all considered as forms of emotional abuse if frequent and sustained (Gervis, 2010). These themselves contribute to an unhealthy training environment (Brackenridge and Rhind, 2010).

Concerns about social isolation and undermined competence are exacerbated by the phenomenon of athlete burnout, which Coakley (1992) identified as a more severe consequence of the social conditions in elite youth sport. Burnout results from excessive demands and the athlete feeling unable to meet them. It is characterized by physical and emotional exhaustion, which is often linked to overtraining, a reduced sense of accomplishment and devaluing of sport participation (Lemyre *et al.*, 2007). Common symptoms include poor sleep quality, lack of energy, chronic fatigue, feelings of helplessness and depression, nausea and frequently being ill (Gould and Dieffenbach, 2003; Lemyre *et al.*, 2007). Burnout is prevalent in youth athletes who were, or had been, involved in intensive and competitive training regimes (Coakley, 1992; Gould *et al.*, 1996). Additionally, Lemyre *et al.* (2007) found that youth athletes were often closer to the critical thresholds for burnout than adult elite athletes, suggesting they may be at higher risk.

Athletic identity

Immersion into the elite sports culture with its performance narrative has been associated with the development of an identity closely aligned to 'athletic role' (e.g., Lamont-Mills and Christensen, 2006). This potentially places at risk the development of a multifaceted well-rounded identity, an important developmental task that often has to be negotiated at a time coinciding with being involved in a TIDS (Wylleman and Lavallee, 2004), at risk. A one-dimensional athletic identity resonates with the behaviors, performance expectations and social norms within the competitive athletic context (e.g., Carless and Douglas, 2013). This typically single-minded identity can result in inadequate coping and disturbances in psychological states when dealing with the inevitable, but commonly temporary, set-backs that accompany high-level sport, such as injury, performance slumps or failures. Moreover, a strong athletic identity can lead to over-commitment to being an athlete at the cost of other identities, which can result in poor physical and mental health, including social isolation (Horton and Mack, 2000). Equally important, an overly developed athletic identity renders athletes ill-prepared for transitioning out of sport when this transition occurs prematurely (due to deselection or career-ending injury; Alfermann, 2000), or naturally (end of career; e.g., Lavallee *et al.*, 1997) (see Chapter 6). Harmful transitions of this sort can result in mental health problems, including identity loss, depression (Douglas and Carless, 2006, 2009), and jeopardized well-being (Sparkes, 1998).

Even though having an athletic identity brings some performance benefits (e.g., increased self-esteem, positive body image, willingness to work hard), its strong association with an overriding performance focus and 'winning at all cost mentality' can pose additional problems, such as the willingness to self-sacrifice or self-harm (Douglas and Carless, 2006; Nixon, 1992). While 'no pain, no gain' narratives persist (Carless and Douglas, 2013), willingness to risk one's health can also be related to the 'toxic jock' (Miller and Hoffman, 2009) side of the athletic identity, often underpinned by masculinity values. Here this refers to the social valuing of physical strength and size, aggressiveness and assertiveness. These values reinforce 'acting tough' in social situations, and often entails 'risk-taking and stoicism in the face of pain and injury' (Miller and Hoffman 2009: 352). TIDS with a particular evolved or inherent social culture, therefore, have the potential to encourage engagement in health compromising behaviors with potential immediate and long-term harm. For example, the risk of developing disordered eating patterns has been highlighted in sports like long-distance running and cycling where a specific body is required or valued. In particular, sports where a high lean body to fat mass ratio is: 1) linked to improved performance, 2) favoured aesthetically (e.g. gymnastics) or 3) provides a competitive advantage by offering a high power-to-weight ratio (e.g., sports working with weight classification such as rowing and wrestling) have been highlighted to increase this risk (Pipe, 2001; Sundgot-Borgen and Torstveit, 2010). Thus, youth athletes with stronger athletic identities may be more likely and more willing engage in such behaviors.

Devalued via deselection

Youth athletes involved in TIDS face the continuous threat of being deselected. Although there is a paucity of research exploring athletes' experiences with deselection, it seems realistic that the negative impacts of deselection could include substantial disruption of mood and psychological state, including feelings of anger, fear, anxiety, depression and humiliation (Brown and Potrac, 2009). Deselected sub-elite young footballers highlighted feeling 'disposed of with little thought or care' (Brown and Potrac, 2009: 152) when they were no longer deemed talented enough to reach the elite status. Even allowing for the almost inevitability of dese-lection from TIDS, it is important that this is handled sensitively, even to the extent that it becomes a requirement to provide direct links to other, possibly non-elite, sporting communities or other developmental opportunities (Bailey *et al.*, 2010).

Psycho-social: a case study of a specific TIDS – promising results?

Conducted in the Berlin/Brandenburg region of Germany, Beckmann *et al.* (2006) is a rare longitudinal study that tracked athletic and psycho-social development in an integrated system of school and elite sport over a six-year period (i.e., ages 12–18 years old). Youth athletes from soccer, volleyball, modern pentathlon, gymnastics, rhythmic gymnastics, judo, martial arts, canoeing, swimming, triathlon, athletics and rowing, were offered the opportunity to attend the sport school, which created the basis for three groups: 1) athletes attending the school but living at home; 2) a group attending the school and living (boarding) on site; and 3) a control group of non-sport students attending a school in the same geographical region with a similar educational program. Repeated assessments were made of the performance prerequisites, (e.g., body composition, endurance and power) and sport performance as well as the development of motivational concepts (i.e., volition, achievement motivation, action vs. state orientation), self-concept, stress and recovery.

Results highlighted that athletes, compared to controls, showed a 'starting point advantage' in social self-concept: they self-reported having more positive relationships with parents and peers. Over time, athletes' physical self-concept also developed more positively, scoring consistently higher on perceptions of sports competence, fitness and athleticism, while these scores decreased amongst controls. Contrary to expectations, athletes experienced neither higher strain nor lower recovery than controls, indicating that the presumption of having a 'double burden' – of school and sport – did not generate higher levels of perceived stress. The authors highlighted that, when managed well, a TIDS could *reduce* overall stress by delivering physical loads as an effective recovery to the mental demands of the program and vice versa. However, boarding athletes – who shared their living and social space with other athletes – seemed to be confronted with a higher availability for social comparison. They paid progressively more attention to nutrition and appearance, which potentially placed them at greater risk for developing body image and eating-related problems.

Interestingly, compared to controls, boarding athletes benefitted in terms of motivational volition. Volition or 'self will' (Elbe *et al.* 2005: 560) refers to the ability to sustain long-term goals and remain invested, and is seen as a constituent of self-regulation (i.e., a learned cognitive skill; Butler and Winne, 1995). Parallel research suggests that talented athletes, compared to non-athletic controls, develop superior self-regulation skills (Toering *et al.*, 2009). Such data indicate the potential of TID for positively impacting psychological functioning and cognitive skill. Importantly, volition development may also be a transferrable asset, contributing to skill and attainment in other life areas, such as school and work attainment. This study provides promise on how an intensive well-balanced system can be structured to bring about positive as opposed to negative outcomes.

Summary

Reflecting the focus and orientation of existing research, the potential negatives of TIDS involvement have perhaps featured more predominantly in this account. This may be because any form of intensified behavior raises concerns about greater risk of negative health outcomes. However, based on the peer-reviewed evidence, there are reasons to be optimistic about the positive contributions a well-developed TIDS can make to health and well-being. Ensuring positive, healthy, youth athlete development appears to hinge on careful and simultaneous balancing of multiple training (e.g., volume and intensity of training), psycho-logical (e.g., sense of autonomy, identity, efficacy), social context (sense of belonging) and cultural (e.g., TIDS values and narratives) factors. There are many potential positive health outcomes that can be achieved, including opportunities for physical activity, social interaction, learning, psychosocial development and exploration. Insights from longitudinal comparative studies like TOYA and Beckman *et al.* (2006) show the potential interaction of such factors on health-related outcomes. In the latter case, an integrated system involving sport, school and living, where resources were optimized, proved to be generally healthy. Importantly, the empirical evidence shows that this system was associated with reducing, or at least not increasing, perceived athlete stress and positively influencing psycho-social skill development. That said, these results might not be generalizable to TIDS in other sports and locations. Collectively, these studies provide several directions for future research and highlight the value of assessing equivalent outcomes in different delivery approaches.

Based on this review, it is reasonable to ask: 'what can be done to improve existing TIDS?' Practitioners directly involved in TID, might primarily review the 'healthiness' of their athlete development systems. This process could be assisted by independent observers, such as sport scientists or practitioners from other TID contexts. Such reviews may be best focused on improving existing practice, and not as an exercise of questioning or applying blame. As part of reviewing, athlete and TIDS monitoring could incorporate the three components of 'positive health': subjective, biological and functionality. Table 3.1 contains some suggestions but they are by no means exhaustive.

Table 3.1 Eight recommendations for healthy youth athlete development in TIDS

Recommendations
1 Monitor (e.g., weekly) athlete motivation (e.g., enthusiasm), confidence and subjective feeling (general positive feeling, sense of belonging) over time (e.g., using standard questionnaires).
2 Monitor training and competition load (i.e., frequency, volume and intensity) using standard recording methods (e.g., coach/athlete training diaries; athlete heart rate and/or GPS tracking; athlete ratings of perceived exertion); integrate rest and complete recovery periods.
3 Monitor athlete psychological, physical and behaviour responses to training and competition load (e.g., sleep quality, resting heart rate, appetite, energy levels, mood disturbance). Check for signs and symptoms of overtraining (e.g., using standard questionnaires).
4 Integrate strength and conditioning and physiotherapist screening prior to increases in training load exposure. Implement prehabilitation programmes to reduce or avoid injury in the biologically maturing athlete.
5 Monitor injury prevalence, type and nature of occurrence across and within TIDS. Integrate preventative steps, track player rehabilitation and recovery interventions.
6 Emphasise 'learning and personal development' in the social climate, as opposed to a winning and performance narratives at the youth athlete stage (e.g., up to 18 years of age).
7 Take a long-term development view. Promote social inclusion and belonging by limiting deselection. Permit long-term periods for health and performance development to occur in youth athletes. Remove emphasis on 'performance', and the accompanying perceptions of threat and fear of deselection.
8 Monitor holistic development. Balance TIDS involvement with development in other activities. Track and facilitate positive social relationships (e.g., peers, parents, family, teachers), education development (e.g., attainment) and engagement in alternative activity (i.e., exploration of interests). See a 'rounded athlete' as positive for health and performance.

Our stance is that TIDS can be described as 'healthy' when youth athletes feel safe, emotionally positive, enthusiastic, motivated to learn, involved and integrated, and where their actions are more self-determined. Poor health seems to emerge when demands are externally imposed, constrained or coerced by an elitist sporting culture and/or performance narrative. Biologically, athletes should be afforded opportunities to develop their physical capacities, within a period associated with physical and maturation change, but in safe progressive training environments where exposure to overtraining and injury risk is actively minimized. Finally, athletic motor and cognitive skills that underpin learning and performance will be acquired, and along with other features of positive health, have the potential to positively transfer into functioning in other daily life activities.

Overall, besides a pure concentration on athletic performance or biological capacity *per se*, those involved in TIDS (e.g., coaches, administrators, etc.) would be wise to monitor and positively impact athlete subjective well-being, as well as

other psycho-social capacities for functionality. When these features are integrated and developed successfully, we hypothesize a reciprocal benefit for
athletic development and performance. Central to this issue, though, are the
philosophical values and motivational stances of TIDS directors and practitioners. Where practitioners hold narrow notions of system purpose, perhaps because
they are overly focused on performance, their notions of 'health and harm' may
remain narrow and medicalized; their concerns may not extend beyond limiting
the incapacity resulting from injury. In contrast, TIDS designed more holistically
will account for a wider array of factors, including individual psychological well-
being, social interactions/settings and cultural context. This way lays the best
chance to reveal and develop the long-term capacities of youth athletes.

References

Alfermann, D. (2000) Causes and consequences of sport career termination', in D.
    Lavallee and P. Wylleman (eds) *Career Transitions in Sport: International
    perspectives*, Morgantown: WV: Fitness Information Technology, 45–58.
Bailes, J. E. and Cantu, R. C. (2001) 'Head injury in athletes', *Neurosurgery,* 48(1): 26–46.
Bailey, D. A., Mckay, H. A., Mirwald, R. L., Crocker, P. R. E. and Faulkner, R. A. (1999)
    'A six-year longitudinal study of the relationship between physical activity and bone
    mineral accrual in growing children: The University of Saskatchewan bone mineral
    accrual study', *Journal of Bone and Mineral Research*, 14(10): 1672–9.
Bailey, R., Collins, D., Ford, P., Macnamara, A., Toms, M. and Pearce, G. (2010)
    Participant Development in Sport: An academic review, Leeds: Sports Coach UK.
Baker, J., Cobley, S. and Schorer, J. (eds) (2012) *Talent Identification and Development in
    Sport: International perspectives*, London: Routledge.
Baxter-Jones, A. D. G. and Helms, P. J. (1996) 'Effects of training at a young age: a review
    of the Training of Young Athletes (TOYA) study', *Pediatric Exercise Science*, 8:
    310–27.
Baxter-Jones, A. D. G. and Maffulli, N. (2002) 'Intensive training in elite young female
    athletes', *British Journal of Sports Medicine*, 36(1): 13–15.
Baxter-Jones, A. D. G., Maffuli, N. and Helms, P. J. (1993) 'Low injury rates in elite
    athletes', *Archives of Disease in Childhood*, 68: 130–2.
Beckmann, J., Elbe, A., Szymanski, B. and Ehrlenspiel, F. (2006) *Chancen und risiken:
    Vom leben im verbundsystem von schule und leistungssport. Psychologische,
    soziologische und sportliche leistungsaspekte* (Auflage 2006 ed.): Bundesinstitut für
    Sportwissenschaft, Bonn.
Brackenridge, C. and Fasting, F. (eds) (2002) *Sexual Harassment and Abuse in Sport:
    International research and policy perspectives*, Whitting & Birch Ltd.
Brackenridge, C. and Rhind, D. (eds) (2010) *Elite Child Athlete Welfare: International
    perspectives*, London: Brunel University Press.
Branta, C. (2010) 'Sport specialization: Development and learning issues', *Journal of
    Physical Education, Recreation, and Dance*, 81: 19–28.
Brown, G. and Potrac, P. (2009) '"You've not made the grade, son": De-selection and
    identity disruption in elite level youth football', *Soccer and Society,* 10(2): 143–59.
Budgett, R. (1998) 'Fatigue and underperformance in athletes: The overtraining
    syndrome', *British Journal of Sports Medicine*, 32(2): 107–10.

Butler, D. L. and Winne, P. H. (1995) 'Feedback and self-regulated learning: A theoretical synthesis', *Review of Educational Research*, 65(3): 245–81.

Caine, D. J. and Golightly, Y. M. (2011) 'Osteoarthritis as an outcome of paediatric sport: an epidemiological perspective', *British Journal of Sports Medicine*, 45(4): 298–303.

Carless, D. and Douglas, K. (2009) '"We haven't got a seat on the bus for you" or "All the seats are mine": Narratives and career transition in professional golf', *Qualitative Research in Sport, Exercise and Health*, 1(1): 51–66.

Carless, D. and Douglas, K. (2013) '"In the Boat" but "Selling Myself Short": Stories, narratives, and identity development in elite sport', *Sport Psychologist*, 27(1): 27–39.

Christensen, M. K. and Sorensen, J. K. (2009) 'Sport of School? Dreams and dilemmas for talented young Danish football players', *European Physical Education Review*, 15(1): 115–33.

Coakley, J. (1992) 'Burnout among adolescent athletes: A personal failure or social problem?', *Sociology of Sport Journal*, 9(3): 271–85.

Cobley, S., Schorer, J. and Baker, J. (2012) 'Identification and development of sport talent: A brief introduction to a growing field of research and practice', in J. Baker, S. Cobley and J. Schorer (eds) *Talent Identification and Development in Sport: International perspectives*, Abingdon, Oxon: Routledge, 1–10.

Cobley, S., Miller, P., Till, K. and McKenna, J. (2013). 'The good and the bad of youth sport today: What about the unforeseen ethical issues?' in S. Harvey and R. Light (eds) *Ethics in Youth Sport: Policy and pedagogical applications*, London, Routledge, 74–91.

Corsellis, J. A., Bruton, C. J. and Freeman-Browne, D. (1973) 'The aftermath of boxing', *Psychological Medicine*, 3: 270–303.

Côté, J. and Hay, J. (2002) 'Children's involvement in sport: A developmental perspective', in J. M. Silva and D. Stevens (eds) *Psychological Foundations of Sport*, Boston: Merrill, 484–502.

Côté, J., Lidor, R. and Hackfort, D. (2009) 'ISSP Position Stand: To sample or to specialize? Seven postulates about youth sport activities that lead to continued participation and elite performance', *International Journal of Sport and Exercise Psychology*, 7(1): 7–17.

Dacyshyn, A. (1999) 'When the balance is gone', in J. Coackley and P. Donnelly (eds) *Inside Sports*, London: Routledge, 214–22.

David, P. (2005) *Human Rights in Youth Sport: A critical review of children's rights in competitive sports*, London: Routledge.

Diehl, K., Thiel, A., Zipfel, S., Mayer, J., Litaker, D. G. and Schneider, S. (2012) 'How healthy is the behavior of young athletes? A systematic literature review and meta-analyses', *Journal of Sports Science and Medicine*, 11(2): 201–20.

Donnelly, P. (1997) 'Child labour, sport labour: Applying child labour laws to sport', *International Review for the Sociology of Sport*, 32(4): 389–406.

Douglas, K. and Carless, D. (2006) 'Performance, discovery, and relational narratives among women professional tournament golfers', *Women in Sport and Physical Activity Journal*, 15(2): 14–27.

Douglas, K. and Carless, D. (2009) 'Abandoning the performance narrative: Two women's wtories of transition from professional sport', *Journal of Applied Sport Psychology*, 21(2): 213–30.

Elbe, A. M., Szymanski, B. and Beckmann, J. (2005) 'The development of volition in young elite athletes', *Psychology of Sport and Exercise*, 6: 559–69.

Elder, G. H. (1998) 'The life course as developmental theory', *Child Development*, 69: 1–12.

Emery, C. A. and Tyreman, H. (2009) 'Sport participation, sport injury, risk factors and sport safety practices in Calgary and area junior high schools', *Journal of Paediatric and Child Health*, 14: 439–44.

Emery, C. A., Meeuwisse, W. H. and McAllister, J. R. (2006) 'Survey of sport participation and sport injury in Calgary and area junior high schools', *Clinical Journal of Sports Medicine*, 16: 20–6.

Field, M., Collins, M.cW., Lovell, M. R. and Maroon, J. (2003) 'Does age play a role in recovery from sports-related concussion? A comparison of high school and collegiate athletes', *The Journal of Pediatrics*, 142(5): 546–53.

Fraser-Thomas, J. L., Côté, J. and Deakin, J. (2005) 'Youth sport programs: an avenue to foster positive youth development', *Physical Education and Sport Pedagogy*, 10(1): 19–40.

Gavett, B. E., Stern, R. A. and McKee, A. C. (2011) 'Chronic traumatic encephalopathy: A potential late effect of sport-related concussive and sub-concussive head trauma', *Clinics in Sports Medicine*, 30(1): 179–90.

Gervis, M. (2010) 'From concept to model: A new theoretical framework to understand the process of emotional abuse in elite child sport', in C. Brackenridge and D. Rhind (eds) *Elite Child Athlete Welfare: International perspectives*, London: Brunel University Press, 60–70.

Gonçalves, C. E. B., Rama, L. M. L. and Figueiredo, A. B. (2012) 'Talent identification and specialization in sport: An overview of some unanswered questions', *International Journal of Sports Physiology and Performance*, 7(4): 390–3.

Gould, D. (1993) 'Intensive sport participation and the prepubescent athlete: Competitive stress and burnout', in B. R. Cahill and A. J. Pearl (eds) *Intensive Participation in Children's Sports*, Champaign, IL: Human Kinetics, 19–38.

Gould, D. and Dieffenbach, K. (2002) 'Overtraining, underrecovery, and burnout in sport', in M. Kellmann (ed.) *Enhancing Recovery: Preventing underperformance in athletes*, Champaign, IL: Human Kinetics, 25–35.

Gould, D. and Dieffenbach, K. (2003) 'Psychological issues in youth sports: Competitive anxiety, overtraining, and burnout', in R. M. Malina and M. A. Clark (eds) *Youth Sports: Perspectives for a new century*, Monterey (CA): Coaches Choice, 149–70.

Gould, D., Udry, E., Tuffey, S. and Loehr, J. (1996) 'Burnout in competitive junior tennis players: A quantitative psychological assessment', *The Sport Psychologist*, 10(4): 322–40.

Gourley, M. M., McLeod, T. C. V. and Bay, R. C. (2010) 'Awareness and recognition of concussion by youth athletes and their parents', *Athletic Training and Sports Health Care: The Journal for the Practicing Clinician*, 2(5): 208–18.

Green, C. (2009) *Every Boy's Dream. English football future on the line*, London: A&C Publishers Ltd.

Greenwald, R. M., Gwin, J. T., Chu, J. J. and Crisco, J. J. (2008) 'Head impact severity measures for evaluating mild traumatic brain injury risk exposure', *Neurosurgery*, 62(4): 789–98.

Güllich, A. and Emrich, E. (2012a) 'Considering long-term sustainability in the development of world class success', *European Journal of Sport Science*, 14 (Supp.1): S383–S397.

Güllich, A. and Emrich, E. (2012b) 'Individualistic and collectivistic approach in athlete support programmes in the german high-performance sport system', *European Journal of Sport and Society*, 9(4): 243–68.

Harmon, K. G., Drezner, J. D., Gammons, M., Guskiewicz, K., Halstead, M., Herring, S., *et al.* (2013) 'American Medical Society for Sports Medicine position statement: Concussion in sport', *Clinical Journal of Sports Medicine*, 23: 1–18.

Hendriksen, K. (2010) 'The ecology of talent development in sport: A multiple case study of succesful athletic talent development environments in Scandinavia', doctoral dissertation. Online at: www.teammangekamp.dk/joomla/images/dokumenter/ henriksen_the_ecology_of_talent_development_in_sport.pdf (accessed 19 March 2014).

Horton, R. S. and Mack, D. E. (2000) 'Athletic identity in marathon runners: Functional focus or dysfunctional commitment?' *Journal of Sport Behavior*, 23(2): 101–19.

Kaleth, A. and Mikesky, A. (2010) 'Impact of early sport specialization: A physiological perspective', *Journal of Physical Education, Recreation, and Dance*, 81: 29–32.

Lamont-Mills, A. and Christensen, S. A. (2006) 'Athletic identity and its relationship to sport participation levels', *Journal of Science and Medicine in Sport*, 9: 472–8.

Lang, M. (2010) 'Intensive training in youth sport: A new abuse of power?' in M. Lang and K.P. Vanhoutte (eds) *Bullying and the Abuse of Power: From the playground to international relations*, Oxford: Freeland Inter-Disciplinary Press, 57–64.

Laure, P. and Binsinger, C. (2005) 'Adolescent athletes and the demand and supply of drugs to improve their performance', *Journal of Sports Science and Medicine*, 3: 272–7.

Lavallee, D., Grove, J. R. and Gordon, S. (1997) 'The causes of career termination from sport and their relationship to post-retirement adjustment among elite-amateur athletes in Australia', *The Australian Psychologist*, 32: 131–5.

Lemyre, P.-N., Roberts, G. C. and Stray-Gundersen, J. (2007) 'Motivation, overtraining, and burnout: Can self-determined motivation predict overtraining and burnout in elite athletes?', *European Journal of Sport Science*, 7(2): 115–26.

Maffulli, N. and Helms, P. (1988) 'Controversies about intensive training in young athletes', *Archives of Disease in Childhood*, 63(11): 1405–7.

Maffulli, N., Baxter-Jones, A. D. G. and Grieve, A. (2005) 'Long term sport involvement and sport injury rate in elite young athletes', *Archives of Disease in Childhood*, 90(5): 525–7.

Malina, R. M. (1994) 'Physical growth and biological maturation of young athletes', *Exercise and Sport Science Reviews*, 22: 389–433.

Malina, R. (2010a) 'Early sport specialization: Roots, effectiveness, risks', *Current Sports Medicine Reports, American College of Sports Medicine*, 9(6): 364–71.

Malina, R. (2010b) 'Physical activity and health of youth', *Science, Movement and Health*, 10(2): 271–7.

Martland, H. S. (1928) 'Punch drunk', *The Journal of the American Medical Association*, 91(15): 1103–7.

Matos, N. and Winsley, R. J. (2007) 'Trainability of young athletes and overtraining', *Journal of Sports Science and Medicine*, 6(3): 353–67.

McGillivray, D., Fearn, R. and McIntosh, A. (2005) 'Caught up in and by the beautiful game: A case study of Scottish professional footballers', *Journal of Sport and Social Issues*, 29(1): 102–23.

McKee, A. C., Cantu, R. C., Nowinski, C. J., Hedley-Whyte, E. T., Gavett, B. E., Budson, A. E., *et al.* (2009) 'Chronic traumatic encephalopathy in athletes: Progressive tauopathy following repetitive head injury', *Journal of Neuropathology and Experimental Neurology*, 68(7): 709–35.

Meeusen, R., Duclos, M., Gleeson, M., Rietjens, G., Steinacker, J. and Urhausen, A. (2006) 'Prevention, diagnosis and treatment of the overtraining syndrome', *European Journal of Sport Science*, 6(1): 1–14.

Miller, H. (1966) 'Mental after-effects of head injury', *Proceedings of the Royal Society of Medicine*, 59(3): 257–61.

Miller, K. E. and Hoffman, J. H. (2009) 'Mental well-being and sport-related identities in college students', *Sociology of Sport Journal*, 26(2): 335–56.

Morris, F. L., Naughton, G. A., Gibbs, J. L., Carlson, J. S. and Wark, J. D. (1997) 'Prospective ten-month exercise intervention in premenarcheal girls: Positive effects on bone and lean mass', *Journal of Bone and Mineral Research*, 12(9): 1453–62.

Myklebust, G. and Bahr, R. (2005) 'Return to play guidelines after anterior cruicate ligament surgery', *British Journal of Sports Medicine*, 39: 127–31.

National Association for Sport and Physical Education (2010) *Guidelines for Participation in Youth Sport Programs: Specialization versus multi-sport participation [Position Statement]*. Restion, VA: National Association for Sport and Physical Education.

Nixon, H. L. (1992) 'A social network anaysis of influences on athletes to play with pain and injuries', *Journal of Sport and Social Issues*, 16(2): 127–35.

Omalu, B. I., Bailes, J., Hammers, J. L. and Fitzsimmons, R. P. (2010) 'Chronic traumatic encephalopathy, suicides and parasuicides in professional American athletes: The role of the forensic pathologist', *The American Journal of Forensic Medicine and Pathology*, 31(2): 130–2.

Pipe, A. (2001) 'The adverse effects of elite competition on health and well-being', *Canadian Journal of Applied Physiology*, 26: S192–S201.

Preamble to the Constitution of the World Health Organization (1946) *Official Records of the World Health Organization*, 2: 100. Genevre: WHO.

Premier League (2011) *Elite Player Performance Plan (EPPP)*, London: Premier League.

Russell, W. D. and Limle, A. N. (2013) 'The relationship between youth sport specialization and involvement in sport and physical activity in young adulthood', *Journal of Sport Behavior*, 36(1): 82–98.

Sagar, S. S., Lavallee, D. and Spray, C. M. (2007) 'Why young elite athletes fear failure: Consequences of failure', *Journal of Sports Sciences*, 25(11): 1171–84.

Seligman, M. E. P. (2008) 'Positive health', *Applied Psychology: An International Review*, 57: 3–18.

Söderman, K., Pietilä, T., Alfredson, H. and Werner, S. (2002) 'Anterior cruciate ligament injuries in young females playing soccer at senior levels', *Scandinavian Journal of Medicine and Science in Sports*, 12: 65–68.

Sparkes, A. C. (1998) 'Athletic identity: An Achilles'heel to the survival of self', *Qualitative Health Research*, 8(5): 644–64.

Steffen, K. and Engebretsen, L. (2010) 'More data needed on injury risk among young elite athletes', *British Journal of Sports Medicine*, 44(7): 485–9.

Stern, R. A., Riley, D. O., Daneshvar, D. H., Nowinski, C. J., Cantu, R. C. and McKee, A. C. (2011) 'Long-term consequences of repetitive brain trauma: Chronic traumatic encephalopathy', *PM&R*, 3(10): S460–S467.

Sundgot-Borgen, J. and Torstveit, M. K. (2010) 'Aspects of disordered eating continuum in elite high-intensity sports', *Scandinavian Journal of Medicine and Science in Sports*, 20: 112–21.

Tenenbaum, G., Stewart, E., Singer, R. N. and Duda, J. (1997) 'Aggression and violence in sport: an ISSP position stand', *The Sport Psychologist*, 11(1): 1–7.

Till, K., Chapman, C., Cobley, S., O'Hara, J. and Cooke, C. (2012) 'Talent identification, selection and development in UK junior Rugby league: An evolving process', in J. Baker, S. Cobley and J. Schorer (eds) *Talent Identification and Development in Sport: International perspectives*, London: Routledge, 106–19.

Tobar, D. A. (2012) 'Trait anxiety and mood state responses to overtraining in men and women college swimmers', *International Journal of Sport and Exercise Psychology*, 10(2): 135–48.

Toering, T. T., Elferink-Gemser, M. T., Jordet, G. and Visscher, C. (2009) 'Self-regulation and performance level of elite and non-elite youth soccer players', *Journal of Sports Sciences*, 27: 1509–17.

Turner, A. P., Barlow, J. H. and Heathcote-Elliott, C. (2000) 'Long term health impact of playing professional football in the United Kingdom', *British Journal of Sports Medicine*, 332–7.

Tveit, M., Rosengren, B. E., Nilsson, J.-Å. and Karlsson, M. K. (2012) 'Former male elite athletes have a higher prevalence of osteoarthritis and arthroplasty in the hip and knee than expected', *American Journal of Sports Medicine*, 40(3): 527–33.

Tveit, M., Rosengren, B. E., Nilsson, J. Å., Ahlborg, H. G. and Karlsson, M. K. (2013a) 'Bone mass following physical activity in young years: a mean 39-year prospective controlled study in men', *Osteoporosis International*, 24(4): 1389–97.

Tveit, M., Rosengren, B. E., Nyquist, F., Nilsson, J. A. N. Å. and Karlsson, M. K. (2013b) 'Former male elite athletes have lower incidence of fragility fractures than expected', *Medicine and Science in Sports and Exercise*, 45(3): 405–10.

Ungerleider, S. (2001) *Faust's gold: Inside the East German doping machine*, New York: Thomas Dunne Books.

Uusitalo, A. L. T. (2001) 'Overtraining. Making a difficult diagnosis and implementing targeted treatment', *The Physician and Sportsmedicine*, 29: 35–50.

Wall, M. and Côté, J. (2007) 'Developmental activities that lead to dropout and investment in sport', *Physical Education and Sport Pedagogy*, 12(1): 77–87.

Wiersma, L. D. (2000) 'Risks and benefits of youth sport specialization: Perspectives and recommendations', *Pediatric Exercise Science*, 12(1): 13–22.

Williams, A. M. and Reilly, T. (2000) 'Talent identification and development in soccer', *Journal of Sports Sciences*, 18(9): 657–67.

Wylleman, P. and Lavallee, D. (2004) 'A developmental perspective on transitions faced by athletes', in M. R. Weiss (ed.) *Developmental Sport and Exercise Psychology: A lifespan perspective*, Morgantown, W.Va: Fitness Information Technology, 503–23.

Yung, P. S. H., Chan, R. H. K., Wong, F. C. Y., Cheuk, P. W. L. and Fong, D. T. P. (2007) 'Epidemiology of injuries in Hong Kong elite badminton athletes', *Research in Sports Medicine*, 15(2): 133–46.

4 Health and the athletic family

Edward Cope, Stephen Harvey and David Kirk

High performance sport places exceptional physical, psychological, and social demands on athletes who participate at this level (Starkes, 2003). In consideration of these demands, the World Health Organization's (WHO's) definition of health as 'a state of complete physical, mental and social well-being and not merely the absence of disease or infirmity' appropriately reflects the holistic nature of the challenge high performance athletes face in their quest to remain 'healthy'. Reaching high performance status depends on a multitude of different factors (Harvey *et al.*, 2013; Samela and Moraes, 2003) that include, but are not limited to, access to quality coaching and facilities (Baker and Horton, 2004), opportunities afforded through geographical location (MacDonald and Baker, 2013), and opportunities to engage in different types of practice activities (Memmert *et al.*, 2010). A key socializing agent in enabling athletes to compete at high performance levels is the family, as families play key roles in helping support athletes' development (Côté, 1999). Whilst WHO's definition of health considers a person's physical, mental, and social well-being, we have interpreted this definition to mean that these three aspects are inextricably linked. In other words, health is constituted by all three components.

Many high performance athletes have cited their parents as a crucial factor in enabling them to reach this level. For example, Michael Owen, the former England international soccer player has on a number of occasions highlighted his family's support as the primary reason why he was able to fulfill his dream of becoming a professional soccer player. Owen suggested his father's attendance at every game served as a 'comfort blanket' for him (*Metro*, 19 March 2013), and outlined how his father left a job he enjoyed for another he disliked so he could attend every one of his son's games. Similarly, former number one world ranked golfer Tiger Woods paid tribute to his parents as he declared that without their love, support, and guidance he would not have achieved such a consistently high level of performance (Woods, 1997). He made reference to his father as being instrumental in his golf development, yet he also stated that without the encouragement and support of his mother away from practice, he would not have developed and maintained his drive to achieve. These examples (among many others) show that the environment created by the family appears to be a key determinant in supporting an athlete's sporting development.

The purpose of this chapter is to review literature investigating the impact families have on the development of athletic performance. In addition, this chapter will, where possible, consider the impact athletic performance has on the health of the 'athletic family'; for the purpose of this chapter we assume the 'athletic family' to include athletes' family members (e.g., parents, siblings, partners) who support them in their pursuit and/or maintenance of high performance sport. To help guide this discussion, we use the Developmental Model for Sport Participation (DMSP) and Self-Determination Theory (SDT) as frameworks. We conclude the chapter with some recommendations as to what constitutes an optimal family environment to enable the development of high performance athletes and the maintenance of their health and the health of their families.

Developmental Model for Sport Participation

Fraser-Thomas *et al.* (2013) suggest levels of family support follow the process of sport socialization outlined within Côté's (1999) DMSP. Specifically, Fraser-Thomas *et al.* outlined three different developmental paths athletes experience as they move from childhood into adulthood; two paths involve high investment sport, while the other leads to recreational involvement. The first path to high investment involves entry into sport through the phases of sampling, specializing, and investment. Fraser-Thomas *et al.* (2013) propose that during the sampling phase, parents help to create a positive learning experience, with the focus being on participation and enjoyment, rather than performance and winning, with siblings likely being involved in sport in a similar manner. Athletes generally go into the specializing phase as they enter their early teenage years. Parent and sibling involvement may continue in much the same fashion as when athletes were in the sampling phase; however, parents may make sacrifices related to finances and time as their child becomes more committed to one or two sports. Athletes typically enter the investment phase in later adolescence, choosing to make a strong commitment to one sport, with aspirations of reaching a high performance level. During this phase, it is probable that parents continue to support their children, with increasing roles surrounding emotional support (e.g., engaging in open communication, providing honest feedback); however, siblings may experience feelings of jealously and rivalry. The second path to high investment involves early specialization, whereby athletes specialize early in one sport, which may place a higher demand on their parents' resources from a young age. Parents in this case may have to be mindful of distribution of resources between children, as this may create friction between siblings.

In our literature review, we have drawn upon findings of empirical studies examining the role of family throughout a range of sport development contexts, as athletes move through various phases of development before they reach a high performance level (Côté and Hay, 2002). As such, we offer an understanding of the influence of the family on athlete development, and the influence of athletes' performance on the health of the athletic family throughout developmental phases, which we believe contributes to understanding how family–athlete relationships may be most effective in these different phases of development. However, given the majority of reviewed studies did not provide details on participants' development pathways, we were unable to distinguish between athletes who had followed a path from sampling to high investment and those who had followed an early specialization pathway. Given this limitation, we use the stated age of athletes in these studies as a means by which to group athletes into different development phases.

Self-Determination Theory

Throughout the chapter, we discuss health from a psychosocial perspective and use SDT (Deci and Ryan, 2000) to explain how the athletic family can support the healthy athletic development of another family member. According to SDT, humans have three innate and developmentally persistent psychological needs, namely those for autonomy, competence, and relatedness (Deci and Ryan, 2000). *Autonomy* refers to the degree to which individuals feel volitional and responsible for their own behavior and, therefore, represents a need for validation of an athlete's actions (Ryan, 1995). Deci and Ryan (1985) argued factors that enhance *autonomy* facilitate intrinsic motivation, whereas those that promote a sense of being controlled (by an external source) diminish it. The need for *competence* concerns the degree to which athletes feel successful in their interactions with their social environment and experience opportunities which allow them to express their capabilities (Ryan and Deci, 2002). Finally, the need for *relatedness* is defined as the extent to which individuals feel a sense of belongingness and connectedness to others in their social environment (Ryan, 1995). For psychological health to be achieved, satisfaction of all three of these needs must be met (Deci and Ryan, 2000).

SDT has been used in a wide variety of sporting and non-sporting contexts to explain how psychological health and well-being of an individual are impacted by their social context. Subsequently, this theory offers an appropriate means by which to understand how the family can either support or thwart an athlete's motivational regulations (Deci and Ryan, 2000), which in turn can impact their physical and social health. Placed on a continuum, at one end is intrinsic motivation, which broadly explains why athletes participate due to their love of playing sport for its own sake. At the other end of the continuum is amotivation, describing the experiences of athletes who cannot recognize why it is they play sport (Quested and Duda, 2011). On the continuum between intrinsic motivation and amotivation is extrinsic motivation (Deci and Ryan, 2000), which can be self-determined or non-self-determined (Deci and Ryan, 2000). The most autonomous form of self-determined motivation is integrated regulation (i.e., participation to satisfy personal needs), followed by identified regulation (i.e., participation for internalized reasons). Non-self-determined extrinsic motivation includes introjected (i.e., participation through feelings of guilt) and external regulations (i.e., participation for rewards). Athletes who participate for non-self-determined reasons could be more at risk of psychological ill-being in one, two, or all of their basic psychological needs of *autonomy*, *competence*, and *relatedness* (Kasser and Ryan, 1996). The family, as the greatest social influence on a young athlete's participation (Fredricks and Eccles, 2005), can impact their self-determined behavior from both a need supporting and need thwarting perspective. In the following sections, we use the DMSP as a framework to discuss how the family can facilitate athletes' self-determined behavior rather than thwart it at each phase of development and, in doing so, ensure athlete psychosocial health and well-being (Deci and Ryan, 2008).

Sampling phase/early specialization phase

It has been proposed that athletes typically engage in the sampling phase or early specialization phase between the ages of 6–12 years (Côté, 1999). Consequently, this section focuses on studies among athletes primarily within this age range. A consistent finding in the research literature among children is that parents have considerable impact on their children's motivation to take part in sport (e.g., Brustad, 1992). Light and colleagues (Light and Curry, 2009; Light and Lemonie, 2010; Light *et al.*, 2013) conducted surveys and interviews with athletes aged 9–12 years focused on what attracted these athletes into sports clubs, and the reasons for their continued participation. One study using questionnaire data showed that of the 115 athletes in a swimming club context, 66 per cent joined because their parents suggested it to them, and 61 per cent stated that their parents influenced their decision to join (Light and Lemonie, 2010). In Light *et al.*'s (2013) study, 57 per cent of swimmers in clubs from France, Germany, and Australia joined their respective swimming clubs because their parents wanted them to. However, few swimmers in both studies felt pressure from their parents to join or even maintain participation. In the soccer club context (Light and Curry, 2009), 11 out of 20 athletes interviewed commented that their dads had enrolled them into the soccer program, with eight of the players mentioning an older sibling as being the reason for their initial participation. Baxter-Jones and Maffulli's (2003) study of talented young sports people concluded that their early involvement was heavily dependent upon their parents introducing them to sport, particularly in the case of swimming, with 70 per cent of athletes sampled citing this as their reason for initially taking part in this sport. A general conclusion from this study was that disinterested or less-motivated parents decreased the likelihood of talented youngsters continuing their participation.

In another recent study, Wheeler (2012) explored the role of family culture in influencing children's sport development. Semi-structured interviews were conducted with at least one parent and their child from eight different families. She found parents supported and encouraged their children to take part in sport because they perceived the children enjoyed it, it gave them the opportunity to make friends, keep fit, and healthy, and to promote future participation. These findings highlight that parental support and encouragement likely reinforce child athletes' self-determined behavior, as parents' reasons for encouraging their children were congruent with their child athletes' own reasons for participating.

They also found that parents who themselves had a background in sport were more likely to become involved in their children's sports participation.

In another qualitative study with 7–11 year old athletes, Keegan *et al.* (2009) found that when parents provided positive feedback, rewarded effort, and provided financial and emotional support, children perceived their intrinsic motivation to be either maintained or increased; however, children perceived their intrinsic motivational levels to decrease when rewards were given for performance outcomes. Defrancesco and Johnson's (1997) study of a prominent American tennis program examining athlete and parents' perceptions of winning and losing also sheds some light on parents' involvement: 64 per cent of athletes indicated that they believed their parents became very upset if they lost a match in which they did not try their hardest; 33 per cent of parents stressed the importance of winning, while 64 per cent indicated that winning was only moderately important. Nonetheless, 67 per cent of parents believed winning was really important to the athletic member of their family. Gould and colleagues' (2008) study examining junior tennis coaches' perspectives of parent behaviors suggests negative parental behaviors include emphasizing winning, attempting to control through becoming over-involved, and being overbearing and pushy. It follows that parents' overemphasis on winning and rewarding of top performances could thwart children's motivation by failing to meet their need for *autonomy* (Deci and Ryan, 2000). However, findings of Gould *et al.*'s studies with junior tennis coaches (2006, 2008) also suggest parents demonstrate a variety of positive behaviors, including a tendency to focus on process rather than outcome goals, emphasize their athletic child's holistic development, adopt a balanced approach that is supportive but not too overbearing, instill key core values such as hard work, and have a positive attitude and keep success in perspective; the facilitation of this type of environment has been suggested to support athletes' intrinsic motivations by meeting children's needs for *autonomy*, *competence*, and *relatedness* (Deci and Ryan, 2000).

Other factors such as socio-economic status and access to facilities may also play a role in elite athlete development. An interesting study conducted by Brockman *et al.* (2009) found parents' provision of financial support, in addition to their co-participation and modeling, served as means of encouraging children of middle to high socioeconomic status (SES) to participate in sports; however, in families of low SES, finances were often seen as a barrier to children's participation in structured sports, with parents encouraging physical activity (versus structured sports) through rewards and other forms of extrinsic motivation. As such, it seems families of low SES may offer less opportunity for children to experience *relatedness, autonomy, and competence* through sport. Nonetheless, not all studies reviewed confirm these findings. For example, Carlson (1988) found in his study with elite and non-elite tennis players that elite players came from families of lower SES backgrounds than those of non-elite players. Carlson's study also highlighted the potential importance of families' communities, as eight of the ten elite players originated from rural areas, whereas nine out of the ten non-elite players grew up in major urban centers. This conflicts with findings from Kirk *et al.*'s (1997b) study, which revealed that living in small geographical regions often limited parents' ability and willingness to support participation, due to lack of access to facilities. MacDonald *et al.* (2009) noted an optimum community size for talent development to be 50,000 to 500,000 persons, which may be considered autonomy supportive in that young children can engage in higher levels of *deliberate play*, activities that are inherently motivating and not necessarily highly structured (Côté and Hay, 2002). More specifically, when engaging in deliberate play, children are given choice and freedom as they assist in modifying rules and creating their own games, making the way sport is played different to its standardized, adult format, and hence potentially more autonomy supportive.

Specializing phase

According to the DMSP, athletes typically progress through the specializing phase between the ages of 12 and 15 years (Côté, 1999); therefore, this section considers studies of athletes primarily within this age range. In Keegan *et al.*'s (2010) examination of social influences in the specializing years, it was found that athletes were more motivated when their parents displayed autonomy supportive behaviors rather than controlling ones. For example, support and encouragement type behaviors from parents had a positive effect on motivation, whereas criticisms and negative feedback had an adverse effect on motivation. In line with these findings, Carlson's (1988) work with elite and non-elite tennis players found elite athletes felt less pressured to succeed than their non-elite counterparts. Collectively, these findings align with SDT, as parents who encourage a self-determined environment appear to promote more positive outcomes (i.e., motivation, performance).

Côté (1999) indicated that as children move through different developmental phases, sport becomes more time consuming, which in turn requires an increase in financial, logistical, and tangible support. This is in line with findings of numerous studies suggesting the importance of parents providing transport, watching their child play, buying equipment and covering transportation costs (Côté, 1999; Fredricks and Eccles, 2005; Kirk *et al.*, 1998; Wheeler, 2012). Gould *et al.*'s (2006) national survey with junior tennis coaches revealed that coaches perceived the best parents were those who provided logistical and financial support. While Côté (1999) found that families who were committed to their athletic child's involvement in sport somehow found a way to financially support their participation, Kirk *et al.*'s (1997a) study showed that parents described matters financially related to sport (i.e., equipment and transportation costs) as obstacles to their athletic child's sport participation. Similarly, Harwood and Knight's (2009) study of tennis parents found that funding their children to be able to play tennis was very stressful. Additional logistical challenges for parents of athletes in this phase of development involve balancing and spending equal amounts of time with all members of the family (i.e., siblings) and other sacrifices to the family's lifestyle (Harwood and Knight, 2009; Kay, 2000).

Investment phase

Typically, athletes move into the investment phase at approximately 15 years of age (Côté, 1999), although this depends on the nature of the sport as some athletes may specialize early as alluded to above. Harwood and Knight (2009) found one of the most stressful aspects of being a tennis parent was watching their child athlete take part in competitions and tournaments. In a study focused on parental behaviors in an elite tennis context, Lauer *et al.* (2010) conceptualized athletes' development as 'smooth', 'difficult', or 'turbulent' based on the behavior and support displayed by parents. Lauer and colleagues suggested that in order for parents to foster a healthy or 'smooth' relationship with their athletic child, they should not over emphasize the importance of tennis at the expense of other areas of their life. For those in the 'difficulty' pathway, more negative parental behaviors emerged as athletes began to specialize in tennis. It was at this point that an imbalance developed between the extents to which athletes were expected by their parents to invest into tennis compared to other life commitments. For those in the 'turbulent' pathway, negative parental behaviors started very early on in an athlete's development, with parents considering tennis to be most important in relation to other aspects of their athletic child's life. This resulted in negative psychosocial outcomes, namely early dropout due to a loss of intrinsic motivation for the sport.

Finally, in a novel study examining high performance athletes' relationships with their romantic partners, Jowett and Cramer (2009) reported athletes found it difficult to detach themselves from their athletic identity, leading to an increase in the likelihood that they would suffer from depression and an untrusting relationship. Conversely, athletes who were able to detach themselves from their athletic identity were more likely to maintain positive relationships with their partners. Of particular interest, however, is that athletes who were unable to detach themselves from their athletic identity actually had an increased ability to compete in elite level sport.

Providing family support for healthy athlete development

In the sections above, positive emotional support, autonomy supportive behaviors, and financial support from parents were consistently cited as important factors contributing to optimal healthy athletic development. Whilst we acknowledge that most data have been generated with athletes in the sampling/early specialization phase, this finding was consistent across all developmental phases. It would thus appear that these factors are essential to facilitating 'health' among high performance developing athletes. These findings are in line with past suggestions that a caring and supportive family environment where sport is not taken too seriously best motivates a child to take part in sport (Allender *et al.*, 2006).

Findings of our review support principles of SDT in that parental aspirations that were congruent with athletes' intrinsic motivations were often associated with positive outcomes, whereas a focus on extrinsic aspirations from parents was often associated with negative outcomes. For example, Keegan *et al.* (2010) found that when parents employed behaviors associated with an autonomy supportive environment, athletes experienced positive health and well-being outcomes. Furthermore, a focus from parents and other family members on values and behaviors that are compatible with athletes' intrinsic motivations were more likely to be internalized when less pressure was placed on the athlete (Grolnick *et al.*, 1997). If the family emphasizes the importance of extrinsic aspirations, athletes' basic psychological needs of *autonomy*, *competence* and *relatedness* will not be met (Deci and Ryan, 2000), which could result in high levels of emotional and physical exhaustion (Adie *et al.*, 2008). Moreover, it has been found that a determinant of burnout in elite adult athletes is the promotion of low self-determined, rather than high self-determined motives (Lonsdale *et al.*, 2009).

Emerging from this review of literature, we propose some tentative suggestions regarding how families can ensure healthy development. First, parental support provided must be congruent with the athlete's phase of development. The conceptual model proposed by Fraser-Thomas *et al.* (2013) provided us with a useful starting point in which to reflect on the family support required at the different phases of the DMSP. For athletes in the sampling phase it is vitally important that the relationships parents form and maintain with their athletic child are positive and supportive (Grolnick *et al.*, 1997). It is also important to note that children require an element of space, freedom, and choice in deciding their sports participation (Mageau and Vallerand, 2003). Consequently, parents have to be mindful of not being overbearing and pushy as this could result in drop out from sport and the associated detrimental health outcomes this brings. In the specializing phase, parents must continue to display autonomy supportive behaviors, while providing the financial and emotional support and resources required to practice and compete. As athletes begin to move into the investment phase, the sporting demands placed on them increase further (Baker *et al.*, 2003). Although, there is less research with athletes at this developmental phase, findings from Jowett and Cramer (2009) highlight the challenges of maintaining positive relationships with partners, given the investment of time and effort required to maintain participating at a high performance level.

Given that the family serves as the primary socializing agent in a young athlete's life (Harvey *et al.*, 2013), families need to be particularly sensitive to the importance of creating an environment that autonomously supports the athlete's motivations for participating. As athletes move through different developmental phases it remains important for parents to create non-pressuring environments where athletes do not feel they have to compete to satisfy their parents' wishes. Throughout development, parental focus should remain on rewarding effort and attitude, as opposed to prioritizing the importance of winning. Furthermore, parents should engage their child athlete in decisions about participation and investment in sport. Athletes should not be driven by feelings of guilt or the desire to please members of their family.

Health of the athletic family

Given the substantive financial and emotional support, and time invested and sacrificed by parents to enable their athletic child to participate in sport, findings regarding parents' stresses and challenges surrounding their child's sport involvement may not seem surprising. While there appears to be a growing focus on parent education in sport, most of this work has focused on parents' appropriate/inappropriate behaviors (e.g., Canada's *Respect in Sport*), highlighting a need for sport organizations to better support parents in the process of developing elite athletes. Moreover, siblings have the potential to provide important emotional support (Davis and Meyer, 2008), as well as act as role models (Côté, 1999). Consequently, one way of dealing with potential sibling jealousies is for parents to provide opportunities for co-participation with all members of the athletic family in certain activities, whether they are sporting or non-sporting pursuits. In addition, parents of multi-child families need to have greater awareness of spending quality leisure time with all their children in order to ensure the health of all family members. This may be especially important in lower SES families, who tend to spend less time co-participating in leisure time physical activity than those of middle and higher SES families (Brockman *et al.*, 2009). Spending leisure time as a family is therefore critical in maintaining the *relatedness* aspect of the self-determination framework suggested in this chapter and should be a primary recommendation for athletic families.

Recommendations for future research

In this chapter we reviewed literature on the role of families in athletes' development and performance through the lens of health. The review highlighted the sparseness of empirical research that focuses in these areas. For example, Harwood and Knight (2009) explained how parents had difficulty balancing their time equally between all siblings, yet no research has been undertaken to find out how siblings experience being part of a family that has a high performing athlete within it. Consequently, we suggest that in addition to generating data to better understand parents' roles, we must also explore roles of other family members.

As outlined above, parents may benefit from additional education and guidance with regard to optimally fostering their elite child athlete's development. Mageau and Vallerand (2003) outlined key behaviors for coaches aiming to create an autonomy-supportive environment that include: 1) providing as much choice as possible within specific limits and rules; 2) providing a rationale for tasks, limits, and rules; 3) inquiring about, and acknowledging, others' feelings; 4) allowing opportunities for athletes to take initiative and work independently; 5) providing non-controlling competence feedback; 6) avoiding overt control, guilt-inducing criticisms, controlling statements, and tangible rewards; and 7) preventing ego-involvement from taking place. Further research is necessary to determine if these characteristics also have relevance for parents of elite young athletes. Additional research is also necessary to better understand the optimal working relationship between parents and coaches to determine their specific roles in facilitating child athletes' holistic development. Such work could tap into effective club policies and philosophies on parent and coach behaviors and interactions. There may also be a niche for interventions studies aimed at better preparing athletes, their parents, and their families for the sport development journey.

In this chapter we also explored how the participation of the athlete impacted the health of the family. Whilst a handful of studies have highlighted general findings, there remains a paucity of research in this area (Davis and Meyer, 2008). The research that has been conducted provides a starting point in which to understand some of the factors that impact the health – or ill health – of parents and siblings. Future research must also consider the multiple perspectives of various family members, with a particular sensitivity to the voices of siblings.

In addition, it is clear that research undertaken with athletes in the specializing and investment stages is underdeveloped. As such, what we know about maintaining the health (particularly the mental health) of a high performance athlete is limited. We welcome research that generates more data about family influence on 'older' high performance athletes, and 'older' high performance athletes' influence on families.

Our final recommendations for future research relates to methodological approaches. We believe that in this area of research, employing mixed methodologies and/or multiple methodologies would be advantageous. Whilst we acknowledge the contribution quantitative and qualitative methods alone have made in advancing our understanding of this research area, we do believe that the use of mixed and/or multiple methodologies will further enhance our understanding of the family in sport. In particular, ethnographic or case study approaches would be especially welcomed given their relevance in being able to deal with the multiple perspectives in need of study. Also, we call for more research of a longitudinal nature, which investigates how family support changes as athletes move through different stages of the DMSP. On a final note, research that deals with the inter-relatedness of family members would offer deeper insights into the health of the athletic family as a whole, and not simply as individual members of that family.

References

Adie, J.W., Duda, J.L., and Ntoumanis, N. (2008) 'Achievement goals, competition appraisals, and the psychological and emotional welfare of sports participants', *Journal of Sport and Exercise Psychology*, 20: 220–35.

Allender, S., Cowburn, G., and Foster, C. (2006) 'Understanding participation in sport and physical activity among children and adults: A review of qualitative studies', *Health Education Research*, 21: 826–35.

Baker, J. and Horton, S. (2004) 'A review of primary and secondary influences on sport expertise', *High Ability Studies*, 15: 211–28.

Baker, J., Côté, J., and Abernethy, B. (2003) 'Learning from the experts: Practice activities of expert decision makers in sport', *Research Quarterly for Exercise and Sport*, 74: 342–7.

Baxter-Jones, A.D.G. and Maffulli, N. (2003) 'Parental influence on sport participation in elite young athletes', *Journal of Sports Medicine and Physical Fitness*, 43: 250–5.

Brockman, R., Jago, R., Fox, K.R., Thompson, J.L., Cartwright, K. and Page, A.S. (2009) '"Get off the sofa and go and play": Family and socioeconomic influences on the physical activity of 10–11 year old children', *BMC Public Health*, 9: 253–9.

Brustad, R. J. (1992) 'Integrating socialisation influences into the study of children's motivation in sport', *Journal of Sport and Exercise Psychology*, 14: 59–77.

Carlson, R. (1988) 'The socialisation of elite tennis players in Sweden: An analysis of the players' background and development', *Sociology of Sport Journal*, 5: 241–56.

Côté, J. (1999) 'The influence of the family in the development of talent in sport', *The Sports Psychologist*, 13: 395–417.

Côté, J. and Hay, J. (2002) 'Children's involvement in sport: A developmental perspective', in J.M. Silva and D. Stevens (eds) *Psychological Foundations of Sport*, Boston, MA: Allyn & Bacon, 484–502.

Davis, N.W. and Meyer, B.B. (2008) 'When siblings becomes competitor: A qualitative investigation of some-sibling competition in elite sport', *Journal of Applied Sport Psychology*, 20: 342–7.

Deci, E.L. and Ryan, R.M. (1985) *Intrinsic Motivation and Self-determination in Human Behavior*, New York: Academic Press.

Deci, E.L. and Ryan, R.M. (2000) 'The "what" and "why" of goal pursuits: human needs and the self-determination of behaviour', *Psychological Inquiry*, 11: 227–68.

Deci, E.L. and Ryan, R.M. (2008) 'Self-determination theory: A macrotheory of human motivation, development, and health', *Canadian Psychology*, 49: 182–5.

DeFrancesco, C. and Johnson, P. (1997) 'Athlete and parents perceptions in junior tennis', *Journal of Sport Behavior*, 20: 29–36.

Fraser-Thomas, J., Strachan, L., and Jeffrey-Tosoni, S. (2013) 'Family influence on children's involvement in sport', in J. Côté and R. Lidor (eds) *Conditions of Children's Talent Development in Sport*, Morgantown, WV: Fitness Information Technology, 179–96.

Fredricks, J.A. and Eccles, J.S. (2004) 'Parental influences on youth involvement in sports', in M. Weiss (ed.) *Developmental Sport and Exercise Psychology: A lifespan perspective*, Morgantown, WV: Fitness Information Technology, 145–65.

Fredricks, J.A. and Eccles, J.S. (2005) 'Family socialisation, gender, and sport motivation and involvement', *Journal of Sport and Exercise Psychology*, 27: 3–31.

Gould, D., Lauer, L., Rolo, C., Jannes, C., and Pennisi, N. (2006) 'Understanding the role parents play in tennis success: A national survey of junior tennis coaches', *British Journal of Sports Medicine*, 40: 632–6.

Gould, D., Lauer, L., Rolo, C., Jannes, C., and Pennisi, N. (2008) 'The role of parents in tennis success: Focus group interviews with junior coaches', *The Sport Psychologist*, 22: 18–37.

Grolnick, W.S., Deci, E.L., and Ryan, R.M. (1997) 'Internalization within the family: The Self-Determination Theory perspective', in J.E. Grusec and L. Kuczynski (eds) *Parenting and Children's Internalization of Values: A handbook of contemporary theory*, Hoboken, NJ: John Wiley & Sons, 135–61.

Harwood, C. and Knight, C. (2009) 'Understanding parental stressors: An investigation of British tennis parents', *Journal of Sport Sciences*, 27: 339–51.

Harvey, S., Jung, H., and Kirk, D. (2013) 'Sociological aspects of talent development', in J. Côté and R. Lidor (eds) *Conditions of Children's Talent Development in Sport*, Morgantown, WV: Fitness Information Technology, 209–30.

Jowett, S. and Cramer, D. (2009) 'The role of romantic relationships on athlete's perform- ance and well-being', *Journal of Clinical Sport Psychology*, 3: 58–72.

Kasser, T. and Ryan, R.M. (1996) 'Further examining the American dream. Differential correlates of intrinsic and extrinsic goals', *Personality and Social Psychology Bulletin*, 22: 80–7.

Kay, T. (2000) 'Sporting excellence: A family affair?', *European Physical Education Review*, 6: 151–69.

Keegan, R.J., Harwood, C.G., Spray, C.M., and Lavallee, D.E. (2009) 'A qualitative inves- tigation exploring the motivational climate in early-career sports participants: Coach, parent and peer influences on sport motivation', *Psychology of Sport and Exercise*, 10: 361–72.

Keegan, R.J., Spray, C., Harwood, C., and Lavellee, D. (2010) 'The motivational atmos- phere in youth sport: Coach, parent, and peer influences on motivation in specializing sport participants', *Journal of Applied Sport Psychology*, 22: 87–105.

Kirk, D., O'Connor, A., Carlson, T., Burke, P., Davis, K., and Glover, S. (1997a) 'Time commitments in junior sport: Social consequences for participants and their families', *Journal of Sport Behaviour*, 20: 51–73.

Kirk, D., Carlson, T., O'Connor, A., Burke, P., Davis, K. and Glover, S. (1997b) 'The economic impact on families of children's participation in junior sport', *The Australian Journal of Science and Medicine in Sport*, 29: 27–33.

Kirk, D., Penney, D., Carlson, T. and Braiuka, S. (1998) *Socio-economic Determinants of Junior Sport Participation in Queensland*, Queensland: University of Queensland Foundation.

Lauer, L., Gould, D., Roman, N., and Pierce, M. (2010) 'How parents influence junior tennis players development: qualitative narratives', *Journal of Clinical Sports Psychology*, 4: 69–92.

Light, R. and Curry, C. (2009) 'Children's reasons for joining sports clubs and staying in them: A case study of a Sydney soccer club', *ACHPER Australia Healthy Lifestyles Journal*, 56: 23–7.

Light, R. and Lemonie, Y. (2010) 'A case study on children's reasons for joining and remaining in a French swimming club', *Asian Journal of Exercise and Sports Science*, 7: 27–33.

Light, R., Harvey, S., and Memmert, D. (2013) 'Why children join and stay in sports clubs: Case studies in Australian, French and German swimming clubs', *Sport, Education and Society*, 18: 550–66.

Lonsdale, C., Hodge, K., and Rose, E. (2009) 'Athlete burnout in elite sport: A self-deter- mination perspective', *Journal of Sport Sciences*, 27: 785–95.

MacDonald, D.J. and Baker, J. (2013) 'Circumstantiated development: Birthdate and birth- place effects on athlete development', in J. Côté and R. Lidor (eds) *Conditions of Children's Talent Development in Sport*, Morgantown, WV: Fitness Information Technology, 197–208.

MacDonald, D.J., Cheung, M., Côté, J., and Abernethy, B. (2009) 'Place but not date of birth influences the development and emergence of athletic talent in American Football', *Journal of Applied Sport Psychology*, 21: 80–90.

Mageau, G.A. and Vallerand, R.J. (2003) 'The coach-athlete relationship: A motivational model', *Journal of Sports Sciences*, 21: 883–904.

Memmert, D., Baker, J., and Bertsch, C. (2010) 'Play and practice in the development of sport specific creativity in team ball sports', *High Ability Studies*, 21: 3–18.

Metro (2013) 'Michael Owen retires from football with touching statement', *Metro*, 19

March 2013. Online at: http://metro.co.uk/2013/03/19/michael-owen-retires-from-football-with-touching-statement-3548559/ (accessed 10 April 2014).

Quested, E. and Duda, J.L. (2011) 'Enhancing children's positive sport experiences and personal development: A motivational perspective', in I. Stafford (ed.) *Coaching Children in Sport*, London: Routledge, 123–38.

Ryan, R.M. (1993) 'Agency and organization: Intrinsic motivation and autonomy, and the self in psychological development', in J.E. Jacobs (ed.) *Nebraska Symposium on Motivation, 1992: Developmental perspectives on motivation*, Lincoln, NE: University of Nebraska Press, 1–56.

Ryan, R. M. (1995) 'Psychological needs and the facilitation of integrative processes', *Journal of Personality*, 63: 397–427.

Ryan, R.M. and Deci, E.L. (2002) 'An overview of Self-Determination Theory: An organismic-dialectical perspective', in E.L Deci and R.M. Ryan (eds) *Handbook of Self-determination Research*, Rochester, NY: Boydell & Brewer, Ltd, 3–36.

Salmela, J.H. and Moraes, L.C. (2003) 'Development to expertise: the role of coaching, families, and cultural contexts', in J.L. Starkes and K.A. Ericsson (eds) *Expert Performance in Sports: Advance in research on sport expertise*, Champaign, IL: Human Kinetics, 275–94.

Starkes, J.L. (2003) 'The magic and the science of sport expertise: Introduction to sport expertise research and this volume', in J.L. Starkes and K.A. Ericsson (eds) *Expert Performance in Sports: Advance in research on sport expertise*, Champaign, IL: Human Kinetics, 3–16.

Wheeler, S. (2012) 'The significance of family culture for sports participation', *International Review for the Sociology of Sport*, 47: 235–52.

Woods, T. (1997) *Training a Tiger: A father's guide to raising a winner in both golf and life*, New York: Harper Collins.

5 Injury risk and long-term effects of injury in elite youth sports

Tanis J. Hastmann-Walch and Dennis J. Caine

Physical activity has important and wide-ranging health benefits. Specifically, in children and youth, physical activity increases cardiovascular fitness and muscular strength, reduces body fat, improves cardiovascular and metabolic disease risk profiles, enhances bone health and reduces symptoms of depression and anxiety (US Department of Health and Human Services, 2009). Similarly, participation in youth sports, including at the elite level, is also associated with the potential for these wide-ranging health benefits. Youth sport participation also addresses an important public health concern related to lack of physical activity. Importantly, youth sport participation has been associated with decreased odds of excessive television viewing and computer/video game use (Lowry *et al.*, 2013), which is related to obesity and potential adverse health outcomes.

Participation in youth sports is increasingly popular and widespread in North America. Trends over recent decades include increased numbers of participants in some sports, particularly girls, increased duration and intensity of training, earlier specialization and year-round training, and increased difficulty of skills practiced (Caine, 2010). These trends appear to extend beyond North American culture, as indicated by the advent of Youth Olympic Games (Ruedl *et al.*, 2012; Steffen and Engebretson, 2010, 2011) where about 3500 athletes from more than 200 National Olympic Committees (NOCs) participated in the first Summer Youth Olympic Games held in Singapore in August 2010. More recently, about 1000 athletes from 69 NOCs participated in the first Winter Youth Olympic Games in Innsbruck, Austria, in January 2012 (Ruedl *et al.*, 2012). The Youth Olympic Games for athletes aged 14–18 years, with its cultural and educational emphasis, is one approach of the International Olympic Committee (IOC) to showcase high-level sports as a catalyst to improving the health of youth (Steffen and Engebretsen, 2011).

Engaging in sports activities at a young age has numerous health benefits, but also carries increased risk of injury. Injuries can counter the beneficial effects of sports participation at a young age if an athlete is unable to continue to participate because of the residual effects of injury. In the short-term, severe injury may require a young athlete to drop out of his or her sport, at least temporarily. In the long term, many talented athletes choose or are forced to give up their promising sports careers (Steffen and Engebretsen, 2010). For example, several studies involving highly competitive young gymnasts attest to the role that injury may play in the early retirement of some of these young athletes (Caine *et al.*, 2003; Dixon and Fricker, 1993; Jackson *et al.*, 1989; Katz and Scerpella, 2003; Singer and Roy, 1984).

To date, few studies have evaluated the long-term health outcomes of youth sports injury (Maffulli *et al.*, 2010, 2011), particularly with respect to elite youth athletes. This chapter employs an epidemiological lens in its examination of the incidence of injury in elite youth sport and will offer a review of current knowledge related to the long-term health outcomes associated with injury incurred during participation in elite youth sport. Due to the paucity of research that actually follows injured elite youth longitudinally, extrapolation related to health outcomes will be made from injury studies of youth athletes as well as of former elite youth athletes, particularly those whose injuries can be traced back to their involvement in elite youth sport. Topics to be covered include incidence of injury, catastrophic injury, physeal injury and growth disturbance, and the residual effects of injuries.

Incidence of injury

Multiple studies of the epidemiology of injury among youth participants involved in recreational and competitive sports have been conducted to provide information on the incidence and distribution of injury affecting this population, as well as to determine potential risk factors for injury (Caine *et al.*, 2006a, 2008). However, there remains a paucity of information on injury risk related to the young athlete competing in elite, high-level sport. If one adopts the predefined age range of 14–18 years, with 'elite' reflecting competition at the national or international level (Steffan and Engebretson, 2010), then a search of the literature reveals eight studies presenting exposure-based (per 1000 hours) data on overall and/or competition injury risk of youth and adolescent elite athletes (see Table 5.1). These studies may be divided into 'seasonal' follow-up (Johnson *et al.*, 2009; Le Gall *et al.*, 2006, 2008; Yung *et al.*, 2007) and tournament studies (European and World Championships) held over multiple years (Hägglund *et al.*, 2009; Junge and Dvorak, 2007; Junge *et al.*, 2004; Waldén *et al.*, 2007).

Injury rates for seasonal studies include soccer (Johnson *et al.*, 2009; Le Gall *et al.*, 2006, 2008) and badminton (Yung *et al.*, 2007). Injury rates for training in these sports ranged from 1.4 to 4.6 injuries per 1000 hours training (Johnson *et al.*, 2009; Le Gall *et al.*, 2008), with injury rates in soccer higher for males (4.6) than for females (3.9) in two studies (Le Gall *et al.*, 2006, 2008). Competition injury rates ranged from 5.9 to 22.4 injuries per 1000 hours, with rates higher for females (22.4) than males (11.2) (Johnson *et al.*, 2009; Le Gall *et al.*, 2006, 2008), and higher rates in soccer than badminton. Overall injury rates (competition and training) were only provided in three studies (Le Gall *et al.*, 2006, 2008; Yung *et al.*, 2007) and ranged from 3.1 to 6.4 injuries per 1000 hours, with injury rates higher for females than males in soccer.

Table 5.1 Incidence rate of injuries sustained by elite young athletes

Reference	Study design	Group studied	Sport	No. of injuries	Rate per 1000 hours training	Rate per 1000 hours competition	Rate per 1000 hours overall
Johnson et al., 2009	Prospective 6 years	Male N=292 9–16 years	Soccer	476	1.4	10.5	
Le Gall et al., 2008	Prospective 8 years	Female N=119 15–19 years	Soccer	619	4.6	22.4	6.4
Le Gall et al., 2006	Prospective 10 years	Male N=528 13–15 years	Soccer	1152	3.9	11.2	4.8
Yung et al., 2007	Retrospective 1 year	M & F N=11 16–21 years	Badminton	37	2.8	5.9	3.1
Hägglund et al., 2009	Prospective	Female U19 N=433	Soccer	43	1.1–7.4	11.7–28.2	4.9–13.5
		Male U19 N=436	Soccer	38	1.5–2.1	16.3–27.8	6.4–13.0
		Male U17 N=433	Soccer	40	1.2–5.6	20.7–28.6	8.4–13.3
Waldén et al., 2007	Prospective	Male U19 N=144	Soccer	17	2.9	30.4	13.4
Junge and Dvorak, 2007	Prospective	Female U19 N=432	Soccer			68–85	
Junge et al., 2004	Prospective	Male U17 N=576	Soccer			51.0–88.1	

Overall injury rates for U19 and U17 European and World soccer championships were generally higher than those reported for seasonal studies and ranged from 4.9–13.5 injuries per 1000 hours exposure (Hägglund *et al.*, 2009; Junge and Dvorak, 2007; Junge *et al.*, 2004; Waldén *et al.*, 2007). Training injury rates at these championships ranged from 1.1–7.4 injuries per 1000 hours (Hägglund *et al.*, 2009; Waldén *et al.*, 2007). In contrast, competition injury rates ranged from 11.7–88.1 injuries per 1000 hours (Hägglund *et al.*, 2009; Junge and Dvorak, 2007; Junge *et al.*, 2004; Waldén *et al.*, 2007). None of these studies provided information on the long-term effects of these injuries.

The injury rates reported for elite youth sports are difficult to compare to injury rates reported for studies of non-elite young athletes due to diversity of study populations, short periods of data collection and small sample sizes in some studies, low response rates and recall bias associated with the use of questionnaires, and variable injury definitions and methods of data collection (Caine *et al.*, 2008). With the exception of soccer, few data are available on the epidemiology of injury among young elite athletes competing in sports that were included in the Youth Summer Olympic Games (Steffen and Engebretsen, 2010). These data show that apart from soccer, little knowledge on injury risk among elite youth athletes involved in summer Olympic sports is available.

Ruedl *et al.* (2012) reported on the nature of incidence of injury incurred by young athletes participating in the first Winter Youth Olympic Games 2012 in Innsbruck, Austria. Among the 1021 registered athletes, a total of 111 injuries were incurred, resulting in a reported incidence of 108.7 injuries per 1000 registered athletes. Unfortunately, this injury rate represents a clinical incidence (number of injuries per 'k' athletes), which does not account for the potential variance in exposure among participants and sports for risk for injury (Knowles *et al.*, 2006). For example, an injured gymnast who is not training in all parts of practice is not at the same risk of incurring injury as compared to a non-injured gymnast. Incidence rate is the preferred measure of incidence in research studies because it can accommodate differences in exposure time of individual athletes.

The lack of epidemiologic injury data on young elite athletes is disturbing, especially given the high volume and intensity of training characteristic of elite sports participation. As van Mechelan *et al.* (1992) argued, sound epidemiologic data are needed to provide an essential basis for identifying the extent of the injury problem, uncovering risk factors and mechanisms for injury, using interventions to reduce the risk or severity of injury, and evaluating the efficacy of injury countermeasures.

Catastrophic injury

The worst-case scenario in youth sports is catastrophic injury. According to the National Center for Catastrophic Sports Injuries (www.unc.edu/depts/nccsi), a catastrophic injury may be direct (brain/spinal cord injury or skull/spinal fracture) or indirect (systemic failure as a result of exertion or by a complication secondary to a non-fatal injury). These injuries are further categorized as fatalities, non-fatal injuries (permanent severe functional disability), and serious injuries (no permanent disability but significant initial injury, for example vertebral fracture without paralysis).

The National Center for Catastrophic Sports Injury Research (NCCSIR) monitors the occurrence of catastrophic injuries in both high school and college sports in the US. While these types of injuries are relatively rare, they can cause permanent neurological deficits or even death (e.g., cardiac death), which can be devastating to the athletes and their families (Zemper, 2010). In addition to the physical pain and injury, catastrophic injuries are associated with depression and mental health problems (Shuer and Dietrich, 1997). The risk of sudden death due to cardiac failure or heat exertion may be of particular concern in elite youth athletes given the volume and intensity of training required for competition at this level.

School sports with the highest direct catastrophic injury rates (per 100,000 participants), and therefore the highest risk level for these types of injuries, are ice hockey, (American) football, gymnastics, wrestling, cheerleading, and lacrosse (Zemper, 2010). Although these are school data it is important to note that some of these sports are also included in national and international youth sport competitions, including the Junior Olympics. There are presently no incidence data on catastrophic injuries among elite young athletes. Nonetheless, there have been some highly publicized spinal cord injuries affecting elite-level gymnasts from China and the US (Cowley and Westly, 1998; Ryan, 1995). Notably, however, a report on injuries sustained during the 2002, 2003, and 2004, USA National Gymnastics Artistic Gymnastics Championships revealed that no gymnasts were treated for catastrophic injuries (Caine and Nassar, 2005). Notably, no catastrophic injuries were reported during the first Winter Youth Olympic Games 2012 in Innsbruck (Ruedl *et al.*, 2012).

Epiphyseal injuries and growth disturbance

As with all growing athletes, elite youth athletes are at risk of incurring growth plate injury. Physeal injuries account for between 15 per cent and 30 per cent of all skeletal injuries in youth (Perron *et al.*, 2002). Disturbed physeal growth as a result of acute epiphyseal plate injury can result in limb length discrepancy, angular deformity, or altered joint mechanics (Ogden, 2000), all of which may affect health adversely. In particular, osteoarthritis may result from chondral damage at the time of growth plate injury, articular incongruity, or joint mal-alignment (Bible and Smith, 2009; Peterson, 2007). Although more elaborate classification systems for describing acute physeal injuries are available, the system most widely used was developed by Salter and Harris (1963). A detailed description and illustration of the injury types is available at the following link: www.niams.nih.gov/Health-infor/Growth-Plate-Injuries/default.asp.

A systematic review of case series literature on epiphyseal plate injuries revealed that 38.3 per cent of 826 acute cases were sport-related, representing a variety of competitive and training levels, and 45 cases (14.2 per cent) were associated with growth disturbance (Caine *et al.*, 2006b). These injuries occur in a variety of sports, although gridiron football is most often reported (Caine *et al.*, 2006b). The peak frequency is consistent with the pubescent growth spurt in each gender (Schuch *et al.*, 2011; Bailey *et al.*, 1989).

Incidence data on acute epiphyseal injuries are lacking for competitive sports, especially elite sports (Caine *et al.*, 2006b). Physeal injury was not included as an injury type or descriptive category in the report of sports injuries sustained during the first Winter Youth Olympic Games in Innsbruck (Ruedl *et al.*, 2012) or the reports of injuries affecting young elite male and female soccer players (Le Gall *et al.*, 2006, 2008).

The available data indicate that the percent of acute epiphyseal injuries may vary from 1–30 per cent in studies of competitive sports injuries (Caine *et al.*, 2006b). Two injury studies of elite and sub-elite Australian gymnasts indicated a clinical incidence of 11.5 to 12.5 injuries per 100 gymnasts (Kolt and Kirkby, 1995, 1999), although there is no information provided on the long-term follow-up of these injuries.

There is also concern that the tolerance limits of the physis may be exceeded by the repetitive physical loading required in many sports, particularly during the adolescent growth spurt (Caine *et al.*, 2006b). Although typical youth overuse injuries such as the common apophyseal injuries and patellofemoral pain are readily recognized and treated with little long-term sequalae, the physis is a site of overuse injury that can be easily overlooked (DiFiori, 2010).

Epiphyseal growth plate stress injuries are thought to develop when repetitive loading of the extremity disrupts metaphyseal perfusion that in turn inhibits ossification of the chondrocytes in the zone of provisional calcification (DiFiori *et al.*, 2006). The hypertrophic zone continues to widen as the chondrocytes continue to transition from the germinal layer to the proliferative zone (Jaramillo *et al.*, 1993). Widening of the physis may be seen radiographically, whereas physeal cartilage extension into the metaphysis has been shown with magnetic resonance imaging (MRI) (Dwek *et al.*, 2009; Jaramillo *et al.*, 1993).

Baseball pitchers were the first youth athletes, more than 50 years ago, to present with physeal stress injury (Dotter, 1953). Since then, multiple case reports have documented stress changes of the proximal humeral physis in youth baseball pitchers (Ricci and Mason, 2004). Often associated with persistent pain in the throwing arm, stress changes of the proximal humeral growth plate, or 'Little League Shoulder', represent a sequelae of repetitive traction and rotational forces across the epiphysis and growth plate (Hansen, 1982).

Similar cases of stress-related proximal humeral physeal widening have been reported in other youth athletes involved in overhead sports including cricket, gymnastics, badminton, sport climbing, swimming, and volleyball (Caine *et al.*, 2006b). There is also a recent report of physeal stress lesions of the clavicle in an elite male gymnast (Carson *et al.*, 2012). However, the most commonly reported upper extremity physeal stress injuries involve the distal radial physes of gymnasts, representing a range of competitive levels, including elite (Caine *et al.*, 2006b). Most reports describe distal radius stress reaction with a radiographically widened and irregular physis, especially on the metaphyseal side. However, one study using MRI, documented physeal cartilage extension into the metaphysis (Dwek *et al.*, 2009).

Cases of stress-related lower extremity physeal injuries involving the proximal tibia, distal femur, distal tibia and fibula, and first metatarsus have been reported in youth athletes representing a broad range of sports that involve running (DiFiori *et al.*, 2006). There is also preliminary evidence that the development of cam-type deformity (excess of bone at the upper surface of the femoral head), secondary to stress-related alteration in the proximal femoral physis during adolescence, may be influenced by impact sports practice in sports such as soccer and elite basketball (Agricola *et al.*, 2012; Siebenrock *et al.*, 2013). Individuals with cam-type deformity may, in turn, be at increased risk of subsequent development of secondary coxarthrosis (Siebenrock *et al.*, 2011).

Although incidence data are lacking, there is evidence of the existence of stress-related physeal injury affecting young athletes representing a variety of sports and training levels, including elite youth. Most of these injuries resolved without growth complication during short-term follow-up. However, there are also reports of stress-related partial and complete epiphyseal closure in athletes representing basketball, baseball, dance, gymnastics, football, rugby, and tennis, and representing a variety of competitive levels, including elite youth athletes (Albanese *et al.*, 1989; Bak and Boeckstyns, 1997; Ejnisman *et al.*, 2007; Howe *et al.*, 1997; Laor *et al.*, 2006; Nanni *et al.*, 2005; Sato *et al.*, 2002; Shih *et al.*, 1995; Shybut *et al.*, 2008). These data are consistent with results from animal studies where prolonged intense physical training may precipitate pathological changes in the physis and, in extreme cases, produce growth disturbance and eventually osteoarthritis (Caine and Golightly, 2011; Caine *et al.*, 2006b).

Residual effects of injury

Osteoarthritis

A public health concern regarding long-term consequences of youth sport injury and sports participation is the risk of development of osteoarthritis (OA) at a relatively young age (Caine and Golightly, 2011; Marshall and Golightly, 2007). OA is a clinical syndrome that results from a progressive loss of articular cartilage accompanied by attempted repair of cartilage, and in many instances the formation of subchondral bone cysts and osteophytes (Buckwalter, 2003). OA is the most common form of arthritis and affects 27 million people in the US, probably reflecting the aging of the population and the obesity epidemic (Lawrence *et al.*, 2008).

Although OA generally affects older adults, injury-mediated OA, or post-traumatic OA, has been observed in former athletes who are young adults and can be linked to injury incurred during participation in youth sports, including physeal injury (Golightly *et al.*, 2011). Based on their review of elite sports participation and OA, Hunter and Ekstein (2009) concluded that elite athletes who perform high-impact activities and put undue stress on the joints increase the risk of hip and knee OA, especially in the presence of a joint injury. The knee, in particular, is the most common joint site for OA and, combined with the ankle, are the leading locations for injury in youth sports (Caine *et al.*, 2006a). Notably, Ruedl and colleagues (2012), reporting on injuries incurred during the first Winter Youth Olympic Games, noted that the most common injury location was the knee (14 per cent).

Not surprisingly, the most common joint site for OA is the knee. At the knee, anterior cruciate ligament (ACL), meniscus, and articular cartilage injuries are closely linked to knee OA (Gelber *et al.*, 2000; Roos, 2005; Theln *et al.*, 2006). Studies of meniscus and ACL injuries suggest a link between previous injury and the development of OA. In a study of 67 Swedish female soccer players with a confirmed ACL injury sustained before 20 years of age, radiographic evidence of OA was present in 51 per cent of the injured knees after 12 years, compared with 8 per cent in the uninjured knees (Lohmander *et al.*, 2007).

Similarly, in 219 male soccer players, 14 years after ACL injury (age range at injury, 16–42 years), the prevalence of radiographic knee OA was 41 per cent in the injured knees versus 4 per cent in the uninjured knees (Von Porat *et al.*, 2004). In long-term follow-up studies of young athletes with meniscus surgery, more than 50 per cent had knee OA and associated pain with functional impairment (Abdon *et al.*, 1990; Dai *et al.*, 1997; Manzione *et al.*, 1983; McNicholas *et al.*, 2000; Medlar *et al.*, 1980; Wroble *et al.*, 1992; Zaman and Leonard, 1981). It is evident that knee injury incurred during youth sport contributes to early onset OA development in some individuals, as supported by animal models of ACL/meniscus injuries and human adult studies (Little *et al.*, 1997; Roos *et al.*, 1998).

Spine of former athletes

Spinal injuries in youth elite athletes are of critical importance due to the devastating consequences and reduced quality of life that accompanies such injuries. Youth are more susceptible to spinal cord injuries due to greater mobility of the spine because of its immaturity. This mobility is due to their undeveloped neck musculature, lax ligaments, shallow angulations of facet joins, and incomplete ossification of their vertebrae (Jagannathan *et al.*, 2006). Understanding the long-term consequences of non-catastrophic spine injuries in youth is necessary to reduce injury, paralysis, bone mineral density changes, and degeneration later in life.

Spine injuries are most common in contact sports, such as football, ice hockey, and wrestling (Bailes *et al.*, 2007). Additionally, youth athletes competing at an elite level often endure high intensity training at an early age. Poor technique, physical preparation, and/or overuse are often the cause of spine injuries that have long-lasting effects (Foster *et al.*, 1989). Disc degeneration is a normal occurrence in aging; however, the process has been shown to occur sooner and with greater pain and/or symptoms in former youth elite athletes (Burnett *et al.*, 1996; Grandhed and Morelli, 1988). Baranto and colleagues (2006) examined back pain and degeneration in young elite divers (aged 10–21) for five years. Results showed that most divers had a history of back pain and new abnormalities, or deterioration of an abnormality at the time of follow-up.

Schmitt *et al.* (2005) examined bone mineral density and degenerative changes of the lumbar spine in former elite track and field athletes. Dual energy x-ray absorptiometry showed that throwers, pole vaulters, and jumpers had higher bone mineral density compared to former marathon athletes. In an earlier study, Schmitt *et al.* (2004) investigated the occurrence of degenerative radiographic changes of the lumbar spine in former elite athletes representing different track and field disciplines. When comparing track and field sports, throwing and jumping athletes had a higher risk of radiographic changes in the lumbar spine compared to runners and jumpers (Schmitt *et al.*, 2004). Elite javelin throwers, exclusively, have been shown to have greater frequency of spondylolysis and spondylolistheis compared to the general population, after 20 years (Schmitt *et al.*, 2001). In contrast, degenerative changes in this population showed only mild changes, comparable to individuals engaged in physical work (Schmitt *et al.*, 2001).

Disc degeneration is a late sign of injury, and is of critical concern to former elite athletes compared to non-athletes (Lundin *et al.*, 2001). This may be a result of sport participation, however, muscular strength (Timpka *et al.*, 2013) and physical activity (Hasler, 2013) have been shown to be protective against back pain, and disability from back pain is less common in athletes compared to non-athletes (Videman *et al.*, 1995). Nevertheless, public health strategies in youth athletes are needed to prevent degenerative changes to the spine and back pain in adulthood.

Concussion

A concussion is defined as "any mild closed head injury involving altered cognitive functioning (e.g., confusion, memory loss, disorientation) or signs or symptoms (e.g., headache, dizziness, balance problems, nausea) or brief loss of consciousness of no longer than one minute following a direct or indirect blow to the head" (Kontos *et al.*, 2013: 718). Sports that are considered high-risk for concussions include football, hockey, wrestling, rugby, soccer, and lacrosse. Any direct blow to the head/face or a blow to the body that transmits a force to the brain can cause a concussion (McCrory *et al.*, 2009).

As a result of their sheer volume and potential for catastrophic injury, pediatric concussions are viewed as a public health concern (Wiebe *et al.*, 2011). More than 250,000 patients aged 8–19 years presented to emergency departments in the US for sport-related concussions between 2001 and 2005 (Bakhos *et al.*, 2010). Gessel and co-workers (2007), using data from the High School Reporting Information Online (RIO), reported that concussions represented 8.9 per cent of all high school injuries. Although gridiron football was the sport associated with the highest rate of concussions among high school athletes, of particular interest are the higher rates of concussions seen in youth female athletes compared to their male counterparts in soccer and basketball (Gessel *et al.*, 2007; Powell and Barber-Foss, 1999; Schulz *et al.*, 2004).

Data on concussions sustained during elite youth sport participation are scarce. During the 2012 Winter Youth Olympic Games in Innsbruck, 10 per cent of all injuries were head injuries and more than two-thirds of these injuries (7.2 per cent) were concussions, with most of these occurring in alpine skiing and snowboarding (Ruedl *et al.*, 2012). Notably, in longitudinal studies of French elite youth soccer players, only two concussions were reported for males (Le Gall *et al.*, 2006) and two for females (Le Gall *et al.*, 2008).

Children and adolescents take longer than adults to recover after a concussion, which underscores the need for a more conservative approach to management and return to play (Guskiewicz and Valovich McLeod, 2011). Cognitive sequelae of concussion, including impaired memory, poor attention, and lack of concentration, may negatively impact a child's ability to learn and attend to schoolwork (Iverson *et al.*, 2006; Kirkwood *et al.*, 2006, 2008; McCrory *et al.*, 2004). Long-term consequences of untreated and unresolved brain trauma experienced during youth sport include physical, psychosocial, and cognitive/memory symptoms, and may result in post-concussion syndrome (Hall and Chapman, 2005). However, a majority of concussions have acute, temporary symptoms that resolve themselves in weeks or months (Sterr *et al.*, 2006).

General conclusions

The health outcomes related to youth elite sport participation emphasize the importance of youth engaging in physical activity and sports, such as increased cardiovascular fitness and muscular strength, reduced body fatness, and many others. However, participation at an elite level at a young age increases risk of injury and severe residual effects, with long-lasting consequences. This review summarized the current knowledge related to adverse effects associated with youth elite sport participation and included: incidence of injury, catastrophic injury, physeal injuries, and growth disturbance, and the residual effects of injury, including osteoarthritis, spine injuries, and concussion. Elsewhere in this text the long-term morbidity and mortality effects are reviewed (Chapter 8).

An increasing number of youth are engaging in elite-level sports, yet, there is a lack of information regarding the incidence and long-term effects of injury to these athletes. Many studies have examined the short-term consequences of elite-level sport participation, with competition injury rates far exceeding training injury rates (Hägglund *et al.*, 2009; Junge and Dvorak, 2007; Junge *et al.*, 2004; Waldén *et al.*, 2007). However, long-term prospective studies are needed to provide a better understanding of the long-term health related effects of injury sustained during elite youth sports participation. Much of the current information related to our knowledge of long-term health outcomes is due to retrospective studies of former elite youth athletes.

Given the life-changing impact injury can have on elite youth athletes, both in the short and long term, the current paucity of well-designed epidemiological studies of all forms of elite youth sports injuries is disturbing. The importance of establishing denominator-based injury surveillance in obtaining an accurate picture of injury risk and severity and as a basis for testing risk factors cannot be overemphasized. Systematic injury surveillance of this highly competitive population is needed to monitor injuries, identify high-risk sports, and ensure new knowledge on injury trends, which can form the basis for further research on injury risk factors, injury mechanisms, and injury prevention. We feel that there is an ethical imperative for elite youth sports governing bodies, both nationally and internationally, to provide incentive and guidance for epidemiological research in all forms of elite youth sport.

References

Abdon, P., Turner, M. S., Pettersson, H., Lindstrand, A., Stenstrom, A. and Swanson, A. J. (1990) 'A long-term follow-up study of total meniscectomy in children', *Clinical Orthopaedics and Related Research*, 257: 166–70.

Agricola, R., Bessems, J., Ginai, A. Z., Heijboer, M. P., van der Heijden, R. A., Verhaar, J A. *et al.* (2012) 'The development of cam-type deformity in adolescent and young male soccer players', *American Journal of Sports Medicine*, 40: 1099–106.

Albanese, S. A., Palmer, A. K., Kerr, D. R., Carpenter, C. W., Lisi, D. and Levinsohn, E. M. (1989) 'Wrist pain and distal growth plate closure of the radius in gymnasts', *Journal of Pediatric Orthopaedics*, 9: 23–8.

Bak, K. and Boeckstyns, M. (1997) 'Epiphysiodesis for bilateral irregular closure of the distal radial physis in a gymnast', *Scandinavian Journal of Medicine and Science in Sports*, 7: 363–6.

Bakhos, L. L., Lockhart, G. R., Myers, R. and Linakis, J. G. (2010) 'Emergency department visits for concussion in young child athletes', *Pediatrics*, 126(3): e550–6.

Bailes, J. E., Petschauer, M., Guskiewicz, K. M. and Marano, G. (2007) 'Management of cervical spine injuries in athletes', *Journal of Athletic Training*, 42(1): 126–34.

Bailey, D. A., Wedge, J. H., McCulloch, R. G., Martin, A. D. and Bernhardson, S. C. (1989) 'Epidemiology of fractures of the distal end of the radius in children as associated with growth', *Journal of Bone and Joint Surgery*, 71: 1225–31.

Baranto, A., Hellstrom, M., Nyman, R., Lundin, O. and Sward, L. (2006) 'Back pain and degenerative abnormalities in the spine of young elite divers: a 5-year follow-up magnetic resonance imaging study', *Knee Surgery, Sports Traumatology, Arthroscopy*, 14(9): 907–14.

Bible, J. E. and Smith, B. G. (2009) 'Ankle fractures in children and adolescent', *Techniques in Orthopaedics*, 24: 211–19.

Buckwalter, J. A. (2003) 'Sports, joint injury, and posttraumatic osteoarthritis', *Journal of Orthopaedic and Sports Physical Therapy*, 33: 578–88.

Burnett, A. F., Khangure, M. S., Elliott, B. C., Foster, D. H., Marshall, R. N. and Hardcastle, P. H. (1996) 'Thoracolumbar disc degeneration in young fast bowlers in cricket: A follow-up study', *Clinical Biomechanics*, 11(6): 305–10.

Caine, D. J. (2010) 'Are kids having a rough time of it in sports?', *British Journal of Sports Medicine*, 44: 1–3.

Caine, D. J. and Golightly, Y. M. (2011) 'Osteoarthritis as an outcome of paediatric sport: An epidemiological perspective', *British Journal of Sports Medicine*, 45: 52–6.

Caine, D. and Nassar, L. (2005) 'Gymnastics injuries', in D. Caine and N. Muffulli (eds) *Epidemiology of Pediatric Sports Injuries*, Medicine and Sport Sciences, 48, Basel: Karger, 18–58.

Caine, D., Knutzen, K. and Howe, W. (2003) 'A three-year epidemiological study of injuries affecting young female gymnasts', *Physical Therapy in Sport*, 4: 10–23.

Caine, D., Caine, C. and Maffulli, N. (2006a) 'Incidence and distribution of pediatric sport-related injuries', *Clinical Journal of Sports Medicine*, 16: 500–53.

Caine, D., DiFiori, J. and Maffulli, N. (2006b) 'Physeal injuries in children's and youth sports: Reasons for concern?', *British Journal of Sports Medicine*, 40: 749–60.

Caine, D., Maffulli, N. and Caine, C. (2008) 'Epidemiology of injury in child and adolescent sports: injury rates, risk factors, and prevention', *Clinical Journal of Sports Medicine*, 27(1): 19–50.

Carson, J. T., McCambridge, T. M., Carrino, J. A. and McFarland, E. G. (2012) 'Case report: bilateral epiphyseal clavicular stress-related lesions in a male gymnast', *Clinical Orthopaedics and Related Research*, 470(1): 307–11.

Cowley, J. and Westly, M. (1998) 'A gymnast's long fall: A minor misstep leaves China's best vaulter paralysed: can new drugs help her walk again?', *Newsweek*, 3 August, 56.

Dai, L., Zhang, W. and Xu, Y. (1997) 'Meniscal injury in children: Long-term results after meniscectomy', *Knee Surgery, Sports Traumatology, Arthroscopy*, 5: 77–9.

DiFiori, J. (2010) 'Overuse injury of the physis: A "growing" problem', *Clinical Journal of Sports Medicine*, 20(5): 336–7.

DiFiori, J., Caine, D. and Malina, R. (2006) 'Wrist pain, distal radial growth plate injury, and ulnar variance in the young gymnast', *American Journal of Sports Medicine*, 34: 840–9.

Dixon, M. and Fricker, P. (1993) 'Injuries to elite gymnasts over 10 yr', *Medicine and Science in Sport and Exercise*, 25(12): 1322–9.

Dotter, W. E. (1953) 'Little leaguer's shoulder-fracture of the proximal humeral epiphyseal cartilage due to baseball pitching', *Guthrie Clin Bull*, 23: 68–72.

Dwek, J. R., Cardoso, F. and Chung, C. R. (2009) 'MR imaging of overuse injuries in the skeletally immature gymnast: Spectrum of soft-tissue and osseous lesions in the hand and wrist', *Pediatric Radiology*, 39: 1310–16.

Ejnisman, B., Andreoli, C. V., Pochini, A. D. C., Monteiro, G. C., Faloppa, F., Cohen, M. and Skap, A. Y. (2007) 'Proximal humeral epiphysiolysis in a gymnast', *Acta Ortopedica Brasileira*, 15: 290–1.

Foster, H., John, D., Elliott, B. C., Ackland, T. and Fitch, K. (1989) 'Back injuries to young fast bowlers in cricket: a prospective study', *British Journal of Sports Medicine*, 23(3): 150–4.

Gelber, A. C., Hochberg, M. C., Mead, L. A., Wang, N. Y., Wigley, F. M. and Klag, M. J. (2000) 'Joint injury in young adults and risk for subsequent knee and hip osteoarthritis', *Annals of Internal Medicine*, 133(5): 321–8.

Gessel, L. M., Fields, S. K., Collins, C. L., Dick, R. W. and Comstock, R. D. (2007) 'Concussions among United States high school and collegiate athletes', *Journal of Athletic Training*, 42(4): 495–503.

Golightly, Y. M., Marshall, S. W. and Caine, D. J. (2011) 'Future shock: Youth sports and osteoarthritis risk', *Lower Extremity Review*, 3(10): 22–7.

Grandhed, H. and Morelli, B. (1988) 'Low back pain among retired wrestlers and heavy-weight lifters', *American Journal of Sports Medicine*, 16(5): 530–3.

Guskiewicz, K. M. and Valovich McLeod, T. C. (2011) 'Pediatric sport-related concussion', *Physical Medicine and Rehabilitation*, 3(4): 353–64.

Hägglund, M., Waldén, M. and Ekstrand, J. (2009) 'UEFA injury study-an injury audit of European championships 2006 to 2008', *British Journal of Sports Medicine*, 43(7): 483–9.

Hall, R. C. and Chapman, M. J. (2005) 'Definition, diagnosis, and forensic implications of postconcussional syndrome', *Psychosomatics*, 46(3): 195–202.

Hansen, N. B. (1982) 'Epiphyseal changes in the proximal humerus of an adolescent baseball pitcher', *American Journal of Sports Medicine*, 10(6): 380–4.

Hasler, C. C. (2013) 'Back pain during growth', *Swiss Medical Weekly*, 143: w13714.

Howe, W. B., Caine, D., Bergman, G. D. and Keeler, L. W. (1997) 'Wrist pain-gymnastics', *Medicine and Science in Sports and Exercise*, 29: S151.

Hunter, D. J. and Eckstein, F. (2009) 'Exercise and osteoarthritis', *Journal of Anatomy*, 214(2): 197–207.

Iverson, G. L., Brooks, B. L., Collins, M. W. and Lovell, M. R. (2006) 'Tracking neuropsychological recovery following concussion in sport', *Brain Injury*, 20(3): 245–52.

Jackson, D. W., Silvino, N. and Reiman, P. (1989) 'Osteochondritis in the female gymnast's elbow', *Arthroscopy*, 5(2): 129–36.

Jagannathan, J., Dumont, A. S., Prevedoo, D. M., Shaffrey, C. I. and Jane, J. A. (2006) 'Cervical spine injuries in pediatric athletes: Mechanisms and management', *Journal of Neurosurgery*, 21(4): E6.

Jaramillo, D., Laor, T. and Zaleske, D. J. (1993) 'Indirect trauma to the growth plate: Results of MR imaging after epiphyseal and metaphyseal injury in rabbits', *Radiology*, 187(1): 171–8.

Johnson, A., Doherty, P. J. and Freemont, A. (2009) 'Investigation of growth, development, and factors associated with injury in elite schoolboy footballers: prospective study', *British Medical Journal*, 338: b490.

Junge, A. and Dvorak, J. (2007) 'Injuries in female football players in top-level international tournaments', *British Journal of Sports Medicine*, 41(Suppl 1): i3–7.

Junge, A., Dvorak, J., Graf-Baumann, T. and Peterson, L. (2004) 'Football injuries during FIFA tournaments and the Olympic Games, 1998–2001: Development and implementation of an injury-reporting system', *American Journal of Sports Medicine*, 32(1Suppl): 80S–89S.

Katz, D. A. and Scerpella, T. A. (2003) 'Anterior and middle column thoracolumbar spine injuries in young female gymnasts. Report of seven cases and review of the literature', *American Journal of Sports Medicine*, 31: 611–16.

Kirkwood, M. W., Yeates, K. O. and Wilson, P. E. (2006) 'Pediatric sport-related concussion: A review of the clinical management of an oft-neglected population', *Pediatrics*, 117(4): 1359–71.

Kirkwood, M. W., Yeates, K. O., Taylor, H. G., Randolph, C., McCrea, M. and Anderson, V. A. (2008) 'Management of pediatric mild traumatic brain injury: A neuropsychological review from injury through recovery', *The Clinical Neuropsychologist*, 22(5): 769–800.

Knowles, S. B., Marshall, S. W. and Guskiewicz, K. M. (2006) 'Issues in estimating risks and rates in sports injury research', *Journal of Athletic Training*, 41: 207–15.

Kolt, G. S. and Kirkby, R. J. (1999) 'Epidemiology of injury in elite and subelite female gymnasts: a comparison of prospective and retrospective findings', *British Journal of Sports Medicine*, 33(5): 312–18.

Kolt, G. S. and Kirkby, R. J. (1995) 'Epidemiology of injuries in Australian female gymnasts', *Sports Medicine, Training and Rehabilitation*, 6: 223–31.

Kontos, A. P., Elbin, R. J., Fazio-Sumrock, V. C., Burkhart, S., Swindell, H., Maroon, J. and Collins, M. W. (2013) 'Incidence of sports-related concussion among youth football players aged 8–12 years', *Journal of Pediatrics*, 163(3): 717–20.

Laor, T., Wall, E. J. and Vu, L. P. (2006) 'Physeal widening in the knee due to stress injury in child athletes', *American Journal of Roentgenology*, 186(5): 1260–4.

Lawrence, R. C., Felson, D. T., Helmick, C. G., Arnold, L. M., Choi, H., Deyo, R. A. *et al.* (2008) 'Estimates of the prevalence of arthritis and other rheumatic conditions in the United States. Part II', *Arthritis and Rheumatism*, 58(1): 26–35.

Le Gall, F., Carling, C., Reilly, T., Vandewalle, H., Church, J. and Rochcongar, P. (2006) 'Incidence of injuries in elite French youth soccer players: A 10-season study', *American Journal of Sports Medicine*, 34(6): 928–38.

Le Gall, F., Carling, C. and Reilly, T. (2008) 'Injuries in young elite female soccer players: An 8-season prospective study', *American Journal of Sports Medicine*, 36: 276–84.

Little, C., Smith, S., Ghosh, P. and Bellenger, C. (1997) 'Histomorphological and immuno-histochemical evaluation of joint changes in a model of osteoarthritis induced by lateral meniscectomy in sheep', *Journal of Rheumatology*, 24(11): 2199–209.

Lohmander, L. S., Englund, P. M., Dahl, L. L. and Roos, E. M. (2007) 'The long-term consequence of anterior cruciate ligament injuries: osteoarthritis', *American Journal of Sports Medicine*, 35(10): 1756–9.

Lowry, R., Lee, S. M., Fulton, J. E, Demissie, Z. and Kann, L. (2013) 'Obesity and other correlates of physical activity and sedentary behaviors among US high school students', *Journal of Obesity*. Online at: www.hindawi.com/journals/jobe/2013/276318/.

Lundin, O., Hellstrom, M., Nilsson, I. and Sward, L. (2001) 'Back pain and radiological changes in the thoraco-lumbar spine of athletes. A long-term follow-up', *Scandinavian Journal of Medicine and Science in Sports*, 11(2): 103–9.

Maffulli, N., Longo, U. G., Gougoulias, N., Loppini, M. and Denaro, V. (2010) 'Long-term health outcomes of youth sports injuries', *British Journal of Sports Medicine*, 44(1): 21–5.

Maffulli, N., Longo, U. G., Spiezia, F. and Denaro, V. (2011) 'Aetiology and prevention of injuries in elite young athletes', *Medicine and Sport Science*, 56: 187–200.

Manzione, M., Pizzutillo, P. D., Peoples, A. B. and Schweizer, P. A. (1983) 'Meniscectomy in children: a long term follow-up study', *American Journal of Sports Medicine*, 11(3): 111–15.

Marshall, S. W. and Golightly, Y. M. (2007) 'Sports injury and arthritis', *North Carolina Medical Journal*, 68(6): 430–3.

McCrory, P., Meeuwisse, W., Johnston, K., Dvorak, J., Aubry, M., Molloy, M. and Cantu, R. (2009) 'Consensus statement on Concussion in Sport 3rd International Conference on Concussion in Sport held in Zurich, November 2008', *Clinical Journal of Sports Medicine*, 19(3): 185–200.

McCrory, P., Collie, A., Anderson, V. and Davis, G. (2004) 'Can we manage sport-related concussion in children the same as in adults?', *British Journal of Sports Medicine*, 38(5): 516–19.

McNicholas, M. J., Rowley, D. I., McGurty, D., Adalberth, T., Abdon, P., Lindstrand, A. and Lohmander, L. S. (2000) 'Total meniscectomy in adolescence: A 30-year follow-up', *Journal of Bone and Joint Surgery (Br)*, 82–B(2): 217–21.

Medlar, R. C., Mandiberg, J. J. and Lyne, E. D. (1980) 'Meniscectomies in children. Report of long term results (mean, 8.3 years) of 26 children', *American Journal of Sports Medicine*, 8(2): 87–92.

Nanni, M., Butt, S., Mansour, R., Muthukumar, T., Cassar-Pullicino, V. N. and Roberts, A. (2005) 'Stress-induced Salter–Harris I growth plate injury of the proximal tibia: First report', *Skeletal Radiology*, 34(7): 405–10.

National Center for Catastrophic Sports Injury Research (NCCSIR) (no date) 'Definition of injury'. Online at: www.unc.edu/depts/nccsi/NCCSIR_injuryterms (accessed 1 July 2013).

Ogden, J. A. (2000) *Skeletal Injury in the Child*, New York: Springer-Verlag.

Perron, A. D., Miller, M. D. and Brady, W. J. (2002) 'Orthopedic pitfalls in the ED: Pediatric growth plate injuries', *American Journal of Emergency Medicine*, 20(1): 50–4.

Peterson, H. E. (2007) *Epiphyseal Growth Plate Fractures*, Berlin: Spring-Verlag.

Powell, J. W. and Barber-Foss, K. D. (1999) 'Traumatic brain injury in high school athletes', *Journal of the American Medical Association*, 282(10): 958–63.

Ricci, A. R. and Mason, D. E. (2004) 'Little league shoulder: Case report and literature review', *Delaware Medical Journal*, 6(1): 11–24.

Roos, E. M. (2005) 'Joint injury causes knee osteoarthritis young adults', *Current Opinion in Rheumatology*, 17(2): 195–200.

Roos, H., Lauren, M., Adalberth, T., Roos, E. M., Jonsson, K. and Lohmander, L. S. (1998) 'Knee osteoarthritis after meniscectomy: Prevalence of radiographic changes after twenty-one years, compared with matched controls', *Arthritis and Rheumatism*, 41(4): 687–93.

Ruedl, G., Schobersberger, W., Pocecco, E., Blank, C., Engebretsen, L.,Soligard, T. *et al.* (2012) 'Sports injuries and illnesses during the first Winter Youth Olympic Games 2012 in Innsbruck, Austria', *British Journal of Sports Medicine*, 46(15): 1030–7.

Ryan, J. (1995) *Pretty Girls in Little Boxes: The making and braking of elite gymnasts and figure skaters*, New York: Doubleday.

Salter, R. B. and Harris, W. R. (1963) 'Injuries involving the epiphyseal plate', *Journal of Bone and Joint Surgery*, 45(3): 587–622.

Sato, T., Shinozaki, T., Fukudo, T., Watanabe, H., Aoki, J., Yanagawa, T. and Takagishi, K. (2002) 'Atypical growth plate closure: a possible chronic Salter and Harris Type V injury', *Journal of Pediatric Orthopedics. Part B*, 11(2): 155–8.

Schmitt, H. and Gerner, J. H. (2001) 'Paralysis from sport and diving accidents', *Clinical Journal of Sports Medicine*, 11(1): 17–22.

Schmitt, H., Brocai, D. R. and Carstens, C. (2001) 'Long-term review of the lumbar spine in javelin throwers', *Journal of Bone and Joint Surgery (Br)*, 83(3): 324–27.

Schmitt, H., Dubljanin, E., Schneider, S. and Schiltenwolf, M. (2004) 'Radiographic changes in the lumbar spine in former elite athletes', *Spine*, 29(22): 2554–9.

Schmitt, H., Friebe, C., Schneider, S. and Sabo, D. (2005) 'Bone mineral density and degenerative changes of the lumbar spine in former elite athletes', *International Journal of Sports Medicine*, 26(6): 457–63.

Schuch, T., Hanson, C., Goodwin, B. J., Romanick, M. and Caine, D. (2011) 'A hospital-based study of pediatric sport and recreational injuries', *Safe Kids Grand Forks Newsletter*, December 2011.

Schulz, M. R., Marshall, S. W., Mueller, F. O., Yang, J., Weaver, N. L., Kalsbeek, W. D. and Bowling, J. M. (2004) 'Incidence and risk factors for concussion in high school athletes, North Carolina, 1996–1999', *American Journal of Epidemiology*, 160(10): 937–44.

Shih, C., Chang, C. Y. and Penn, I. W. (1995) 'Chronically stressed wrists in adolescent gymnasts: MR imaging appearance', *Radiology*, 195(3): 855–59.

Shuer, M. L. and Dietrich, M. S. (1997) 'Psychological effects of chronic injury in elite athletes', *Western Journal of Medicine*, 166(2): 104–9.

Shybut, T. B. and Rose, D. J., Strongwater, A. M. (2008) 'Second metatarsal physeal arrest in an adolescent flamenco dancer: A case report', *Foot and Ankle International*, 29(8): 859–62.

Siebenrock, K. A., Behning, A., Mamisch, T. C. and Schwab, J. M. (2013) 'Growth plate alteration precedes cam-type deformity in elite basketball players', *Clinical Orthopaedics and Related Research*, 471(4): 1084–91.

Siebenrock, K. A., Ferner, F., Noble, P. C., Santore, R. F., Werlen, S. and Mamisch, T. C. (2011) 'The cam-type deformity of the proximal femur arises in childhood in response to vigorous sporting activity', *Clinical Orthopaedics and Related Research*, 469(11): 3229–40.

Singer, K. M. and Roy, S. P. (1984) 'Osteochondrosis of the humeral capitellum', *American Journal of Sports Medicine*, 12(5): 351–60.

Steffen, K. and Engebretsen, L. (2010) 'More data needed on injury risk among young elite athletes', *British Journal of Sports Medicine*, 44: 480–5.

Steffen, K. and Engebretsen, L. (2011) 'The Youth Olympic Games and a new awakening for sports and exercise medicine', *British Journal of Sports Medicine*, 45(16): 1251–2.

Sterr, A., Herron, K. A., Hayward, C. and Montaldi, D. (2006) 'Are mild head injuries as mild as we think? Neurbehavioral concomitants of chronic postconcussion syndrome', *BMC Neurology*, 6: 7. Doi:10.1186/1471-2377-6-7.

Theln, N., Holmberg, S. and Thelin, A. (2006) 'Knee injuries account for the sports related increased risk of knee osteoarthritis', *Scandinavian Journal of Medicine and Science in Sports*, 16(5), 329–33.

Timpka, S., Petersson, I. F., Zhou, C. and Englund, M. (2013) 'Muscle strength in adolescent men and future musculoskeletal pain: a cohort study with 17 years of follow-up', *BMJ Open*, 3(5).

US Department of Health and Human Services (2008) 'Physical activity advisory committee report', Washington, DC: US Department of Health and Human Services. Online at: www.health.gov/PAGuidelines/Report/ (accessed 31 October 2009).

Videman, T., Sarna, S., Crites Battie, M., Koskinen, S., Gill, K., Paananen, H. and Gibbons, L. (1995) 'The long-term effects of physical loading and exercise lifestyles on back-related symptoms, disability, and spinal pathology among men', *Spine*, 20(6): 699–709.

van Mechelan, W., Hobil, H. and Kemper, H. (1992) 'Incidence, severity, aetiology and prevention of sports injuries: A review of concepts', *Sports Medicine*, 14(2): 82–9.

Von Porat, V., Roos, E. M. and Roos, H. (2004) 'High prevalence of osteoarthritis 14 years after an anterior cruciate ligament tear in male soccer players: A study of radiographic and patient relevant outcomes', *Annals of the Rheumatic Diseases*, 63(3): 269–73.

Waldén, M., Hägglund, M. and Ekstrand, J. (2007) 'Football injuries during European Championships 2004–2005', *Knee Surgery, Sports Traumatology, Arthroscopy*, 15(9): 1155–62.

Wiebe, D. J., Comstock, R. D. and Nance, M. L. (2011) 'Concussion research: A public health priority', *Injury Prevention*, 17(1): 69–70.

Wroble, R. R., Henderson, R. C., Campion, E. R., el-Khoury, G. Y. and Albright, J. P. (1992) 'Meniscectomy in children and adolescents. A long-term follow-up study', *Clinical Orthopaedics and Related Research*, 279: 180–9.

Yung, P. S., Chan, R. H., Wong, F. C., Cheuk, P. W. and Fong, D. T. (2007) 'Epidemiology of injuries in Hong Kong elite badminton athletes', *Research in Sports Medicine*, 15(2): 133–46.

Zaman, M. and Leonard, M. A. (1981) 'Meniscectomy in children: Results in 59 knees', *Injury*, 12(5): 425–8.

Zemper, E. D. (2010) 'Catastrophic injuries among young athletes', *British Journal of Sports Medicine*, 44: 13–20.

Section II

Elite sport participation over the lifecourse

6 In the name of performance

Threats, belittlement, and degradation

Ashley Stirling and Gretchen Kerr

Elite athletes are often pushed to their limits, both physically and mentally, in the name of athletic excellence (Tofler and DiGeronimo, 2000; Tofler *et al.*, 1996). When this occurs, and the sole focus for an athlete's participation in sport is performance attainment, the health of the athlete in this environment can be jeopardized. In this chapter, the sport–health relationship is critiqued through the lens of athlete maltreatment. In particular, research to date on athletes' experiences of emotional abuse in the coach–athlete relationship is reviewed and discussed in relation to the consequences for athletes' emotional health. Throughout the chapter, the experience of emotional abuse in the coach–athlete relationship is problematized, but questions are raised about whether positive outcomes such as performance and personal growth may be derived from these experiences. From the onset we would like to highlight that while this chapter provides a critique of the potential positive and negative health consequences of athletes' experiences of emotional ill-treatment, it is our perspective that under no circumstance should emotionally harmful coaching practices be condoned in sport.

The literature is replete with examples of athletes experiencing overuse injuries, exploitation, eating disorders, academic sacrifices, sexual abuse, and other forms of maltreatment (David, 2005). Looking specifically at examples of emotional harm in the coach–athlete relationship, former US Olympic gymnast Dominique Moceanu recalled how her father-coach physically and mentally abused her as she trained (Raboin, 1999). In a recent report entitled 'Help! My coach is a screamer!,' Goldberg (2012) highlighted a case of emotional ill-treatment:

> Basketball practice wound down and what usually happened, happened once again. Coach lost it for the umpteenth time that week. Stopping practice he began to yell at the top of his lungs, 'Stupid, f'en freshman! What an *&%#+#@ idiot! Can't you get the damn play right!? What is your *%##!!@@@ problem!!? Are you f'en stupid or what!?' The athlete, who actually was a very talented ball player shrunk backwards, turning bright red. His eyes began to water as he fought back tears.

In Canada, in the youth sport of hockey, one parent posted the following letter on an online coaching blog:

> Coach, my son is on a team where the coach is always yelling at the players for making a mistake. My son is having a hard time dealing with this and is so afraid to make a mistake, for fear of being scolded.
>
> (Pitter, 2010)

Another parent reported a similar story describing her child's experience in the sport of swimming:

> My 10-year-old son was bullied recently. He was told that he was an 'embarrassment.' He was told to 'shut up.' He was yelled at and scolded in a tone of voice tinged with disgust and disdain. He was told he would be punished for any mistakes he or his peers made in the future. Surprisingly, this didn't happen at school. The bully wasn't even a peer of his. The bully was his swim coach, a young lady of perhaps 26. She was desperately trying to motivate her swimmers to swim fast in the big meet the next day. And this was her attempt at motivation.
>
> (Schinnerer, 2009)

Addressing the question: 'Is high performance sport a healthy pursuit?,' we begin this chapter with a historical overview of concerns for athletes' emotional health, followed by a review of the literature on athlete emotional abuse. The normalization of athletes' emotionally abusive experiences in the high performance sport environment is highlighted, along with research on the negative implications of emotionally abusive coaching practices on athletes' emotional health and well-being. The chapter will conclude with an exploration of the potential for growth to be gleaned from the experience of emotional abuse, including whether or not some athletes excel in the context of an emotionally abusive developmental approach.

Emotional health is defined as 'a state of wellbeing in which the individual realizes his or her own abilities, can cope with the normal stresses of life, can work productively and fruitfully, and is able to make a contribution to his or her community' (World Health Organization, 2004). Associated with emotional health are feelings of self-esteem, self-worth, contentment, security, sense of control, and motivation. Emotional health encompasses the ability to develop psychologically, intellectually, and spiritually, resolve problems and setbacks, and have meaningful social interactions and connections with others. Conversely, poor emotional health is associated with distress and psychosocial impairment (Canadian Institute for Health Information, 2009). Common correlates of poor emotional health include mood disorders, anxiety, addictions and substance abuse, and antisocial behavior (Canadian Institute for Health Information, 2009).

Historical concerns for athletes' emotional health

Long before the issue of athlete emotional abuse was identified as a topic of focus in sport science research, several researchers reported general links between athletes' sport participation and various aspects of emotional health. Interestingly, a wealth of research exists supporting both the positive and negative impact of sport participation on athletes' emotional health.

A number of positive associations have been reported between athletes' sport involvement and expressions of self-worth, self-esteem, and enhanced mood (Eime *et al.*, 2013). Researchers have reported a positive relationship between the self-esteem levels of those who participate in sport compared with those who do not participate in sports (Coalter, 2007; Fraser-Thomas *et al.*, 2005; Slutzky and Simpkins, 2009). This is particularly the case for female youth (Adams-Blair, 2002; Debate *et al.*, 2009). Others have reported that participation in competitive sport is linked positively with motivation levels, both in sports and in school (Umbach *et al.*, 2006). Lower stress (Fraser-Thomas *et al.*, 2005) and depression scores (Carl, 2001; Sabo *et al.*, 2009) have also been reportedly found in adolescent athletes compared with non-athletes. In sum, there is a substantial body of research that suggests a positive link between sport participation and healthy emotional development. The bulk of this research, however, has been conducted in youth sport contexts at sub-elite levels of sport. Looking specifically at research on the positive correlates of intercollegiate student athletes' sport participation, enhanced confidence, motivation, sense of empowerment, and self-esteem have been reported (Blinde *et al.*, 1993; Chen *et al.*, 2010; Woodruff and Schallert, 2008). Further research is required on the emotional health benefits of high performance elite-level sport participation.

In contrast, researchers have also identified potential negative impacts of participation in sport on athletes' emotional health. As a few examples, researchers of the competitive climate of organized youth sport have suggested that the overemphasis on winning may decrease the enjoyment and motivation of child participants (Coakley, 2001; Ogilvie, 1979; Orlick, 1973; Orlick and Botterill, 1975). The emphasis on winning performances in sport has been criticized for the consequences it can have on athletes' emotional health as evident in the significant levels of stress and performance-related anxiety reported by many competitive athletes (Hanton *et al.*, 2005; Jones and Hardy, 1990; Mellalieu *et al.*, 2009; Passer, 1983; Scanlan, 1986; Scanlan *et al.*, 2005; Thatcher and Day, 2008). Furthermore, researchers have reported that well-trained athletes can suffer from overtraining and burnout which can be expressed in the form of depression, chronic fatigue, devaluation, and increased mood disturbances (Lonsdale *et al.*, 2009; Puffer and McShane, 1992; Richardson *et al.*, 2008). Taken together, this research suggests that sport participation has the potential to enhance or hinder an athlete's emotional health.

One of the critical determinants of whether or not an athlete benefits emotionally from his or her sport participation is the nature of the coach–athlete relationship. Numerous researchers have proposed that the interpersonal relationship between the coach and athlete has a significant positive influence on the athlete's health and development in sport, including: the athlete's social development (Jowett, 2005; Smith and Smoll, 2007), athletic performance, perceived satisfaction, and psychological well-being (Antonini-Philippe and Seiler, 2006;

Jowett and Cockerill, 2003; Jowett and Frost, 2007). Referring to the potential negative influence of the coach–athlete relationship on an athlete's emotional health, when the athletes' participation in sport was encouraged or pushed by an external person such as a coach, it was associated with a variety of negative mood states including total mood disturbance, depression-dejection, fatigue, tension-anxiety, and anger-hostility (Stirling and Kerr, 2006). Other researchers have highlighted that external pressures from a coach can be internalized and reproduced by the athletes themselves, thus increasing the negative consequences of such behaviors (Bartholomew *et al.*, 2009). Interestingly, in the same study described above, when the athletes' efforts in sport were driven internally, no association with negative mood states was seen (Stirling and Kerr, 2006).

Building on this research, and the previous research on the potential consequences of winning-centered philosophies in sport, the negative implications of sport participation on emotional health may be attributed in part to the expectations placed on athletes by authority figures in sport, and the associated harmful training behaviors used to push athletes to achieve higher levels of sporting success. This line of thinking has led to a more focused exploration of the specific coaching practices that may hinder athletes' emotional health, with a sub-set of these harmful coaching behaviors being termed 'athlete emotional abuse.'

Athlete emotional abuse

Emotional abuse, defined as a pattern of emotionally harmful behaviors within a critical relationship (Stirling and Kerr, 2008), includes such examples as: persistent demeaning comments, name-calling, belittlement, and acts of humiliation. Although athletes may experience a range of emotionally harmful behaviors in sport, the term emotional abuse is used to describe a very specific set of harmful behaviors within the coach–athlete relationship – namely those behaviors that have the potential to cause emotional harm (i.e. spurning, terrorizing, belittling, humiliating, threatening, exploiting/corrupting, and/or deny emotional responsiveness), occur on a repeated basis, and exist within a coach–athlete relationship in which the athlete depends on the coach for his/her sense of self-worth and fulfillment of needs in the same way that a child would depend upon a parent (Stirling, 2009). Importantly, while the coach may deliberately use harmful coaching practices, his/her actions may not intend to harm the athlete and the coach may not realize the implications of the harmful coaching practices.

Initial research on abuse in sport focused almost exclusively on sexual abuse and harassment, with research on athlete emotional abuse emerging more recently (Stirling, 2009). While both forms of athlete abuse can occur within the coach–athlete relationship, they differ in many ways. Namely, athlete sexual abuse is initiated from a coach's desire to dominate the athlete, and for this to occur he (or she) must overcome various internal and external inhibitors (Brackenridge, 1997). Athlete sexual abuse is generally associated with a grooming process in which an athlete is targeted and inappropriate coaching transgressions of a sexual nature occur between the coach and the athlete. Most individuals in sport would agree to the inappropriateness of sexually abusive coach–athlete relations, and as such athlete sexual abuse occurs in private spaces and secrecy is secured in the athlete so that he/she is hesitant to report such experiences to others (Cense and Brackenridge, 2001).

Emotional abuse, by contrast, occurs for very different reasons. There are two distinct origins for the use of emotionally abusive coaching practices; expressive and instrumental. Expressive origins of emotional abuse refer to a coach's emotionally abusive behaviors that result from heightened emotions and a lack of emotional control, for example, when a coach yells derogatory remarks at an athlete out of anger or frustration during an important game/competition. Emotionally abusive coaching behaviors may also be used for instrumental reasons as a way to shape/manage an athlete's behavior. For example, a coach may exert emotionally harmful behaviors towards the athlete as a way to push the athlete to improve his/her performance in sport (Stirling, 2013). Interestingly, in cases of instrumental emotional abuse the coach is often well-intentioned, may not realize the harmful effects of the emotional ill-treatment, and may believe that this is the best method to develop athletic talent (Stirling, 2013). Although stakeholders in sport may not condone these practices, they often occur in public spaces where they are readily witnessed by others and are rationalized as a necessary approach for elite athlete development (Stirling, 2011).

Whatever it takes: the normalization of emotional abuse

Although research on emotional abuse in sport is relatively new, a number of studies have suggested that emotionally abusive coaching practices are commonly accepted as a required part of developing top performing athletes (Gervis and Dunn, 2004; Stirling and Kerr, 2007). Boocock's (2002) report on child abuse in swimming in the UK revealed that violent or improper behaviors of a coach are often accepted as a part of the regular training routine. Likewise, Bringer *et al.* (2001: 229) wrote about the influence of a winning or performance focus on the vulnerability of athletes to abuse: 'Athletes learn to subject themselves to anything that might assist them in pursuit of medals...Ultimately these behaviors contribute to an environment that normalizes abuse and disempowers athletes.'

Tofler and DiGeronimo (2000: 24) explained that abusive situations can result when adults get wrapped up in their own sporting ambitions for their child and fail to question the coaching practices used to achieve these goals: 'At this level the child is at risk of becoming an objectified and exploited instrument of the adult's goals. These goals are pursued with little regard for short- and long-term physical and emotional morbidity or even mortality.' Cook and Cole (2001) explained that the needs and rights of athletes can be overlooked when the goal of winning overshadows other reasons for participating in sport, therefore placing athletes in a position of vulnerability to abuse. Likewise, Donnelly (1993: 114) stated:

... the body has become an instrument, an object to be worked on, trained, tuned, and otherwise manipulated in order to achieve performance. Those close to the athlete (coaches, trainers, commentators) and even athletes themselves refer to the athlete's body as if it or the performance it produces exists distinct from the person (in some cases even substituting for the person). Detachment of the body and its performance from the person legitimizes the use of drugs and other techniques, even violation and abuse, in the name of improved performance.

Across numerous studies, emotionally abusive coaching practices are reportedly the most common form of athlete abuse, thus suggesting a certain level of acceptance (Alexander *et al.*, 2011; Gravely and Cochran, 1995; Kirby and Greaves, 1996; Stirling and Kerr, 2010; Stirling *et al.*, 2012). The power held by the coach, as a result of his or her position of authority, expertise, past successes, and access to resources and opportunities (Tomlinson and Strachan, 1996) has previously been described by athletes as equivalent to that held by a parent (Stirling and Kerr, 2009), a priest (Brackenridge, 1997), and a master (Crosset, 1986). Stirling and Kerr (2009) found that the coach's power reportedly promoted the athletes' acceptance of harmful coaching behaviors and inhibited reporting of abusive experiences.

Furthermore, unlike sexual abuse, emotionally abusive coaching practices tend to occur in public, observed by parents, other adult coaches and administrators, thus suggesting an acceptance of these behaviors by several stakeholders as a normal or expected part of the training process (Stirling, 2011). Kerr and Stirling (2012) interviewed parents on their perceptions of their child's experiences of athlete emotional abuse. This study found that similar to athletes, parents are socialized into the culture of elite sport and the acceptance of disconcerting coaching practices, thus becoming silent bystanders to their children's experiences of emotional abuse (Kerr and Stirling, 2012). This lack of recognition of athlete emotional abuse as being problematic has also been reported among other authorities in sport such as coaches (Stirling, 2013), sport medical practitioners (Stirling and Kerr, 2008; Stirling *et al.*, 2011) and sport administrators (Stirling, 2011).

Implications of emotionally abusive coaching practices on athletes' emotional health

Although emotional abuse is commonly rationalized as a necessary part of elite athlete development (Gervis and Dunn, 2004; Kerr and Stirling, 2012; Stirling and Kerr, 2007), it does not occur without consequence. According to one study, athletes' interpretations and responses to emotionally abusive coaching practices seem to vary across the sport career and depend upon how well the athlete is performing. Emotionally abusive coaching practices appear to be normalized by the athletes for the bulk of their careers, by the end of their athletic careers, or upon retirement, the athletes report their coach's practices as problematic

(Stirling and Kerr, 2007). In this same study, athletes discussed the effects of athlete emotional abuse. Athletes explained that the first time they were degraded by their coach they were upset, but after the athletes recovered from the initial harmful incident, they became accustomed to their coaches' emotional ill-treatment and came to recognize it as a common part of training. Within the high performance sport environment, the use of emotionally abusive coaching practices was reportedly normalized as a required coaching method used to enhance athletic performance. It appeared that as long as the athletes perceived their sporting performances positively, they continued to rationalize their experience of athlete emotional abuse and described few consequences of the emotional abuse on their emotional health. As soon as athletic performance was compromised, however, athletes reportedly suffered increasingly negative effects in response to their emotionally abusive experiences. Some of the negative implications on emotional health reported at this stage included emotional upset, depressed mood, self-dislike, disordered eating, interactions with friends, and engagement in rebellious behavior (Stirling and Kerr, 2007).

This research is interesting as it explains why emotionally abusive coaching practices are so readily normalized as an appropriate approach to athlete development – as long as the athlete is performing well, the emotional abuse has little to no effect. Given that the negative effects of the emotional ill-treatment may not be evident until the end of an athlete's career or until following retirement from sport, the coach may not recognize the negative consequences of the behavior. A vicious cycle then occurs in which high performing athletes experience emotionally abusive coaching practices due to a belief that this is how high performance athletes should be coached. If the athlete performs well as is not affected by the emotional ill-treatment, the coach's behavior seems to have created a positive outcome for the athlete and is therefore readily justified. It should be noted that no research has been conducted to date on the effects of these behaviors on sport performance, but preliminary research has suggested that compared to controlling motivational approaches, which could be used to describe athlete emotional abuse when used for instructional purposes, autonomy-supportive coaching behaviors lead to greater peak performance (Adie *et al.*, 2008; Gillet *et al.*, 2010). Returning to research on the negative consequences of athlete emotional abuse, Gervis and Dunn (2004) conducted retrospective interviews with adults who had been identified as elite athletes between the ages of 8 and 16 years. Specifically, they were asked about their experiences of, and emotional responses to, their coach's negative behavior, focusing specifically on the emotionally abusive coaching behaviors of belittling, humiliating, shouting, scapegoating, rejecting, isolating, threatening, and ignoring. Of the athletes interviewed, a greater frequency of negative emotional responses was reportedly experienced at the most elite levels of sport. As well, several athletes reported a residual negative effect of these experiences ten years later. The negative emotional responses reported by athletes in this study included feeling depressed, low self-worth, low self-confidence, loneliness, anger, and emotional withdrawal.

In a subsequent investigation, Gervis (2009) developed the 22-item Sport

Emotional Response Questionnaire (SER-Q), which measures the frequency of negative (i.e., emotionally abusive) coach behavior, athletes' emotional response, and perceived effect on performance. Using this questionnaire, Gervis (2009) surveyed 543 athletes and reported no significant differences in the frequency of emotionally abusive coaching behaviors according to the athlete's gender, type of sport, and the coach's gender. However, more frequent negative coaching behaviors reportedly occurred at the national and international levels compared to the recreation, club, and regional level, thus suggesting that negative coaching behaviors were most common at the highest level of sport. Looking at the impact of these experiences on athletes' emotional health, a greater negative emotional response to these experiences was also reported among the international-level and national-level athletes. Interestingly, Gervis (2009) reported that as the frequency of emotionally abusive coaching increased, so did the perceived negative effects.

Further examining the specific outcomes of emotional abuse in sport, semi-structured interviews were conducted with 14 retired elite athletes on the perceived effects of their experiences of emotional abuse in the coach–athlete relationship (Stirling and Kerr, 2013). In this study, athletes described several negative psychological effects of their emotionally abusive experiences including emotional upset, anger, low self-efficacy, low self-esteem, and anxiety. Negative training effects reported by the athletes included decreased motivation, reduced enjoyment, impaired focus, and difficulty with skill acquisition. Athletes reportedly experienced performance decrements as a direct consequence of their coach's emotionally harmful behavior.

Though the research to date on athlete emotional abuse may be interpreted to suggest several negative health consequences, further research on this topic is warranted. Given the exploratory nature of the sport-related research, small sample sizes, focus on athletes' perceived experiences, and reliance on self-reported outcomes rather than more objective assessment of emotional consequences (Gervis and Dunn, 2004; Stirling and Kerr, 2007, 2008, 2013), the findings should be viewed as preliminary data upon which to base further research.

Interestingly, some athletes have reported positive effects such as an enhanced sense of accomplishment and athletic performance as a result of experiences of emotional abuse within the coach–athlete relationship (Stirling and Kerr, 2013). More specifically, some athletes reported heightened motivation to succeed in response to emotionally abusive coaching behaviors. Although these athletes represented a small percentage of the sample and further research is needed, these findings prompt one to consider the complexity of the relationship between a coach's emotional ill-treatment and an athlete's responses to these practices. That some athletes reportedly experienced benefits from abusive experiences is consistent with the research on adversarial growth in which positive changes are incurred as a result of struggling with adverse situations (Linley and Joseph, 2004). This research will be addressed in the next section along with the question: 'Can some athletes advance their performance and emotional well-being as a result of experiences of athlete emotional abuse, and if so, what contributes to this growth?'

Potential for adversarial growth?

The process by which positive outcomes are incurred as a result of struggling with adverse and potentially traumatic challenges is called adversarial growth (Joseph and Linley, 2005). It is proposed that through experiences of trauma and adversity, some individuals not only recover, but thrive and are propelled to higher levels of functioning than existed prior to the adversity (Joseph and Linley, 2005; Linley and Joseph, 2004, 2011; Sheldon *et al.*, 2002). A growing body of research has demonstrated growth in response to such adversity as accidents and natural disasters, illness, bereavement, war and conflict, sexual abuse, and assault (see Joseph and Linley, 2006).

More recently, research has begun to explore the construct of adversarial growth in the sport environment. Tamminen and colleagues (2013) examined the influence of adverse athletic experiences on the potential for growth among five elite female athletes, including incidents of performance slumps, coach conflicts, bullying, eating disorders, injuries, and sexual abuse within the coach–athlete relationship. The researchers reported that participants experienced feelings of isolation, emotional disruption, and questioning of their athletic identity and athletic self-efficacy as a result of their adverse experiences. These experiences, however, were also a source for growth for the athletes in realizing their strength, gaining perspective, and gaining a desire to help others. This research, however, did not examine the impact of adverse athletic experiences on specific characteristics of emotional health such as sense of self, sense of control, motivation, and sense of connectedness with others; nor did it examine the long-term implications of the athletes' adverse experiences on emotional health. Inevitably, one could also question the degree of adversity experienced with these challenges, with the effects of being sexually abused, for example, being quite different from those associated with performance slumps.

In a recent article on trauma and talent in sport, Collins and MacNamara (2012) argued that overcoming real-life challenges is a precursor to high-level achievement. In their critique, Collins and MacNamara suggested that structured trauma such as playing in an older age group, out of position, being set higher expectations than peers, military-style challenges, deselection from certain events, or relocation for training camps may be used as a developmental tool for facilitating personal development within talent pathways. They emphasized that development from these challenging experiences, however, should not be left to chance, emphasizing the importance of confidence and skill building debriefs. While the challenging experiences examined in their review, undoubtedly, present valuable teachable moments and developmental opportunities, they are a far cry from what would typically be called traumas; nor would they likely be associated with affective responses comparable to those potentially elicited by emotionally abusive experiences.

Although these studies represent a constructive first step in the exploration of adversarial growth in the sport environment, they share many of the conceptual and methodological weaknesses that exist in the non-sport adversarial growth literature. For example, despite the documented importance of an individual's appraisal and subjective experience in affecting adversarial growth, there appear to be significant conceptual differences between adverse challenges such as performance slumps and deselection for example, and what may be considered as universal traumas such as terrorist attacks and sexual assault, which rely less on individual appraisal. Further, the lack of pre-event data, over-reliance on self-reports, and a lack of objective measures of growth (Linley and Joseph, 2004) leave much room for future research on adversarial growth in general and growth in the sport environment more specifically.

Returning to research specifically on the topic of athlete emotional abuse, although some athletes have reportedly experienced an enhanced sense of accomplishment and greater athletic performance in response to emotionally abusive coaching practices (Stirling and Kerr, 2013), it is advised that these findings be interpreted with caution, in part, because they are based on the self-reports of a small number of athletes who also reported several harmful effects. It is also unclear as to whether the expressed positive impact of the athlete emotional abuse is truly reflective of adversarial growth or merely a further indicator of the widespread acceptance of these harmful coaching practices as a required part of the athlete development process. It is our opinion that these findings are likely explained by the later assertion.

Linley and Joseph (2004) proposed that adversarial growth may simply reflect adherence to a cultural script (2004: 19) insofar as many of us are led to believe that some good comes from the bad things in life. The sport environment and associated 'sport ethic' (Hughes and Coakley, 1991) is characterized by similar dogma, including the need to push through limits, playing through pain and injury, and making sacrifices for the sport and the team. Hughes and Coakley (1991) note that the sport ethic itself is not necessarily a bad thing. Rather, it is the unquestioned acceptance of it and excessive over conformity to it that is problematic. In the same way, the competitive climate of sport may not in itself be concerning, but the over conformity of the athlete to performance-based values, and a lack of questioning of coaching practices used in the pursuit of athletic success, may lead to the normalization and rationalization of athlete emotional abuse.

Also of worthy consideration is the tendency of those in the psychology field to consider experiences in a binary fashion – that emotional responses are either positive or negative when in reality, the human experience is certainly far more complex than such a binary categorization suggests. As Joseph and Linley (2006: 1050) write, '...we are reminded by trauma that the dialectical forces of positive and negative, loss and fulfillment, suffering and growth, may often go hand in hand.' Similarly, Linley and Joseph (2004) indicated that growth and distress represent separate and independent constructs rather than opposite ends of the same continuum; as such, it is possible that some athletes may experience adversarial growth from emotionally abusive coaching practices, but that they may also and simultaneously experience distress. This relationship warrants further attention to more fully understand the health implications of sport participation.

Finally, it is important to emphasize that no research has been conducted specifically on the potential psychological growth that may result from or in spite of athlete emotional abuse, and as such, no claims can be made. Further, there is a need for longitudinal empirical research on the time-course or trajectory of adversarial growth in non-sport or sport environments.

Regardless of any potential adversarial growth that may occur from an athlete's harmful experiences, emotionally abusive coaching practices must not be condoned. The more humane and poignant consideration is the athletic and personal accomplishments that may be achievable in an environment free of abusive experiences. In other words, how might elite athletes be challenged in a developmentally appropriate and harm-free manner to elicit positive personal growth and ensure a positive impact on athlete emotional health? This stands as an important future area of research.

Conclusion

In critiquing the sport–health relationship through the lens of athlete maltreatment, the potential for negative emotional health consequences resulting from athletes' experiences of emotional abuse in the coach–athlete relationship is undisputed. However, while recognizing the potential for harm as a consequence of emotionally abusive experiences, some high performance athletes have claimed that they experience success, personally and athletically, as a result of their emotionally abusive experiences. Whether or not some athletes experience adversarial growth as an outcome of their emotionally abusive experiences is unknown at this point and is perhaps an irrelevant question given that harmful coaching practices are not to be condoned.

Far more empirical research is needed to more fully understand the relationship between athletes' sport participation and their emotional health. The empirical research on emotional abuse in sport is arguably in a stage of infancy. As such, much more work is needed to further our understanding of the processes by which emotionally abusive coaching practices are normalized as well as the consequences of such practices for athletes. More specifically, some questions to be addressed in future research include: What are the short- and long-term effects of athlete emotional abuse? Do any factors mitigate athletes' experience of emotionally abusive coaching practices and/or the associated consequences of such experiences? Does the apparent normalization of emotionally abusive coaching practices moderate their harmful influences? In what ways may the balance of healthy or appropriate and unhealthy or inappropriate coaching practices mitigate or moderate the effects of emotionally abusive experiences? What are healthier methods of producing successful athletes? Future work should also focus on ways in which coaches can be educated, monitored, and encouraged to provide learning environments that facilitate healthy growth and development for elite sport participants, both personally and athletically.

References

Adams-Blair, H. (2002) 'The importance of physical education and sport in the lives of young females', *International Sports Journal*, 6: 45–50.

Adie, J. W., Duda, J. L., and Ntoumanis, N. (2008) 'Autonomy support, basic need satisfaction and the optimal functioning of adult male and female sport participants: A test of basic needs theory', *Motivation and Emotion*, 32: 189–99.

Alexander, K., Stafford, A., and Lewis, R. (2011) 'The experiences of children participating in organized sport in the UK', *The University of Edinburgh/NSPCC Child Protection Research Unit*. Online at: www.nspcc.org.uk/Inform/research/findings/experiences_children_sport_main_report_wdf85014.pdf (accessed 19 March 2014).

Antonini-Phillipe, R. and Seiler, R. (2006) 'Closeness, co-orientation and complementarity in coach-athlete relationships: What male swimmers say about their male coaches', *Psychology of Sport and Exercise*, 7: 159–71.

Bartholomew, K. J., Ntoumanis, N., and Thorgersen-Ntoumani, C. (2009) 'A review of controlling motivation strategies from a self-determination theory perspective: Implications for sports coaches', *International Review of Sport and Exercise Psychology*, 2: 215–33.

Blinde, E. M., Diane E. Taub, D. E., and Han, L. (1993) 'Sport participation and women's personal empowerment: Experiences of the college athlete', *Journal of Sport and Social Issues*, 17: 47–60.

Boocock, S. (2002) 'NSPCC report reveals concerns over child abuse in swimming'. Online at: www.nspcc.org.uk (accessed 20 March 2014).

Brackenridge, C. (1997) '"He owned me basically…" Women's experience of sexual abuse in Sport', *International Review for the Sociology of Sport*, 32: 115–30.

Bringer, J., Brackenridge, C., and Johnston, L. (2001) 'The name of the game: A review of sexual exploitation of females in sport', *Current Women's Health Reports*, 1: 225–31.

Canadian Institute for Health Information (2009) *Improving the Health of Canadians: Exploring positive mental health*, Ontario: Canadian Population Health Initiative.

Carl, S. (2001) 'Depression, body image, and self-esteem as a function of sports participation among male and female adolescents', unpublished dissertation, Hofstra University, Long Island, New York.

Cense, M. and Brackenridge, C. (2001) 'Temporal and developmental risk factors for sexual harassment and abuse in sport', *European Physical Education Review*, 7: 61–79.

Chen, S., Snyder, S., and Magner, M. (2010) 'The effects of sport participation on student-athletes' and non-athletes' social life and identity', *Journal of Issues in Intercollegiate Athletics*, 3: 176–93.

Claussen, A. H. and Crittenden, P. M. (1991) 'Physical and psychological maltreatment: relations among types of maltreatment', *Child Abuse and Neglect*, 15: 5–18.

Collins, D. and MacNamara, A. (2012) 'The rocky road to the top: Why talent needs trauma', *Sports Medicine*, 42: 907–14.

Coakley, J. (2001) 'Sports and children: Are organized programs worth the effort?', in J. Coakley (ed.) *Sport in Society: Issues and controversies*, 7th edn, Toronto: McGraw Hill, 109–37.

Coalter, F. (2007) *A Wider Social Role for Sport: Who's keeping the score?*, London, UK: Routledge.

Cook, D. and Cole, C. (2001) 'Kids and sport', *Journal of Sport and Social Issues*, 25: 227–8.

Crosset, T. (1986) 'Male coach–female athlete relationships', paper presented to the Norwegian Confederation of Sport Conference on Coaching Female Top-Level Athletes, Sole, Norway, November 15–16.

David, P. (2005) *Human Rights in Youth Sport: A critical review of children's rights in competitive sports*, New York: Routledge.

Debate, R. D., Pettee Gabriel, K., Zwald, M., Huberty, J., and Zhang, Y. (2009) 'Changes in psychosocial factors and physical activity frequency among third- to eighth-grade girls who participated in a developmentally focused youth sport program: A preliminary study', *Journal of School Health*, 79: 474–84.

Donnelly, P. (1993) 'Problems associated with youth involvement in high performance sport', in B. Cahill and A. Pearl (eds) *Intensive Participation in Children's Sports: American Orthopaedic Society for Sports Medicine*, Champaign, IL: Human Kinetics, 95–127.

Eime, R. M., Young, J. A., Harvey, J. T., Charity, M. J., and Payne, W. R. (2013) 'A systematic review of the psychological and social benefits of participation in sport for children and adolescents: Informing development of a conceptual model of health through sport', *International Journal of Behavioral Nutrition and Physical Activity*, 10: 98.

Fraser-Thomas, J. L., Côté, J., and Deakin, J. (2005) 'Youth sport programs: an avenue to foster positive youth development', *Physical Education and Sport Pedagogy*, 10: 19–40.

Gervis, M. (2009) 'An investigation into the emotional responses of child athletes to their coach's behaviour from a child maltreatment perspective', unpublished dissertation, Brunel University, Uxbridge, United Kingdom.

Gervis, M. and Dunn, N. (2004) 'The emotional abuse of elite child athletes by their coaches', *Child Abuse Review*, 13: 215–23.

Gillet, N., Vallerand, R. J., Amoura, S., and Baldes, B. (2010) 'Influence of coaches' autonomy support on athletes' motivation and sport performance: A test of the hierarchical model of intrinsic and extrinsic motivation', *Psychology of Sport and Exercise*, 11: 155–61.

Goldberg, A. (2012) 'Yelling/anger in sports', *Competitive Advantage*. Online at: www.competitivedge.com/yellinganger-sports (accessed 19 March 2014).

Gravely, A. R. and Cochran, T. R. (1995) 'The use of perceptual data to assess intercollegiate athletics', paper presented at the 35th Annual Forum of the Association for Institutional Research, Boston, Massachusetts, May 28–31.

Gross, A. B. and Keller, H. R. (1992) 'Long-term consequences of childhood physical and psychological maltreatment', *Aggressive Behavior*, 18: 171–85.

Hanton, S., Fletcher, J., and Coughlan, G. (2005) 'Stress in elite sport performers: A comparative study of competitive and organizational stressors', *Journal of Sport Sciences*, 23: 1129–41.

Hughes, R. and Coakley, J. (1991) 'Positive deviance among athletes: The implications of overconformity to the sport ethic', *Sociology of Sport Journal*, 8: 307–25.

Jones, J. G. and Hardy, L. (1990) *Stress and Performance in Sport*, New York: John Wiley & Sons Ltd.

Joseph, S. and Linley, P.A. (2005) 'Positive adjustment to threatening events: An organismic valuing theory of growth through adversity', *Review of General Psychology*, 9: 262–80.

Joseph, S. and Linley, P. A. (2006) 'Growth following adversity: Theoretical perspectives and implications for clinical practice', *Clinical Psychology Review*, 26: 1041–53.

Jowett, S. (2005) 'The coach–athlete partnership', *The Psychologist*, 18: 412–15.

Jowett, S. and Cockerill, I. M. (2003) 'Olympic medalists' perspective of the athlete–coach relationship', *Psychology of Sport and Exercise*, 4: 313–31.

Jowett, S. and Frost, T. C. (2007) 'Race/Ethnicity in the all male coach–athlete relationship: Black footballers' narratives', *Journal of International Sport and Exercise Psychology*, 3: 255–69.

Kerr, G. A. and Stirling, A. E. (2012) 'Parents' reflections on their child's experiences of emotionally abusive coaching practices', *Journal of Applied Sport Psychology*, 24: 191–206.

Kirby, S. and Greaves, L. (1996) 'Foul play: Sexual harassment in sport', paper presented at the Pre-Olympic Scientific Congress, Dallas, Texas, USA, July 11–15.

Linley, P. A. and Joseph, S. (2004) 'Positive change following trauma and adversity: a review', *Journal of Traumatic Stress*, 17: 11–21.

Linley, P. A. and Joseph, S. (2011) 'Meaning in life and posttraumatic growth', *Journal of Loss and Trauma*, 16: 150–9.

Lonsdale, C., Hodge, K., and Rose, E. (2009) 'Athlete burnout in elite sport: A self-determination perspective', *Journal of Sport Sciences*, 27: 785–95.

Mellalieu, S. D., Neil, R., Hanton, S., and Fletcher, D. (2009) 'Competition stress in sport performers: Stressors experienced in the competition environment', *Journal of Sport Sciences*, 27: 729–44.

Ogilvie, (1979) 'The child athlete: Psychological implications of participation in sport', *The Annals of the American Academy of Political and Social Science*, 445: 47–58.

Orlick, T. (1973) 'Children's sport – A revolution is coming', *CAHPHER Journal*, 39: 12–14.

Orlick, T. and Botterill, C. (1975) *Every Kid Can Win*, Chicago, IL: Nelson Hall.

Passer, M. (1983) 'Fear of failure, fear of evaluation, perceived competence and self-esteem in competitive trait anxious children', *Journal of Sport Psychology*, 5: 172–88.

Pitter (2010) 'The yelling coach', *Sweet Hockey Training*. Online at: http://sweethockeytraining.com/category/ask-coach-pitter/ (accessed 19 March 2014).

Puffer, J. C. and McShane, J. M. (1992) 'Depression and chronic fatigue in athletes', *Clinics in Sports Medicine*, 11: 327–38.

Raboin, S. (1999) 'A family torn apart', *USA Today*, 9 December, 1C–2C.

Richardson, S. O., Anderson, M. B., and Morris, T. (2008) *Overtraining Athletes: Personal journeys in sport*, Champaign, IL: Human Kinetics.

Sabo, D., Miller, K., Melnick, M. and Heywood, L. (2009) *Her Life Depends On It: Sport, Physical Activity, and the Health and Well-Being of American Girls II*, East Meadow, NY: Women's Sports Foundation.

Scanlan, T. (1986) 'Competitive stress in children', in M. Weiss and D. Gould (eds) *The 1984 Olympic Scientific Congress proceedings, volume 10: Sport for children and youth*, Champaign, IL: Human Kinetics, 107–13.

Scanlan, T., Babkes, M. L., and Scanlan, L. A. (2005) 'Participation in sport: A developmental glimpse at emotion', in J. L. Mahoney, R. W. Larson, J. S. Eccles (eds) *Organized Activities as Contexts of Development: Extra-curricular activities, after-school and community programs*, New Jersey, NY: Lawrence Erlbaum & Associates, 275–301.

Schinnerer, J. (2009) 'The consequences of verbally abusive athletic coaches', *Psych Central*. Online at: http://psychcentral.com/lib/2009/the-consequences-of-verbally-abusive-athletic-coaches/ (accessed 19 March 2014).

Sheldon, K. M., Kasser, T., Smith, K., and Share, T. (2002) 'Personal goals and psychological growth: testing an intervention to enhance goal attainment and personality integration', *Journal of Personality*, 70: 5–31.

Slutzky, C. B. and Simpkins, S. D. (2009) 'The link between children's sport participation and self-esteem: Exploring the mediating role of sport self-concept', *Psychology of Sport and Exercise*, 10: 381–9.

Smith, R. E. and Smoll, F. L. (2007) 'Social-cognitive approach to coaching behaviours', in S. Jowett and D. Lavallee (eds) *Social Psychology in Sport*, Champaign, IL: Human Kinetics, 75–90.

Stirling, A. E. (2009) 'Definition and constituents of maltreatment in sport: Establishing a conceptual framework for research practitioners', *British Journal of Sports Medicine*, 43: 1091–9.

Stirling, A. E. (2011) 'Initiating and sustaining emotional abuse in the coach–athlete relationship: Athletes', parents', and coaches' reflections', unpublished doctoral dissertation, University of Toronto, Toronto, Ontario, Canada.

Stirling, A. E. (2013) 'Understanding the use of emotionally abusive coaching practices', *International Journal of Sports Science and Coaching*, 8(4): 625–40.

Stirling, A. E. and Kerr, G. A. (2006) 'Perfectionism and mood states among recreational and elite athletes', *Athletic Insight*, 8: 13–27.

Stirling, A. E. and Kerr, G. A. (2007) Elite female swimmers' experiences of emotional abuse across time', *Journal of Emotional Abuse*, 7: 89–113.

Stirling, A. E. and Kerr, G. A. (2008) 'Defining and categorizing emotional abuse in sport', *European Journal of Sport Science*, 8: 173–81.

Stirling, A. E. and Kerr, G. A. (2009) 'Abused athletes' perceptions of the coach–athlete relationship', *Sport in Society*, 12: 227–39.

Stirling, A. E. and Kerr, G. A. (2010) 'Sport psychology consultants as agents of child protection', *Journal of Applied Sport Psychology*, 22: 305–19.

Stirling, A. E. and Kerr, G. A. (2013) 'The perceived effects of elite athletes' experiences of emotional abuse in the coach–athlete relationship', *International Journal of Sport and Exercise Psychology*, 11: 87–100.

Stirling, A. E., Bridges, E., Cruz, E. L., and Mountjoy, M. (2011) 'Canadian Academy of Sport and Exercise Medicine position statement: Abuse, harassment, and bullying in sport', *Clinical Journal of Sport Medicine*, 21: 385–91.

Stirling, A. E., Kerr, G. A., and Cruz, L. C. (2012) 'An evaluation of Canada's National Coaching Certification Program's "Make Ethical Decisions" coach education module', *International Journal of Coaching Science*, 6: 45–60.

Tamminen, K. A., Holt, N. L., and Neely, K. C. (2013) 'Exploring adversity and the potential for growth among elite female athletes', *Psychology of Sport and Exercise*, 14: 28–36.

Thatcher, J. and Day, M. C. (2008) 'Re-appraising stress appraisals: The underlying properties of stress in sport', *Psychology of Sport and Exercise*, 9: 318–35.

Tofler, I. and DiGeronimo, T. (2000) *Keeping Your Kids Out Front Without Kicking Them From Behind: How to nurture high-achieving athletes, scholars, and performing artists*, San Francisco, CA: Jossey-Bass.

Tofler, I. R., Stryer, B. K., Micheli, L. J., and Herman, L. R. (1996) 'Physical and emotional problems of elite female gymnasts', *New England Journal of Medicine*, 335: 281–83.

Tomlinson, P. and Strachan, D. (1996) *Power and Ethics in Coaching: National Coaching Certification Program*. Ottawa, ON: Coaching Association of Canada.

Umbach, P. D., Palmer, M. M., Kuh, G. D., and Hannah, S. J. (2006) 'Intercollegiate athletes and effective educational practices: winning combination or losing effort?', *Research in Higher Education*, 47: 709–33.

Woodruff, A. L. and Schallert, D. L. (2008) 'Studying to play, playing to study: Nine college student-athletes' motivational sense of self', *Contemporary Educational Psychology*, 33: 34–57.

World Health Organization. (2004) *Promoting Mental Health: Concepts; emerging evidence; practice*, Geneva: WHO.

7 Transitional challenges and elite athletes' mental health

*Paul Wylleman, Nathalie Rosier and
Paul De Knop*

In fact, it was on the second day of the Olympics that I said to Matthew, 'I'm definitely going to retire. There's no question about it. There's no way I can do this again. I want you to know that'... So I ended my career formally with an early morning press conference on 31 October... I have no intention of going out in a boat again... That chapter in my life had now come to a close with no sadness, no regrets... After the Olympics, it was time to re-evaluate myself and think about me as an individual, not as part of a team being organized by a coach.

> Rower Steve Redgrave after winning his fifth gold Olympic medal at the
> 2000 Sydney Olympic Games (Redgrave and Townsend, 2001: 303–7)

I have unfortunately no good news. I spent the last days undergoing various medical tests and they have confirmed that my elbow has been damaged... I have rarely been spared from the pain, those last months were very hard. Time has passed, and the doubts have grown... I'm in shock, of course... it is now clear and I accept that my career here... finally ends. I will need time to process all this...

> Seven Grand Slam winning tennis player Justine Henin (Henin, 2011)

All elite athletes will inevitably face the end of their athletic career. While for some this may seem to be an almost 'matter-of-fact' rational process, for others this transition may bring about a period of emotional turmoil and self-doubts impacting the retiree's mental health. In fact, on average, one retired elite athlete in six (13–20 per cent) (Wippert and Wippert, 2008; Wylleman *et al.*, 1993) has been found to experience a wide range of psychological, interpersonal, social, and financial problems as well as a range of negative or even traumatic experiences (e.g., alcohol and substance abuse, acute depression, eating disorders, identity confusion, decreased self-confidence, attempted suicide) during as well as after athletic retirement (Alfermann, 1995; Grove *et al.*, 1998; Lavallee *et al.*, 2000).

As researchers delved further into the impact of this transition, they found that throughout their athletic career, athletes also experienced other types of transitions that had a marked influence on, among other factors, their mental functioning. For rower Steve Redgrave, for example, these included winning his first Olympic medal, establishing a new rowing partnership, deciding not to retire after his fourth gold medal, experiencing turbulent periods in his marriage, and his 'date with destiny' at the 2000 Olympic Games when going for his fifth gold medal (Redgrave and Townsend, 2001). The transition into motherhood led US Olympic swimmer Dara Torres to realize that "becoming a mother changes everything . . . to define your values, to figure out who you are" (Torres and Weil, 2009: 79) and that when she returned to competitive swimming she was "a mom first and a swimmer second" (87). Facing a possible career-ending neck injury meant for English Rugby Union player Jonny Wilkinson not only going into surgery, but also confronting the possibility of not playing, which "does odd things to your head . . . It is funny how quickly you can begin to doubt yourself" (Wilkinson, 2006: 181). As these examples reveal, current as well as retired elite athletes clearly perceive how their mental functioning is impacted not only by the (impending) end of their career, but actually by a set of transitions that are related to sports as well as to other domains of their lives. It is this possible negative impact of transitions that seems to be counterintuitive to the general assumption that elite athletes are or should be psychologically healthy (Moore, 2012).

The purpose of this chapter is to consider how transitions may affect elite athletes' mental health. For the purpose of this chapter, we will consider mental health as "a state of successful performance of mental function, resulting in productive activities, fulfilling relationships with other people, and the ability to adapt to change and to cope with adversity" (US Department of Health and Human Services, 1999: 4). An overview is provided of how research into the impact of athletic retirement as 'end-of-career' transition led to research acknowledging that elite athletes face a range of health-influencing multilevel 'within-career' transitions. This is followed by three case examples as illustrations of how transitional challenges may influence elite athletes' mental functioning. The chapter concludes with some recommendations aimed at providing elite athletes with support in order to optimize the way in which they cope with transitional challenges.

A lifespan perspective on athletic career transitions

The concept of transitions has become a major research topic (e.g., Alfermann and Stambulova, 2007; Bruner *et al.*, 2008; Pummell *et al.*, 2008; Wylleman *et al.*, 2004), as has athlete service provision throughout transitions (e.g., Brewer and Petitpas, 2005; Hays, 2009; Lavallee and Andersen, 2000; Orlick, 2008). Originally focused on the process of retirement from competitive sports and the occurrence of (sub-)clinical problems during the 1960s–1970s (e.g., Haerle, 1975; Hallden, 1965; Mihovilovic, 1968), the end-of-career transition was approached as a singular event compared to retirement from the workforce, or even to the process of dying (Lavallee, 2000). Both comparisons were found to be flawed due to their non-sport specific character, their presumption of career termination as being an inherently negative event requiring considerable adjustment, and to their neglect of life after athletic retirement (Wylleman *et al.*, 1999).

As research-based knowledge grew during the 1980s–1990s, more insight was gained into some of the major causes (e.g., age, de-selection, injury, free choice) for athletic career termination (Ogilvie and Taylor, 1993), while, at the same time, awareness grew suggesting not all causes for termination were strictly athletic in nature; for example, finishing an academic career, marital relationships and family planning, or developing a vocational career were also found to play an important role (Allison and Meyer, 1988; Blinde and Greendorfer, 1985; Swain, 1991). Research also revealed that a combination of causes contributed to terminating the athletic career and that the adjustment process to post-athletic life was mediated by the voluntariness with which athletes retired, as well as by the degree of preparation for a life after sport (e.g., Alfermann and Gross, 1997; Webb *et al.*, 1998; Wheeler *et al.*, 1996).

Based upon these findings, career end became seen more as a transitional process rather than as a singular event (McPherson, 1980). This process was conceptualized, for example, in the Model of Human Adaptation to Transition (Charner and Schlossberg, 1986; Schlossberg, 1981, 1984) that identified three major sets of factors interacting during a transition, namely: 1) the characteristics of the individual experiencing the transition; 2) the perception of the particular transition (e.g., role change, affect, occurrence of stress); and 3) the characteristics of the pre- and post-transition environments. In an effort for more sport-specificity, Taylor and Ogilvie (1998) formulated the Athletic Career Termination model which considered the process of the career termination transition in terms of: 1) the causal factors that initiate the career transition process, 2) the developmental factors related to transition adaptation, 3) the coping resources that affect the responses to career transitions, 4) the quality of adjustment to career transition, and 5) possible treatment issues for distressful reactions to career transition. It is clear that following the development of these models, experts better recognized factors related to the impact the transitional process could have on elite athletes' mental health, and took into account mechanisms (i.e., coping resources, treatment) that could be considered in order to prevent and/or counteract possible negative effects of retirement.

As knowledge about the transitional process grew, so did the insight not only that athletes faced different transitions at various points throughout their athletic careers (Wylleman *et al.*, 1999) but that these transitions could be categorized in function of their degree of predictability. More specifically, during a normative transition athletes generally progress in a predictable and anticipated way from one stage to another (e.g., junior to senior level, progressing from regional to national-level competitions, from active participation into discontinuation from competitive sport). A non-normative transition, however, does not occur in a set plan or schedule but is the result of important events that take place in an individual's life, which are generally unpredicted, unanticipated, and involuntary (e.g., a season-ending injury, the loss of a personal coach, an unanticipated 'cut' from the team, or not going to the Olympic Games due to political reasons). While perhaps less obvious, a non-normative transition may also include non-transitions, which are key transitions expected to happen but which (un)expectedly do not occur. For example, Dutch long track skater Sven Kramer, who won gold and bronze at the 2010 Winter Olympic Games in Vancouver, looked back with a strong feeling of disappointment at these Games as he unexpectedly failed (due to a mistake in lane change) to win the gold medal in the 10,000 meters, defining this non-occurring event as "one of the most important moments" in his life (Grijsbach, 2010). Remakably, this event repeated itself during the 2014 Winter Olympic Games in Sochi where Kramer, as favorite, wanted to redeem himself after four years but was now beaten for the gold in the same event (by a compatriot!).

Past research has clearly shown that athletes face a combination of both types of transitions throughout their athletic careers (e.g., Bloom, 1985; Salmela, 1994; Sinclair and Orlick, 1993; Stambulova, 1994, 2000; Wylleman *et al.*, 1993). Moreover, as each normative transition leads elite athletes from one stage to another, several different athletic career models have been developed identifying normative career stages and their accompanying transitions. For example, while Salmela (1994) described three normative career stages (i.e., from initiation to development, from development to perfection, from perfection to career termination), Stambulova (1994, 2000) identified a six-point transition model including, for instance, the transition of beginning sports specialization, and from amateur sports to professional sports. As these models allowed the identification of those normative transitions all athletes were expected to experience during their athletic career, they could also be used to envisage how to prepare athletes for, and support them during, up-coming transitions (e.g., from junior to senior level) and thus decrease the likelihood of negative impacts on their mental health. While clearly very beneficial, this approach did not allow elite athletes to prepare for those non-normative events (including the non-transitions).

While the concept of normative athletic transitions and stages broadened the understanding of the athletic career development, it was argued that transitions needed to be delineated not only in terms of their predictability, but also in terms of the developmental context in which they occurred (Wylleman and Lavallee, 2004). A need existed for a 'whole career/whole person approach' (Alfermann and Stambulova, 2007), which took into account transitions and stages athletes also faced in other domains of development (e.g., psychological, psychosocial) and that influenced their athletic development (Wylleman *et al.*, 1999). In 2004, Wylleman and Lavallee presented a 'lifespan' model that later was elaborated into the Holistic Athletic Career model (Wylleman *et al.*, 2013a). This model provided a description of the nature and types of transitions athletes may face throughout and after their athletic career (including stages of initiation, development, mastery, and discontinuation) at different levels of development (i.e., athletic, psychological, psychosocial, academic, vocational, financial). Taking into account its normative perspective on the athletic career, experiential knowledge showed that this model enabled athletes to better prepare for and cope with the concurrent, interactive and reciprocal effects of their transitions in different domains of their lives (Wylleman *et al.*, 2013b).

As it became increasingly clear that elite athletes faced career transitional challenges throughout their athletic careers (e.g., critical life events, life challenges, personal issues, and situational stressors in multiple contexts of development) (Bouchetal Pellegri *et al.*, 2006; Bruner *et al.*, 2008; Pummell *et al.*, 2008), research focused to a greater degree on the mechanisms underlying the possible negative effects of transitions on elite athletes' mental functioning. Experts viewed a transitional challenge as containing the basis for a developmental conflict between what athletes are (or were) and what they want (or believe they ought) to be (Alfermann and Stambulova, 2007). It is this conflict that leads to a process of changes in elite athletes' emotions, cognitions, behaviors, and relationships (Schlossberg, 1981), thus influencing athletes' mental functioning in activities, in relationships, and in their ability to adapt to change and to cope with adversity (US Department of Health and Human Services, 1999).

The process of coping was elaborated by Stambulova (1997, 2003) in her athletic career transition model. She emphasized that the process of the transitional challenge starts for elite athletes with the demands posed to them in order to progress in their development, which stimulates them to mobilize resources and to find ways to cope (Alfermann and Stambulova, 2007). She suggested demands include all factors that may interfere with the development of the athlete (e.g., lack of parental support, combining a study and academic career, first year senior), while resources include all internal and external factors that may facilitate the coping process (e.g., parental support, effective use of mental skills, financial support). The balance between demands and resources and the effective use of resources determines the extent to which athletes are able to cope with the transitional challenge. The process of coping can be effective and lead to a successful transition; it can also be ineffective and lead to a crisis-transition. If elite athletes are able to cope effectively with these transitional challenges, then it can be assumed that they will progress in their development (e.g., by successfully initiating a post-athletic career, by coping with elite sport and motherhood); if not, then elite athletes will be confronted with a crisis or undergo an unsuccessful transition that may lead to a decline in mental health, including sub-clinical or clinical problems (e.g., adjustment problems, psychological disorders; Alfermann and Stambulova, 2007). In this latter case, the use of psychological interventions may aid athletes in successfully coping with the transition; however, if psychological interventions are not effective or if the athlete does not receive psychological support, then the athlete may be confronted with consequences of an unsuccessful transition, which may include decline of athletic performance, overtraining and injuries, and clinical issues (Stambulova, 1994). Failure to cope has been shown to lead to negative consequences, including social losses (Ben-Zur, 2002), depressed mood (Kendler *et al.*, 1998, 1999; Kessler, 1997), changes in locus of control (Braukmann and Filipp, 1995; Eriksen and Ursin, 1999), or physical and psychological symptoms (Ben-Zur, 2002; Theorell *et al.*, 1999).

Elite athletes in transitions

Research during the past three decades has shown that transitions may impact elite athletes' mental functioning not only during retirement nor only in their athletic development, but actually, throughout their athletic career. The possible impact of transitions on elite athletes is illustrated through the three examples described in this section, using a 'whole career/whole person' perspective (Wylleman *et al.*, 2013a). While elite athletes are confronted with a mix of normative and non-normative transitions throughout their career, the following three examples were chosen as major normative transitions occurring near the start, during and at the end of Olympians' athletic careers. While the impact posed by each transition is touched upon throughout each example, a more general overview of the influence of transitional challenges on elite athletes' mental health is part of the conclusion.

The junior-to-senior transition

Towards the end of adolescence, most elite athletes face the transition from elite junior to senior level of competition. As this transition is an institutionalized part of the fabric of competitive sports, it can be considered as normative. The significance of this transition is clearly reflected in the low proportion of athletes successfully progressing to the elite senior level. For example, only between 17 and 27 per cent of elite junior athletes in track and field in Belgium and Germany (Bussmann and Alfermann, 1994; Vanden Auweele *et al.*, 2004) and approximately one junior elite athlete in three in Australia (Australian Sport Commission, 2003) make this transition.

Junior athletes, in their final year, have their last opportunity to win a title within their own age category (e.g., World Junior Championships, Youth Olympic Games) and thus gain credit for a possible professional contract or senior team selection the following year. As such, final-year juniors often challenge themselves to perform to their maximum before taking the actual step to senior level. This need for maximum performances may lead to heightened levels of frustration, anxiety, and stress due to a long period of increased (self-imposed) performance expectations, or may even end in burnout if the expected level of athletic achievements is not reached (e.g., Pummell *et al.*, 2008; Schinke, 2014). This impact on final-year juniors' mental health may be accompanied by a physical overload or overtraining. This is especially relevant as research has shown that the possibility of athletic injury increases throughout the athletic career (Australian Sports Commission, 2003) and specifically during the period of transition from final year junior to first year senior (Orchard and Seward, 2002). Taking into account that an injury carries great emotional cost for athletes (Heil, 2000), psychological outcomes may lead to depressive symptoms, especially at the time of injury onset for athletes with a high athletic identity (Manuel *et al.*, 2002).

In their early senior years, elite athletes are normally confronted with higher standards of training and competition (Bruner *et al.*, 2008; Lorenzo *et al.*, 2009;

Pummell *et al.*, 2008) and may, as a result, experience a change from having been at the top end as junior elite athletes to being at a lower level of athletic prowess and/or achievement as first-year senior athletes (Bussmann and Alfermann, 1994). This change in level of perceived competence may have a strong impact on athletes' self-image and athletic identity (Brewer *et al.*, 2000) and may make novice senior athletes feel 'entrapped in', rather than 'attracted to' senior elite levels of competition. This impact on elite athletes' self-identity may be reinforced by the concurrent challenges they face during their transition from adolescence to young adulthood which require them to develop their own adult identity as well as stronger self-regulatory skills, and skills to cope with unexpected situations, higher expectations and pressures (Wylleman *et al.*, 2013a). Elite athletes may thus become vulnerable to symptoms of burnout as reflected in physical, emotional, and/or social withdrawal from what they formerly perceived to be enjoyable (Raedeke, 1997). This withdrawal can lead to emotional and physical exhaustion, reduced accomplishment, and sport devaluation, and eventually to the dropout of the athlete from elite sport (Cresswell and Eklund, 2007; Gould *et al.*, 1996; Raedeke and Smith, 2001).

On a psychosocial level, relations with significant others also develop or change. For instance, towards the onset of the junior–senior transition, coaches may become more personally involved in their athletes' development, emphasize more technical proficiency, and expect more hard work and discipline from athletes (Lorenzo *et al.*, 2009). Many athletes may also move away from home (e.g. into a professional football academy, their own private accommodation, or student housing), possibly leading to other challenges such as leaving family, friends, club, or elite sport school coach and having to adapt to a novel psychosocial environment (e.g. students, new teammates, new coach; Lorenzo *et al.*, 2009). As a result, parental roles and athletes' perceptions of parental involvement also change (e.g., Wylleman *et al.*, 2007). As young adults, romantic relationships may become a more permanent part of athletes' lives (Wylleman and Lavallee, 2004); however, athletes' strong and almost exclusive focus on their elite sport career may have a strong impact on their social network, as the number and frequency of interactions with their significant others may decrease, leading to feelings of isolation.

As final-year junior elite athletes generally make the transition out of secondary education (MacNamara and Collins, 2010), they may also face challenges at the academic and/or vocational level. For instance, while some may choose to end their academic pursuits and go for a (professional) sport career, others may continue into higher education. In view of the value attributed by parents and by society to an academic education and taking into account the risks (e.g. career-ending injury) and disadvantages (e.g. unfulfilled academic potential, lack of financial security and stability) of elite sport, many novice senior athletes may prefer to continue their academic development (Reints *et al.*, 2008; Reints and Wylleman, 2009; Wylleman and De Knop, 2001). As 'elite student athletes' they will have to cope with challenges that differ strongly from those in secondary education, including, for example, the need to be more personally involved in developing their own academic career, to cope with the relative high degree of freedom to (not) attend academic activities (e.g., classes), to have a more systematic planning of study (e.g., re-scheduling exams), to be fully committed to direct time to academic activities, or to be able to cope with changing social environments (De Knop *et al.*, 1999; Donnelly, 1993).

Finally, this transition has implications on a financial level; research has shown that some novice senior athletes may benefit from a contract as a (semi-)professional athlete on the basis of their athletic potential, while others will have to finance the expenses associated with their development at a senior level themselves (or often via their parents) (Reints, 2011). This reliance on parental financial support may thwart elite athletes' perception of independence and self-control.

The Olympic Games as transition

When athletic achievements bring individuals to world level, many senior elite athletes aspire to successfully compete at the Olympic Games, as it is seen to represent the pinnacle of an athletic career. Competing at the Olympic Games should be considered a transitional challenge as it confronts (especially first-time) Olympians with a diversity of (novel) demands requiring a process of coping that can be effective and lead to a successful transition (i.e., when athletes perform to the best of their ability during the Olympic Games) or, when ineffective, lead to a crisis-transition. In order to prepare elite athletes for a successful participation at the Olympic Games it is important to understand the demands that confront them. While previous research generally focused on the demands of psychological skills in view of actual Olympic competition (e.g., Gould *et al.*, 2002; Greenleaf *et al.*, 2001; Pensgaard and Duda, 2002), a need also existed to gain a better understanding of Olympic participation from a developmental (i.e., before and after Olympic Games) as well as a holistic perspective (e.g., psychosocial level) (Wylleman *et al.*, 2010).

Using a qualitative study with four first-time Olympic athletes, Wylleman and colleagues (Wylleman *et al.*, 2012) showed that these novice Olympians perceived transitional challenges in different domains to occur during, as well as before and after the 2008 Beijing Olympic Games. Challenges perceived at the athletic level included, amongst others, changes in physical and technical preparation and in training routines (frequency and load) as well as coping with jetlag and climate change. These latter issues were perceived to affect athletes' mental functioning (e.g., tiredness) in such a way that support was required to specifically prepare physically and mentally for the effects of jetlag (e.g., Waterhouse *et al.*, 1997) and fatigue (e.g., Hung *et al.*, 2008). After returning from the Olympic Games, these Olympians were also found to take a longer break away from their sport in comparison to other major competitions. This may reflect the need to re-establish a more balanced mental functioning, for example, by returning to their daily routines or to focus on goals in other domains of interest (e.g., studies), put on hold in the run up to the Olympic Games.

While challenges at the athletic level were to be expected, these novice Olympians perceived most challenges to actually occur at the psychological level. These included, for example, an increase in self-confidence and greater identification with the role of Olympian not only before but also after the Olympic Games. Identifying as being part of the Olympic family led to a stronger athletic identity as well as to a greater self-awareness of the influence elite sport had on these athletes' personal lives.

Athletes also highlighted that before and during the Olympic Games they experienced increased isolation while in the holding camp and the Olympic village, as their contact with parents, family, partner and/or peers decreased significantly. In view of the need for a supportive environment to optimize Olympians' mental functioning (e.g., Gould *et al.*, 2002; Jowett and Cramer, 2009), adapting to the more secluded social world of the holding camp and the Olympic village was considered an important transitional challenge. In fact, this seclusion led to another challenge at the psychological level, namely the major challenge of boredom. The long and continuous wait for their first competition challenged athletes' mental functioning perhaps even more than the relatively short period of pre-competition pressure and tension. In order to cope with the challenge of boredom in-between training, eating, and recuperating, Olympians chose to 'keep sane' through increased interaction within their own group, and by focusing on the social aspects of their Olympic experience (e.g., making their own personal video, focusing on the way in which other athletes experienced their Olympic participation). In this way, they were able to create a controlled and stimulating 'safe haven'.

For some, the increased contact with parents, family, partner, and/or peers after returning home from the Olympic Games was perceived to be a (unexpected) challenge as they had to cope with an 'inundation' of social requirements (e.g., parties, press meetings, sponsorship activities) when they were actually looking to settle back down in their own, pre-Games' daily routines. This perceived lack of personal time, or of the control of it, both before as well as after the Olympic Games, may be overwhelming both mentally and physically, resulting in feelings of isolation and loneliness, and possibly leading athletes to psychological maladjustment (Storch *et al.*, 2005; Tracey and Corlett, 1995).

The elite sport to retirement transition

Annually 5–7 per cent of athletes are reported to retire from elite sport (North and Lavallee, 2004). The transitional challenges faced by retiring/retired elite athletes include, amongst others, adjusting to a new life and a new lifestyle following the sport career in which they are suddenly 'like everyone else', missing the sport atmosphere and the competition, dealing with bodily changes and changes in subjective well-being, and adapting to a new social status and vocational responsibilities (e.g., Cecić Erpič *et al.*, 2004; Stephan *et al.*, 2007).

Career termination may lead retiring athletes to experience a sense of loss of personal competence and mastery, social recognition, and enjoyment; they may also feel withdrawn from the sport atmosphere, and miss the numerous satisfying social relationships resulting from competing at the international sport level (Lavallee *et al.*, 2010; Murphy, 1995; Scanlan *et al.*, 1989; Taylor and Ogilvie, 2001). The retiring athlete must also handle significant changes in identity and lifestyle, while trying to cope with a future that requires new skills and competences in order to achieve optimal psychological well-being. Further, retiring athletes must deal with bodily changes, financial changes, and adapt to a new social status and vocational responsibilities. As a result, athletes may alter how they engage in life, which in turn may lead to behavioral deactivation and result in dysphoric mood and a heightened sense of hopelessness (Gardner and Moore, 2006).

Not all elite athletes will experience retirement as traumatic, as many will naturally evolve through this transition. However, athletes retiring with an especially high athletic identity may be in need of professional assistance (Gardner and Moore, 2006), as they are more likely to adapt poorly to career termination, and potentially fall prey to major depression or even suicidal behavior (Baum, 2006; Chartrand and Lend, 1987). While the rate of retired athletes experiencing depressive symptoms is found to be fairly similar to that of the general population, the impact of these symptoms may become compounded by high levels of physical pain (e.g., related to the long-term physical strain and injuries they incurred through sport), putting retired athletes at a higher risk of significant difficulties with sleep, social relationships, finances, and exercise and fitness, or even at an increased risk for suicide (Schwenk *et al.*, 2007).

Particular to the vocational challenges faced by former elite athletes is the phenomenon of 'occupational delay' (Naul, 1994). Those elite athletes who continue as full-time elite athletes after graduating from higher education may actually have few, if any, opportunities to actively employ and further extend the knowledge and skills gained through their education. When retiring from elite sport, these athletes may therefore lack the relevant professional knowledge, skills, experience, and relational networks that others may have acquired via, for example, summer jobs, vocational or in-service training, or part-time employment. The 'delay' between individuals' acquisition of their knowledge and skills and the moment in which they actually put these to use may thus be too long for retired elite athletes to start vocations or attain vocational success. Due to this occupational delay, retired elite athletes may thus need to return to higher (postgraduate) education or to basic vocational training in order to gain (up-to-date or new) professional knowledge and skills.

Retired elite athletes who are successful in entering the job market may find themselves 'at the bottom of the ladder', confronted not only with lower wages in comparison to their non-athletic peers, but also lower than expected wages on the basis of their age, resulting in younger aged co-workers or colleagues who may have seniority over them. Moreover, former elite athletes may (e.g., due to lack of financial stability) turn to their family of origin for support, or even return home to live with their parents, which may lead to interpersonal (or intergenerational) problems. Taking into account these challenges, it should not be surprising that vocational training is an important part of career support services enhancing the quality of the post-athletic career (Reints and Wylleman, 2009).

Practical implications and recommendations

Using athletic retirement and its possible traumatic effect on elite athletes' mental health as a point of departure, this chapter first aimed to create awareness of the different concurrent, interactive, and reciprocal transitions elite athletes face in different domains of life throughout their athletic career. Three examples of transitions specific to Olympic athletes were used to illustrate some of the effects these transitional challenges may have on elite athletes' mental functioning. It must be clear that these three examples, as well as other transitions can influence elite athletes' mental health as the accompanying challenges result in developmental conflicts that affect these athletes' mental function. Depending upon elite athletes' ability to cope with transitions, and the support they receive throughout, these challenges may lead to a range of psychological, interpersonal, social, and financial crises or even traumatic experiences (Stambulova *et al.*, 2009).

More important however is that the developmental and holistic perspectives on elite athletes' careers as described in this chapter allow for the identification of several normative transitions, whose predictable character creates an opportunity for athletes to prepare for them. Taking into account that a transition develops as a process consisting of different transitional challenges concurrently influenced by different domains of development, athletes may decrease the possible negative impact of transitions in three ways. First, crisis-prevention interventions (e.g., education management, life skills training, lifestyle management, career management, financial management, health management) may provide athletes support when foreseeing or being confronted with transitional challenges and when planning or actively trying to mobilize resources to cope with these challenges. Second, crisis-coping interventions (e.g., counselling, clinical psychology therapy) can assist athletes when faced with an ineffective transitional process and thus when heading for or being confronted with a transitional crisis. It is only when these coping interventions fail that interventions may include a third approach of psychotherapeutic or clinical interventions. A worldwide survey of 27 career assistance providers including lifestyle coaches, sport psychology consultants, and career management professionals showed that services are generally aimed at preparing elite athletes for upcoming transitions (during as well as after the athletic career) including, for example, education management, life skills training and lifestyle management, career management, financial management, and health management (Reints, 2011).

It is of course important to fully take into account the individual differences among elite athletes, and more particularly, the occurrence of non-normative transitions as illustrated by legendary tennis player Pete Sampras. In his autobiography, he explicitly stated that he wanted to acknowledge the events that "aren't the things that come to most people's minds at the mention of my name" (i.e., the death of his mentor and coach stricken by cancer, losing a close friend to a tragic accident, versus 14 Grand Slam titles), as he wanted to "reveal what they meant and how they affected me" (Sampras, 2008: x). Pete Sampras' comments reinforce that career assistance services cannot always be tailor-made nor can they be delivered with a 'just-in-time' approach (Stambulova, 2010). Therefore, the delivery of programs to increase the self-regulatory competences of elite athletes is certainly recommended. An example is Danish and colleagues' 'life development interventions' (LDIs) (Danish *et al.*, 1995), which emphasize continuous growth and development across the lifespan and provide athletes with supportive strategies (i.e., before and during a transition) as well as counselling strategies (i.e., after a transition). Wylleman (1999) also presented an educational program for talented athletes who, from the moment they enter competitive sport, are educated about (future) transitions and proactively learn the skills required to cope with transitional challenges they may face throughout their athletic career. Using a developmental and holistic perspective, athletes master skills throughout their career including time management, transitions, media, relationships, financial management, and networking skills (Wylleman and Reints, 2014). Both programs emphasize a lifespan perspective on coping with transitional challenges and thus provide for the reported long-term career development needs of athletes coming through the elite athlete system (North and Lavallee, 2004).

Finally, experiential knowledge shows that coaches and support staff also play an important role in the way athletes are able to cope with transitional challenges. Coaches and support staff should be made fully aware of the significance and impact of the multilevel transitions as elite athletes progress throughout their athletic careers. The use of a generic framework as the Holistic Athletic Career model may assist coaches and support staff in acquiring this insight (Alfermann and Stambulova, 2007; Wylleman *et al.*, 2013a). Furthermore, as transitions influence athletes' development in different domains, an interdisciplinary approach is required covering elite athletes' multilevel needs throughout their athletic career. This approach can be supported by a 'transition coach' who assists elite athletes in preparing for specific transitional challenges, and provides the appropriate multidisciplinary support enabling elite athletes to use in an optimal way their own coping skills during as well as after each transition, thus reducing the possible negative impact on their mental health.

References

Alfermann, D. (1995) 'Career transitions of elite athletes: Drop-out and retirement', in R. Vanfraechem-Raway and Y. Vanden Auweele (eds) *Proceedings of the Ninth European Congress of Sport Psychology*, Brussels: European Federation of Sports Psychology FEPSAC, 828–33.

Alfermann, D. and Gross, A. (1997) 'Coping with career termination: It all depends on freedom of choice', in R. Lidor and M. Bar-Eli (eds) *Proceedings of the Ninth World Congress on Sport Psychology*, Netanya: Wingate Institute for Physical Education and Sport, 65–7.

Alfermann, D. and Stambulova, N. B. (2007) 'Career transitions and career termination', in G. Tenenbaum and R. C. Eklund (eds) *Handbook of Sport Psychology*, 3rd edn, New York: Wiley, 712–36.

Allison, M. T. and Meyer, C. (1988) 'Career problems and retirement among elite athletes: The female tennis professional', *Sociology of Sport Journal*, 5: 212–22.

Australian Sports Commission. (2003) *How Do Elite Athletes Develop? A look through the 'rear-view mirror'. A preliminary report from the National Athlete Development Survey (NADS)*, Canberra, Australia: Australian Sports Commission.

Baum, A. (2006) 'Eating disorders in the male athlete', *Sports Medicine*, 36: 1–6.

Ben-Zur, H. (2002) 'Coping, affect, and aging: The roles of mastery and self-esteem', *Personality and Individual Differences*, 32: 357–72.

Blinde, E. M. and Greendorfer, S. L. (1985) 'A reconceptualization of the process of leaving the role of elite athlete', *International Review for Sociology of Sport*, 20: 87–93.

Bloom, B. S. (ed.) (1985) *Developing Talent in Young People*, New York: Ballantine.

Bouchetal Pellegri, F., Leseur, V. and Debois, N. (2006) *Carrière sportive. Projet de vie.* Paris, éditions INSEP, coll. Entraînement.

Braukmann, W. and Filipp, S.-H. (1995) 'Personale Kontrolle und die Bewältigung kritischer Lebenereignisse [Personal control and the management of critical life events]', in S.H. Filipp (ed.) *Kritische lebensereignisse*, Weinheim: Beltz. 233–51.

Brewer, B. W. and Petitpas, A. J. (2005) 'Returning to self: The anxieties of coming back after injury', in M. Andersen (ed.) *Sport Psychology in Practice*, Champaign, IL: Human Kinetics, 93–108.

Brewer, B. W., Van Raalte, J. L. and Petitpas, A. J. (2000) 'Self-identity issues in sport career transitions', in D. Lavallee and P. Wylleman (eds) *Career Transitions in Sport: International perspectives*, Morgantown, WV: Fitness Information Technology, 29–43.

Bruner, M. W., Munroe-Chandler, K. J. and Spink, K. S (2008) 'Entry into elite sport: A preliminary investigation into the transition experiences of rookie athletes', *Journal of Applied Sport Psychology*, 20: 236–52.

Bussmann, G. and Alfermann, D. (1994) 'Drop-out and the female athlete: A study with track-and-field athletes', in D. Hackfort (ed.) *Psycho-social Issues and Interventions in Elite Sport*, Frankfurt: Lang, 89–128.

Cecić Erpič, S. C., Wylleman, P. and Zupani, M. (2004) 'The effect of athletic and non-athletic factors on the sports career termination process', *Psychology of Sport and Exercise*, 5: 45–59.

Charner, I. and Schlossberg, N. K. (1986) 'Variations by theme: The life transitions of clerical workers', *The Vocational Guidance Quarterly*, 212–24.

Chartrand, J. M. and Lent, R. W. (1987) 'Sports counseling: Enhancing the development of the student-athlete', *Journal of Counseling and Development*, 66: 164–7.

Cresswell, S. L. and Eklund, R. C. (2007) 'Athlete burnout: A longitudinal qualitative study', *The Sport Psychologist*, 21: 1–20.

Danish, S. J., Petitpas, A. J. and Hale, B. D. (1995) 'Psychological interventions: A life developmental model', in S. M. Murphy (ed.) *Sport Psychology Interventions*, Champaign, IL: Human Kinetics, 19–38.

De Knop, P., Wylleman, P., Van Hoecke, J. and Bollaert, L. (1999) 'Sports management – A European approach to the management of the combination of academics and elite-level sport', in S. Bailey (ed.) *Perspectives – The interdisciplinary series of physical education and sport science. Vol. 1. School sport and competition*, Oxford: Meyer & Meyer Sport, 49–62.

Donnelly, P. (1993) 'Problems associated with youth involvement in high-performance sport', in B. R. Cahill and A. J. Pearl (eds) *Intensive Participation in Children's Sports*, Champaign, IL: Human Kinetics, 95–126.

Eriksen, H. R. and Ursin, H. (1999) 'Subjective health complaints: Is coping more important than control?' *Work and Stress*, 13: 238–52.

Gardner, F. and Moore, Z. (2006) *Clinical Sport Psychology*, Champaign, Il.: Human Kinetics.

Gould, D., Tuffey, S., Udry, E. and Loehr, J. (1996) 'Burnout in competitive junior tennis players: I. A quantitative psychological assessment', *The Sport Psychologist*, 10: 322–40.

Gould, D., Greenleaf, C., Guinan, D. and Chung, Y. (2002) 'A survey of U.S. Olympic coaches: Factors influencing athlete performances and coach effectiveness', *The Sport Psychologist*, 16: 229–50.

Greenleaf, C., Gould, D. and Dieffenbach, K. (2001) 'Factors influencing Olympic performance: Interviews with Atlanta and Nagano U.S. Olympians', *Journal of Applied Sport Psychology*, 13: 154–84.

Grijsbach, M. (2010) 'Vancouver 2010: de mislukte Spelen van Sven Kramer'. Online at: www.rnw.nl/nederlands/article/vancouver-2010-de-mislukte-spelen-van-sven-kramer.

Grove, J. R., Lavallee, D., Gordon, S. and Harvey, J. H. (1998) 'Account-making: A model for understanding and resolving distressful reactions to retirement from sport', *The Sport Psychologist*, 12: 52–67.

Haerle, R. K. (1975) 'Career patterns and career contingencies of professional baseball players: An occupational analysis', in D. W. Ball and J. W. Loy (eds) *Sport and Social Order*, Reading, MA: Addison-Wesley, 461–519.

Hallden, O. (1965) 'The adjustment of athletes after retiring from sport', in F. Antonelli (ed.) *Proceedings of the First International Congress of Sport Psychology*, Rome: International Society of Sport Psychology, 730–3.

Hays, K. F. (2009) *Performance Psychology in Action: A casebook for working with athletes, performing artists, business leaders, and professionals in high-risk occupations*, Washington, DC: American Psychological Association.

Heil, J. (2000) 'The injured athlete', in Y. L. Hahn (ed.) *Emotions in Sport*, Champaign, IL: Human Kinetics, 245–66.

Henin, J. (2011) 'End of career…', Facebook. Online at: www.facebook.com/note.php?note_id=10150092010499306 (accessed 10 April 2014).

Hung, T.-M., Lin, T.-C., Lee, C.-L. and Chen, L.-C. (2008) 'Provision of sport psychology services to Taiwan archery team for the 2004 Athens Olympic Games', *International Journal of Sport and Exercise Psychology*, 6: 308–18.

Jowett, S. and Cramer, D. (2009) 'The role of romantic relationships on athletes' performance and well-being', *Journal of Clinical Sports Psychology*, 3: 58–72.

Kendler, K. S., Karkowski, L. M. and Prescott, C. A. (1998) 'Stressful life events and major depression: Risk period, long-term contextual threat, and diagnostic specificity', *The Journal of Nervous and Mental Disease*, 186: 661–9.

Kendler, K. S., Karkowski, L. M. and Prescott, C. A. (1999) 'Causal relationship between stressful life events and onset of major depression', *The American Journal of Psychiatry*, 156: 837–41.

Kessler, R. C. (1997) 'The effects of stressful life events on depression', *Annual Review of Psychology*, 48: 191–214.

Lavallee, D. (2000) 'Theoretical perspectives on career transitions in sport', in D. Lavallee and P. Wylleman (eds) *Career Transitions in Sport: International perspectives*, Morgantown, WV: Fitness Information Technology, 1–27.

Lavallee, D. and Andersen, M. B. (2000) 'Leaving sport: Easing career transitions', in M. B. Andersen (ed.) *Doing Sport Psychology*, Champaign, IL: Human Kinetics, 249–60.

Lavallee, D., Nesti, M., Borkeles, E., Cockerill, I. and Edge, A. (2000) 'Intervention strategies for athletes in transition', in D. Lavallee and P. Wylleman (eds) *Career Transitions in Sport: International perspectives*, Morgantown, WV: Fitness Information Technology, 111–30.

Lavallee, D., Sugnhee, P. and Tod, D. (2010) 'Career termination', in S. J. Hanrahan and M. B. Andersen (eds) *Routledge Handbook of Applied Sport Psychology: A comprehensive guide for students and practitioners*, New York, NY: Routledge, 242–9.

Lorenzo, A., Borrás, P. J., Sánchez, J. M., Jiménez, S. and Sampedro, J. (2009) 'Career transition from junior to senior in basketball players', *Revista de Psicologia del Deporte*, 18 (suppl.): 309–12.

MacNamara, Á. and Collins, D. (2010) 'The role of psychological characteristics in managing the transition to university', *Psychology of Sport and Exercise*, 11(5): 353–62.

Manuel, J. C., Shilt, J. S., Curl, W. W., Smith, J. A., DuRant, R. H., Lester, L. and Sinal, S. H. (2002) 'Coping with sports injuries: An examination of the adolescent athlete', *Journal of Adolescent Health*, 31: 391–3.

McPherson, B. D. (1980) 'Retirement from professional sport: the process and problems of occupational and psychological adjustment', *Sociological Symposium*, 30: 126–43.

Mihovilovic, M. (1968) 'The status of former sportsmen', *International Review of Sport Sociology*, 3: 73–93.

Moore, Z. E. (2012) 'Counseling performers in distress', in S. M. Murphy (ed.) *The Oxford Handbook of Sport and Performance Psychology*, New York, NY: Oxford University Press, 527–44.

Murphy, S. (1995) 'Transitions in competitive sport: Maximizing individual potential', in S. M. Murphy (ed.) *Sport Psychology Interventions*, Champaign, IL: Human Kinetics, 331–46.

Naul, R. (1994) 'The elite athlete career: Sport pedagogy must counsel social and professional problems in life development', in D. Hackfort (ed.) *Psycho-social Issues and Interventions in Elite Sport*, Frankfurt: Lang, 237–58.

North, J. and Lavallee, D. (2004) 'An investigation of potential users of career transition services in the United Kingdom', *Psychology of Sport and Exercise*, 5: 77–84.

Ogilvie, B. C. and Taylor, J. (1993) 'Career termination issues among elite athletes', in R. N. Singer, M. Murphey and L. K. Tennant (eds) *Handbook of Research on Sport Psychology*, New York: Macmillan, 761–75.

Orchard, J. W. and Seward, H. (2002) 'Epidemiology of injuries in the Australian Football League, seasons 1997–2000', *British Journal of Sports Medicine*, 36: 39–44.

Orlick, T. (2008) *In Pursuit of Excellence*, 4th edn, Champaign, IL: Human Kinetics.

Pensgaard, A. M. and Duda, J. L. (2002) '"If we work hard, we can do it". A tale from an Olympic (gold) medallist', *Journal of Applied Sport Psychology*, 14: 219–36.

Pummell, B., Harwood, C. and Lavallee, D. (2008) 'Jumping to the next level: A qualitative examination of within-career transition in adolescent event riders', *Psychology of Sport and Exercise*, 9: 427–47.

Raedeke, T. D. (1997) 'Is athlete burnout more than just stress? A sport commitment perspective', *Journal of Sport and Exercise Psychology*, 19: 396–417.

Raedeke, T. D. and Smith, A. L. (2001) 'Development and preliminary validation of an athlete burnout measure', *Journal of Sport and Exercise Psychology*, 23: 281–306.

Redgrave, S. and Townsend, N. (2001) *A Golden Age*, London, UK: BBC Worldwide Ltd.

Reints, A. (2011) 'Development and validation of a model of careertransition and the identification of variables of influence on ending the career among elite athletes', unpublished thesis, Vrije Universiteit Brussel.

Reints, A. and Wylleman, P. (2009) 'Investigation of athlete career support services required by and currently offered to (former) elite athletes', in *Proceedings of the Congrès International de Psychologie du Sport*, Paris, France: SFPS – INSEP, 01-03.07.09, 41.

Reints, A., Wylleman, P. and Dom, L. (2008) 'Kwalitatief onderzoek naar relatie tussen beroepsgerichte na-carrièreplanning en huidige beroepssituatie van Vlaamse ex-topjudoka's [Qualitative research into the relationship between profession-oriented past-career planning and current professional situation of Flemish former elite judokas]', during the Congres VSPN 'Van wetenschap naar praktijk'. Amsterdam, the Netherlands: Vereniging Sportpsychologie Nederland – VUAmsterdam.

Salmela, J. H. (1994) 'Learning from the development of expert coaches', *Coaching and Sport Science Journal*, 1: 1–11.

Sampras, P. (2008) *A Champion's Mind: Lessons from a life in tennis*, New York: Crown Publishers.

Scanlan, T. K., Ravizza, K. and Stein, G. L. (1989) 'An in-depth study of former elite figure skaters: 1. Introduction to the project', *Journal of Sport and Exercise Psychology*, 11: 54–64.

Schinke, R. (2014) 'Adaptation', in R. Eklund and G. Tenenbaum (eds) *Encyclopedia of Sport and Exercise Psychology*, Sage, 9–10.

Schlossberg, N. K. (1981) 'A model for analyzing human adaptation to transition', *The Counseling Psychologist*, 9: 2–18.

Schlossberg, N. K. (1984) *Counseling Adults in Transition: Linking practice with theory*, New York: Springer.

Schwenk, T. L., Gorenflo, D. W., Dopp, R. R. and Hipple, E. (2007) 'Depression and pain in retired professional football players', *Medicine and Science in Sports and Exercise*, 39: 599–605.

Sinclair, D. A. and Orlick, T. (1993) 'Positive transitions from high-performance sport', *The Sport Psychologist*, 7: 138–50.

Stambulova, N. (1997) 'Sports career transitions', in J. Bangsbo and B. Saltin (eds) *Proceedings of the 2 Annual Congress of the European College of Sport Sciences*, Copenhagen, Denmark: ECSS, 88–9.

Stambulova, N. (2003) 'Symptoms of a crisis-transition: A grounded theory study', in N. Hassmen (ed.) *SIPF Yearbook 2003*, Örebro, Sweden: Örebro University Press, 97–109.

Stambulova, N. (2010) 'Counseling athletes in career transitions: The five-step career planning strategy', *Journal of Sport Psychology in Action*, 1: 95–105.

Stambulova, N. B. (1994) 'Developmental sports career investigations in Russia: A post-perestroika analysis', *The Sport Psychologist*, 8: 221–37.

Stambulova, N. B. (2000) 'Athlete's crises: a developmental perspective', *International Journal of Sport Psychology*, 31: 584–601.

Stambulova, N., Alfermann, D., Statler, T. and Côté, J. (2009) 'ISSP position stand: Career development and transitions of athletes', *International Journal of Sport and Exercise Psychology*, 7: 395–412.

Stephan, Y., Torregrosa, M. and Sanchez, X. (2007) 'The body matters: Psychophysical impact of retiring from elite sport', *Psychology of Sport and Exercise*, 8: 73–83.

Storch, E.A., Storch, J. B., Killiany, E. M. and Roberti, J. W. (2005) 'Self-reported psychopathology in athletes: A comparison of intercollegiate student-athletes and non-athletes', *Journal of Sport Behavior*, 28: 86–98.

Swain, D. A. (1991) 'Withdrawal from sport and Schlossberg's model of transitions', *Sociology of Sport Journal*, 8: 152–60.

Taylor, J. and Ogilvie, B. C. (1998) 'Career transition among elite athletes: Is there life after sports?', in J. M. Williams (ed.) *Applied Sport Psychology: Personal growth to peak performance*, Mountain View, CA: Mayfield, 429–44.

Taylor, J. and Ogilvie, B. C. (2001) 'Career termination among athletes', in R. Singer, H. Hausenblas and C. Janelle (eds) *Handbook of Sport Psychology*, 2nd edn, New York, NY: Wiley & Sons, 672–91.

Theorell, T., Blomkvist, V., Lindh, G. and Evengård, B. (1999) 'Critical life events, infections, and symptoms during the year preceding chronic fatigue syn-drome (CFS): An examination of CFS patients and subjects with a nonspecific life crisis', *Psychosomatic Medicine*, 61: 304–10.

Torres, D. and Weil, E. (2009) *Age Is Just a Number: Achieve your dreams at any stage in your life*, New York: Broadway Books.

Tracey, J. and Corlett, J. (1995) 'The transition experience of first-year university track and field student athletes', *Journal of The Freshman Year Experience*, 7: 82–102.

US Department of Health and Human Services (1999) *Mental Health: A report of the Surgeon General*, Tockville, MD: US Department of Health and Human Services, Substance Abuse and Mental Health Services Administration, Center for Mental Health Services, National Institutes of Health, National Institute of Mental Health.

Vanden Auweele, Y., De Martelaer, K., Rzewnicki, R., De Knop, P. and Wylleman, P. (2004) 'Parents and coaches: A help or harm? Affective outcomes for children in sport', in Y. Vanden Auweele (ed.) *Ethics in Youth Sport*, Leuven, Belgium: Lannoocampus, 179–93.

Waterhouse, J., Reilly, T. and Atkinson, G. (1997) 'Jet-lag', *The Lancet*, 350: 1609–14.

Webb, W. M., Nasco, S. A., Riley, S. and Headrick, B. (1998) 'Athlete identity and reactions to retirement from sports', *Journal of Sport Behavior*, 21: 338–62.

Wheeler, G. D., Malone, L. A., VanVlack, S., Nelson, E. R. and Steadward, R. D. (1996) 'Retirement from disability sport: a pilot study', *Adapted Physical Activity Quarterly*, 13: 382–99.

Wilkinson, J. (2006) *Jonny Wilkinson. My World*, London: Headline.

Wippert, P.-M. and Wippert, J. (2008) 'Perceived stress and prevalence of traumatic stress symptoms following athletic career termination', *Journal of Clinical Sport Psychology*, 1–16.

Wylleman, P. (1999) *A Career Assistance Program for Elite and Student-athletes*, during the Workshop Career Transitions, Copenhagen, Denmark: Olympic Team Denmark, 8 December 1999.

Wylleman, P. and De Knop, P. (2001) 'Providing quality management in the combination of academics and high level sport', in *Book of Proceedings of the 9th European Congress on Sport Management*, Vitoria-Gasteiz, Spanje: European Association for Sport Management, 364–5.

Wylleman, P. and Lavallee D. (2004) 'A developmental perspective on transitions faced by athletes', in M. Weiss (ed.) *Developmental Sport and Exercise Psychology: A lifespan perspective*, Morgantown, WV: Fitness Information Technology, 507–27.

Wylleman, P. and Reints, A. (2014) 'Career assistance programs', in R. Eklund and G. Tenenbaum (eds) *Encyclopedia of Sport and Exercise Psychology*, Thousand Oaks: SAGE publications, 106–9.

Wylleman, P., De Knop, P., Menkehorst, H., Theeboom, M. and Annerel, J. (1993) 'Career termination and social integration among elite athletes', in S. Serpa, J. Alves, V. Ferreira and A. Paula-Brito (eds) *Proceedings of the Eighth World Congress of Sport Psychology*, Lisbon: International Society of Sport Psychology, 902–6.

Wylleman, P., Lavallee, D. and Alfermann, D. (eds) (1999) *FEPSAC Monograph Series. Career transitions in competitive sports*, Lund: European Federation of Sport Psychology FEPSAC.

Wylleman, P., Lavallee, D. and Theeboom, M. (2004) 'Successful athletic careers', in C. Spielberger (ed.) *Encyclopedia of Applied Psychology*, vol. 3, New York: Elsevier, 511–17.

Wylleman, P., De Knop, P., Verdet, M. C. and Cecic-Erpic, S. (2007) 'Parenting and career transitions of elite athletes', in S. Jowett and D. Lavallee (eds) *Social Psychology in Sport*, Champaign, IL: Human Kinetics, 233–48.

Wylleman, P., Harwood, C. G., Elbe, A.-M., Reints, A. and de Caluwé, D. (2010) 'A perspective on education and professional development in applied sport psychology', *Psychology of Sport and Exercise*, 10: 435–46.

Wylleman, P., Reints, A. and Van Aken, S. (2012) 'Athletes' perceptions of multilevel changes related to competing at the 2008 Beijing Olympic Games', *Psychology of Sport and Exercise*, 13: 687–92.

Wylleman, P., Reints, A. and De Knop, P. (2013a) 'A developmental and holistic perspective on athletic career development', in P. Sotiaradou and V. De Bosscher (eds) *Managing High Performance Sport*, New York, NY: Routledge, 159–82.

Wylleman, P., Reints, A. and De Knop, P. (2013b) 'Athletes' careers in Belgium. A holistic perspective to understand and alleviate challenges occurring throughout the athletic and post- athletic career', in N. Stambulova and T. Ryba (eds) *Athletes' Careers Across Cultures*, New York, NY: Routledge – ISSP, 31–42.

8 Sport and longevity

Does being an elite athlete result in longer life?

Joseph Baker, Nick Wattie and Srdjan Lemez

The short- and medium-term health consequences resulting from participation in elite and high performance sport are varied, ranging from negative outcomes such as rates of injury (Dubravcic-Simunjak *et al.*, 2003), predisposition to developmental deficiencies (e.g., Osgood Schlatter disease; Kujala *et al.*, 1985), and/or psychological/behavioral conditions such as disordered eating (e.g., Sundgot-Borgen and Torstveit, 2004) to positive outcomes such as improved youth development (e.g., Fraser-Thomas *et al.*, 2005) and involvement in healthy behaviors (e.g., increased fruits/vegetables and decreased alcohol/smoking; Pate *et al.*, 2000). Much less research has focused on the long-term health effects of participation in high performance sport. In this chapter we consider the relationship between participation as elite or professional athletes and arguably the ultimate health outcome – longevity (i.e., lifespan). The issue of lifespan length introduces a host of other concerns such as lifespan length versus quality (e.g., is morbidity the more relevant outcome?). Unfortunately, research in this area is in its infancy and many of these issues are beyond the scope of this chapter. In the sections that follow, we focus on summarizing the limited research done to date on participation in high performance sport and lifespan length while highlighting important areas for further investigation.

Studies of mortality and professional sport

Given the almost overwhelming evidence supporting the positive relationship between involvement in physical activity, exercise and sport, and increased health (see Hardman and Stensel, 2009), common sense would suggest that participation in sport, typically among the most vigorous forms of physical activity, should lead to a longer lifespan. However, we actually know very little about the experience of being an elite and/or professional athlete and its resultant effects on health (see also Chapter 5 by Hastmann-Walch and Caine) and mortality.

In the popular media, several concerning cases of suicide and depression in ex- or current elite athletes have captured a significant amount of attention (e.g., the NFL's Junior Seau and the NHL's Rick Rypien); however, these cases seem incongruent with the empirical evidence. Table 8.1 presents a summary of existing studies of mortality in elite sporting samples. The earliest exploration of this

Table 8.1 Studies on mortality and longevity of elite/professional athletes (>1990)

Study	Focus	N	Results/conclusions
Abel and Kruger, 2004	Left-handed MLB players	6038	No significant differences in longevity related to handedness
Abel and Kruger, 2005a	Longevity of MLB players	2604	MLB players lived an average of 4 years longer than age-matched controls. Career length was not a factor
Abel and Kruger, 2005b	Baseball HOFs	3573	Median post-induction survival for HOFs was 5 years shorter than for non-inducted players
Abel and Kruger, 2006a	The healthy worker effect	4492	LE: 4.8 years longer; career length incrementally increased longevity (1900–1939 debut)
Abel and Kruger, 2006b	The healthy worker effect in professional football; debut <1940	1512	Football players lived 6.1 years longer; career length significantly and incrementally increased longevity (+ 5.5 years for one season; + 6.7 years for 4+ seasons). Position was not a predictor
Barnwell, 2012 (Grantland article);	Baseball versus football, 1959–1988	4582	12.8% of football players had died (N=3088) compared to 15.9% of baseball players (N=1494)
Baron et al. 2012	NFL players from 1959–1988	3439	Players had increased overall longevity (SMR=0.53), but those with a playing time BMI >30 kg/m2 had twice the risk of CVD mortality compared to other players. African-American players and defensive linemen had 42% higher CVD mortality
Belli and Vanacore, 2005	Mortality in top league Italian soccer players, 1960–1996	350	High risk for ALS was found. A possible connection between dietary supplements or PEDs and ALS pathogenesis exists
Gajewski and Poznańska, 2008	Mortality of top Polish Olympic athletes, 1924–2000	1689 males; 424 females	Greater overall longevity in male (n=1689; SMR=0.50) and female (n=424; SMR=0.73) Olympians
Grimsmo et al., 2011	Mortality and CV morbidity among long-term endurance cross-country skiers	122	Total deaths were 31% compared with 40% in the general male population. BMI and average systolic blood pressure were predictors of later appearance of CVD

Study	Description	n	Findings
Kuss et al., 2011	Longevity of German soccer players from 1908–2006	812	Reduced longevity for players was found; mainly driven by the mortality of internationals from the earlier half of the observation period (e.g., poorer medical care, WWII, etc.)
Menotti et al., 1990	Life expectancy in national Italian track and field athletes	983	Greater overall longevity in males (SMR=0.73; n=700) and females (SMR=0.48; n=283); (active>1940)
Pärssinen et al., 2000	Premature mortality of Finnish power-lifters due to anabolic agents, 1977–1982	62	Mortality in 12-year follow-up was 12.9% (3.1% for controls); 4.6 times higher risk of death. Causes: suicide, myocardial infarction, hepatic coma, and non-Hodgkin's lymphoma
Reynolds and Day, 2012	MLB players, 1900–1999	14,360	Mortality risk for MLB players increased with age and decreased over time except in the 1950–1969 and 1980–1999 periods. Players had greater life expectancy in all periods compared to the general population
Saint Onge et al., 2008	MLB players, debuts between 1902–2004	6,772	Compared to 20-year-old US males, MLB players can expect almost 5 additional years of life
Sarna et al., 1993	1920–1965 Finnish track and field, skiing, soccer, hockey, weightlifting, and shooting	2,613	Mean LE for endurance sports was 75.6; team sports, 73.9; power sports, 71.5. Increased LEs mainly explained by basketball, boxing, wrestling, decreased cardiovascular mortality (referents, 69.9 LE)
Taioli, 2007	Mortality rates of professional Italian soccer players, 1975–2003	5,389	SMRs: circulatory system (0.41), cancer (0.31), and immune deficiency (0.24); car accidents (2.23), ALS (18.18); overall (0.68)
Zwiers et al., 2012	Mortality in former Olympic athletes, 1896–1936 (known death date)	9,889	High intensity disciplines did not bring a survival benefit compared with low intensity exercise. Increased mortality among athletes with high risk of bodily collision (HR = 1.11)

Note: * All studies used the general population as the control/comparison group and male athletes unless otherwise specified. ALS = amyotrophic lateral sclerosis; BMI = body mass index; CV = cardiovascular; CVD = cardiovascular disease; HOFs = Hall of Famers; HR = hazard rate/ratio of death; LE = life expectancy; PEDs = performance enhancing drugs; SMR = standardized mortality ratio.

phenomenon (Hartley and Llewellyn, 1939) focused on longevity of rowers; moreover, a significant proportion of the research has focused on baseball players, arguably due to consistency in historical records in this sport. Former Major League Baseball (MLB) players live an average of four years longer than the general population's age-matched controls, particularly those who had longer careers (Abel and Kruger, 2005a; 2006a; see also Reynolds, 2012). However, players inducted into the Baseball Hall of Fame had lifespans that were five years shorter than non-inducted players (Abel and Kruger, 2005b), a concept we return to later in this chapter.

Similar general longevity benefits have also been noted in professional American football players. However, Baron and colleagues' (Baron *et al.*, 2012) analysis of National Football League (NFL) players between 1959 and 1988 noted that while athletes had longer lifespan than comparators from the general population, those with a playing time body mass index (BMI) of >30 kg/m² had a significantly higher risk of cardiovascular disease (CVD) mortality (Baron *et al.*, 2012). Moreover, they found significant position and race/ethnicity effects; defensive linemen and African-American players had increased CVD mortality risk (Baron *et al.*, 2012). Unfortunately, the possible mechanisms explaining these increased risks were not identified in the Baron *et al.* study and may be confounded by the tendency for racial/ethnic groups to play specific positions (a phenomenon known as 'racial stacking'; Woodward, 2004).

Interestingly, emerging evidence suggests MLB players have worse survival rates than NFL players (Barnwell, 2012). The lower incidence of early mortality in NFL players relative to MLB players and the general population may be attributed to specific moderators of the professional athlete and longevity relationship. Although a high score on the BMI scale generally indicates a higher body fat percentage, a study on 129 retired NFL players concluded that only 13 out of the 87 who were classified as obese were in fact obese based on their body fat percentage (Hyman *et al.*, 2012). Additionally, despite their overall size, both active and retired NFL players showed a lower prevalence of impaired fasting glucose (Tucker *et al.*, 2009). These findings provide an important portrayal of NFL players' post-retirement and general health practices, and may give some indication into retired players' maintenance of healthy active lifestyles. A non-physical moderator of mortality that may also be overlooked in professional sport cohorts is the incidence of smoking cigarettes; both retired and active NFL players have a much lower incidence of smoking (Tucker *et al.*, 2009), which has been a robust contributor of early mortality (Thun *et al.*, 2013). Similarly, the unique culture of baseball has historically included the prevalent use of smokeless tobacco (i.e., 'spit or chewing tobacco'; Eaves, 2011), which is also associated with an increased risk of CVD (see Piano *et al.*, 2010) and immune system dysfunction (see Willis *et al.*, 2012).

A caveat to Baron and colleagues' (2012) NFL mortality investigation is that it excludes the impact playing football has on quality of life. Although empirical data are only just emerging, popular media has exposed mental illness concerns from brain trauma and other trauma-induced diseases to the public (see King and

Gagné, 2012). A recent longitudinal study of active and retired NFL players found significant decreases in normal brain function in most neuropsychological tests, which corroborates the higher prevalence of depression, drug-use, and potential consequent suicide reported in the popular media (Amen *et al.*, 2011). Importantly, as this discussion continues, it will be important to contextualize both quantitative and qualitative data on player mortality trends as they provide a more accurate portrayal of life quality prior to death.

Although most previous research has considered single sports, some of the most intriguing findings in this area come from cross sports comparisons. Ex-elite athletes who represented Finland between 1920 and 1965 had lower mortality rates than the general population, but the nature of the sport influenced the extent of the mortality benefit (Sarna *et al.*, 1993). Athletes gained between 1.6 years (power sports) and 5.7 years (endurance) longer lifespan compared to age-matched controls (average life expectancy 69.9 years; Sarna *et al.*, 1993), suggesting that aerobic sports provide additional benefits to anaerobic sports. Intriguingly, Zwiers *et al.*'s (2012) study of mortality in Olympic athletes participating between 1896 and 1936 found no benefit to participating in sports with high cardiovascular intensity compared with low cardiovascular intensity sports, although there was an increased mortality risk among athletes participating in sports with high degrees of physical contact compared to those participating in non-contact Olympic sports.

Mechanisms of lifespan benefit in former elite athletes

Almost all of the research in this area has focused on descriptive mortality trends in athlete populations and, as a result, there has been little investigation of the specific mechanisms driving these effects; however, related evidence from normal populations can provide the basis for informed speculation. As in normal populations, longevity gains are the result of many factors (psychological, physical, social, etc.) reflecting the dynamic interplay of genetic and environmental factors in determining human health. In former athletes, mechanisms such as structural/systematic and participation/performance factors may provide answers regarding why benefits in life expectancy occur. For example, Teramoto and Bungum's (2010) literature review on the mortality and longevity of elite/professional athletes noted a trend towards endurance (long-distance runners and cross-country skiers) and mixed-sports (i.e., not endurance-oriented sports including soccer, ice-hockey, and basketball players, track and field jumpers, runners, and hurdlers) athletes having longer survival rates than the general population. Given the strong relationship between participation in aerobic exercise and decreases in CVD, diabetes, obesity, among other negative health outcomes (Hardman and Stensel, 2009), it is possible that the form and duration of the exercise dose may determine the ultimate effect on mortality.

Similarly, differences in morbidity profiles between elite/professional athletes and their age-matched non-athlete counterparts may, at least partially, explain the increased longevity of high performance athletes. Several studies of former elite/professional athletes note arthritis and lower back pain as the most prevalent morbidities in their post-athlete lives (e.g., Nicholas *et al.*, 2007; Räty *et al.*, 1997; Tveit *et al.*, 2012) and while these ailments clearly affect indicators of quality of life, they likely have less of an impact on longevity than other morbidities common in the general population such as CVD. Bäckmand *et al.* (2006) found that ex-athletes had a significantly lower prevalence of heart disease and diabetes than controls, while Kujala *et al.* (2003a) noted a lower prevalence of cancer and cancer mortality. The lower prevalence of morbidities that are highly correlated with mortality may play an important role in explaining the superior longevity outcomes in former elite/professional athletes.

Regardless of the mechanism of the effect, it would be short-sighted to suggest that any mortality benefits seen in former elite athletes are solely the result of their training and lifestyles prior to, and during, their athletic careers. Although there have been no investigations of how lifestyle habits of ex-elite athletes contribute to morbidity and mortality outcomes, these factors will be influential. Continued participation in sport and physical activity will have important implications for maximizing health as athletes age. It is interesting to note that participation opportunities in endurance-based sports are much more readily available for aging athletes, which may relate to the extended lifespans of former elite endurance athletes – they have greater opportunities to continue their careers at the post-elite level.

Sport precocity, career length, and mortality

There is also evidence that elite athletes are not a homogenous group with respect to mortality trends. Contextual factors noted earlier, such as sport type (baseball vs. football), appear to have unique influences on athlete mortality. The *precocity-longevity hypothesis* proposed by McCann (2001) asserts that the factors related to early achievement might also cultivate early death. This hypothesis has its root in research on eminent persons in fields such as politics (presidents, prime ministers and governors), academia (distinguished psychologists), law and entertainment as well as among Nobel Prize winners (McCann, 2001, 2003). These investigations (see Table 8.2) have noted that individuals who achieved a notable career milestone at a younger age (i.e., precociously) typically die at a *younger* age than peers who achieved career milestones later in life. For example, McCann (2001) reported that the correlation between a person's age at winning the Nobel Prize and lifespan ranged from 0.27 to 0.74, depending on the category the Prize was awarded in (e.g., Peace, Literature, Medicine, etc.).

To date the precocity-longevity hypothesis has received limited attention in studies on *athlete* mortality, which may be important since athlete populations exhibit distinctive trends compared to other occupations. Recent research using the *New York Times* obituary archive suggests eminent athletes have shorter lifespans compared to eminent persons in non-athletic occupations, such as artists, writers, professionals, academics, and politicians (Epstein and Epstein, 2013).

In one of the few studies of this phenomenon in athletes, Abel and Kruger (2007) used age at MLB debut as a marker of precocity and observed that for

Table 8.2 Contemporary studies on career precocity and mortality

Study	Focus	N	Results/conclusions
Abel and Kruger, 2007	Precocity-longevity in MLB players (age of MLB debut)	3760	Every year a baseball player debuted before the average age of 23.6 years decreased lifespan by 0.24 years. Among Hall of Fame inductees the correlation between debut age and lifespan was 0.48 (and 0.09 among age-matched peers not in the Hall of Fame)
McCann, 2001	Precocity-longevity in 23 samples of eminent politicians, monarchs, popes, US supreme court justices, Nobel Prize winners, psychologists, and Oscar winners (age of achievement)	1026	Results supported the hypothesis that younger age of notable achievement was related to shorter lifespan. Positive correlations were observed between age of achievement and lifespan (e.g., 0.30 to 0.75 for politicians, 0.27 to 0.74 for Nobel Prize winners)
McCann, 2003	Precocity-longevity among a sample of male US governors (age of election)	1672	Age of election was positively correlated with lifespan (0.37)

every year before the mean debut age (23.6 years) a player debuted, his lifespan decreased by 0.24 years – even after statistically controlling for life expectancy at debut year, career length, position, and BMI. Interestingly, this relationship was most pronounced among pitchers and outfielders (compared with catchers or infielders). However, in comparison to the precocity-longevity effects (correlation coefficients) noted by McCann, those for baseball players appear to be less pronounced (ranging from 0.05 to 0.07). Abel and Kruger (2007) also observed that baseball players voted into the MLB Hall of Fame debuted approximately two and half years *earlier* than their age-matched peers not in the Hall of Fame. However, the correlation between debut age and lifespan was 0.48 among Hall of Famers, but only 0.09 among age-matched peers not in the Hall of Fame (Abel and Kruger, 2007). Although these effects require replication and further exploration, they suggest that beginning a professional sporting career at a younger age is associated with a shorter lifespan *and* that this relationship may be most pronounced among the most exceptional athletes (i.e., Hall of Famers).

Mechanisms of the precocity-longevity effect

As noted earlier, all work in this area has been descriptive so explanations for precocity-longevity effects are purely speculative; however, the potential role of stress has been at the forefront of discussion. It has been hypothesized (e.g., McCann, 2001) that stress, possibly associated with the pressure to achieve (or of achieving) precociously, may have adverse consequences in the form of stress-related disease later in life. Indeed, it has been suggested that experiencing psychological or social stress activates physiological responses, and "stress-related disease emerges, predominantly, out of the fact that we so often activate a physiological system that has evolved for responding to acute physical emergencies, but we turn it on for months on end" (Sapolsky, 2004: 6).

Considerable research attention has been devoted to the topic of stress and coping in sport (e.g., Kowalski, 2007). Over the course of their development, an athlete must cope with frequent physiological and psychological changes in arousal and performance-related emotions, as well as anxiety related to competition/performance demands (Hoar, 2007). Furthermore, the stress related to fear of physical injury and the injury recovery process (see Wiese-Bjornstal, 2004; Williams *et al.*, 2001) is highly relevant to sport performers. Many athletes also experience significant stress at the end of their career as they transition out of sport, regardless of whether they retired on their own terms or due to external factors such as injury (Taylor and Ogilvie, 2001). Despite research on psychological and social stress in athletes, the link between stress and precocity-longevity effects remains hypothetical.

It has also been suggested that these effects are the result of statistical artefacts. For example, an athlete who achieves a notable career achievement at a younger age (e.g., a most valuable player award at age 25) also has more years in which they could die than an athlete who achieves the same career achievement at a later age. This has been termed the *life expectancy bias* (Abel and Kruger, 2007; McCann, 2001). In addition, a form of *selection bias* may exist if a study sample only includes deceased persons (e.g., Simonton, 1988). When a sample does not include the high achievers/eminent persons who are still alive it may result in a skewed average age toward young achievers, and this may artificially inflate, or distort, the relationship between career precocity and lifespan. While studies have attempted to control for these artefacts (e.g., Abel and Kruger, 2007; McCann, 2003), they remain important methodological considerations going forward, and highlight just some of the complexities of working with historical data (see Simonton, 2003).

Future research directions

As noted several times in this short chapter, empirical investigations of lifespans of former high performance athletes have been limited; as a result, conclusions are not possible. However, the relative abundance of historical records in many sports, particularly those with valid and reliable online databases, provides fertile ground for considerable future research. In this section, we use previous work to highlight several intriguing directions for further work in this area.

Determining differences between sports and individuals

As noted above, in the limited between sport comparisons conducted, there seem to be important differences between sports. Understanding when and why these differences occur may provide important data for identifying the mechanism(s) of increased longevity. For instance, are greater benefits associated with sports that are primarily aerobic versus those that are primarily anaerobic? How do other variables such as sport-sanctioned body contact (e.g., American football, boxing, and ice-hockey) affect mortality benefits? It may also be important to explore differences between males and females. Although women typically have higher life expectancies than men, the inverse was observed among a sample of eminent persons (Epstein and Epstein, 2013).

Determining differences within sports

A related issue concerns differences between positions/roles on a team. Abel and Kruger's work indicated no differences in longevity among MLB players and this finding was supported by Redwood *et al.*'s (2013) preliminary study of mortality in high performance rugby union players. Given the clear performance differences between members of a team in many sports, it may be factors other than the intensity of the physical activity stimulus that explain the mortality benefit. Similarly, studies designed to explore differences between levels of competition (e.g., elite versus sub-elite versus recreational) may provide further insight regarding whether participation in elite sport provides superior benefits to other forms of participation.

Gaining an understanding of athlete lifespan, particularly outside their high performance career

Several studies discussed above have noted the need to consider factors independent of athletes' high performance careers, as such factors might affect athletes' health profiles after their high performance careers end. As a result, involvement in high performance sport may reflect the influence of other variables more directly related to health and longevity. Consider the following issues, for example:

- Socioeconomic status, which is strongly related to health outcomes in later life (Adler and Ostrove, 1999) as well as to involvement in high performance sport (Kamphuis *et al.*, 2008).
- Social factors that come from athletes' involvement in elite sport, such as access to superior forms of healthcare.
- Involvement in preventive health behaviors after playing careers end, such as physical activity and exercise.
- Involvement in other activities during their sports career (e.g., occupations), particularly in amateur and semi-professional sports where salaries are considerably lower than those enjoyed by contemporary professional athletes.
- Psychological factors that might affect predisposition to sporting success that in turn might also affect health outcomes, such as the ability to regulate stress and/or manage emotion.

These factors, among others, may drive or constrain young athletes' initial attraction to, and their experience during, high performance sport. Understanding the influence of general lifestyle variables such as these might shed important light on the mechanisms driving these effects.

Understanding the mechanisms of the precocity-longevity relationships

The consistent trend towards early achievement resulting in earlier death is alarming and the lack of understanding regarding the mechanism of these effects is a critical limitation of work in this area.

Determining how historical changes affect mortality outcomes

Of the limited studies that have been conducted, all have examined athletes from sports that have undergone significant historical change. The notion of today's 'professional' or 'elite' athlete is dramatically different from the same careers generations ago. It is possible that these changes over time have influenced the relationships between elite sport participation and mortality outcomes.

Implications for general population

It will be important to determine whether the relationships between elite sport involvement and mortality benefits have any implications for non-elite athletes who make up the vast majority of the general population. It is entirely possible, even likely, that the very factors that facilitated their development into high performance athletes, such as superior fitness-related genotypes, explain their extended lifespans.

Better theory and superior designs

Ultimately, answers to the issues noted above will require better theoretical models and superior study designs that incorporate potential moderators of these effects such as socioeconomic status, sex, preventive health behaviors, etc. Parcelling out these various influences will require more advanced statistical approaches such as multi-level and/or structural equation modeling, survival analysis, in addition to established methods like ANCOVA, which have generally not been used in this type of research previously. Furthermore, it will be important to determine how these effects change over time as sport systems and athlete developmental patterns continue to evolve.

Conclusions

Understanding the long-term implications of involvement in high performance sport is necessary for the formation of comprehensive, evidence-based models of athlete development. Moreover, a complete model of athlete development will require an understanding of how involvement in high performance sport affects aspects of lifespan health like injury, morbidity, and quality of life, in addition to longevity. The preliminary evidence reviewed in this chapter suggests that high performance athletes have longer lifespans than members of the general population; however, developing understanding of the relationships between high-level sport participation, longevity, and other health indicators such as quality of life and life satisfaction will require considerably greater research involvement than has been conducted to date. Once developed, however, this information may be of great interest to athletes, coaches, and other sport stakeholders.

References

Abel, E. L. and Kruger, M. L. (2004) 'Left-handed major-league baseball players and longevity re-examined', *Perceptual and Motor Skills*, 99: 990–2.

Abel, E. L. and Kruger, M. L. (2005a) 'Longevity of major league baseball players', *Research in Sports Medicine*, 13: 1–5.

Abel, E. L. and Kruger, M. L. (2005b) 'The longevity of baseball hall of famers compared to other players', *Death Studies*, 29: 959–63.

Abel, E. L. and Kruger, M. L. (2006a) 'The healthy worker effect in major league baseball revisited', *Research in Sports Medicine*, 14: 83–7.

Abel, E. L. and Kruger, M. L. (2006b) 'The healthy worker effect in professional football', *Research in Sports Medicine: An International Journal*, 14: 239–43.

Abel, E. L. and Kruger, M. L. (2007) 'Precocity predicts shorter life for major league baseball players: Confirmation of McCann's precocity-longevity hypothesis', *Death Studies*, 31: 933–40.

Adler, N. E. and Ostrove, J. M. (1999) 'Socioeconomic status and health: What we know and what we don't', *Annals of the New York Academy of Science*, 896: 3–15.

Amen, D. G., Newberg, A., Thatcher, R., Jin, Y., Wu, J., Keator, D. and Willeumier, K. (2011) 'Impact of playing American professional football on long-term brain function', *The Journal of Neuropsychiatry and Clinical Neurosciences*, 23: 98–106.

Bäckmand, H., Kaprio, J., Kujala, U. M., Sarna, S. and Fogelholm, M. (2006) 'Physical and psychological functioning of daily living in relation to physical activity. A longitudinal study among former elite male athletes and controls', *Aging Clinical and Experimental Research*, 18: 1–10.

Barnwell, B. (2012) 'Mere mortals', *Grantland*. Online at: www.grantland.com/story/_/id/8274392/comparing-mortality-rates-football-baseball (accessed 16 August 2012).

Baron, S. L., Hein, M. J., Lehman, E. and Gersic, C. M. (2012) 'Body mass index, playing position, race, and the cardiovascular mortality of retired professional football players', *The American Journal of Cardiology*, 109: 889–96.

Belli, S. and Vanacore, N. (2005) 'Proportionate mortality of Italian soccer players: Is amyotrophic lateral sclerosis an occupational disease?', *European Journal of Epidemiology*, 20: 237–42.

Dubravcic-Simunjak, S., Pecina, M., Kuipers, H., Moran, J. and Haspl, M. (2003) 'The incidence of injury in elite junior figure skaters', *American Journal of Sports Medicine*, 31: 511–17.

Eaves, T. (2011) 'The relationship between spit tobacco and baseball', *Journal of Sport and Social Issues*, 35: 437–42.

Epstein, C. R. and Epstein, R. J. (2013) 'Death in the *New York Times*: The price of fame is a faster flame', *Quarterly Journal of Medicine* 106: 517–21.

Fraser-Thomas, J., Côté, J. and Deakin, J. (2005). 'Youth sport programs: An avenue to foster positive youth development', *Physical Education and Sport Pedagogy*, 10: 49–70.

Gajewski, A. K. and Poznańska, A. (2008) 'Mortality of top athletes, actors and clergy in Poland: 1924–2000 follow-up study of the long term effect of physical activity', *European Journal of Epidemiology*, 23: 335–40.

Grimsmo, J., Maehlum, S., Moelstad, P. and Arnesen, H. (2011) 'Mortality and cardiovascular morbidity among long-term endurance male cross country skiers followed for 28–30 years', *Scandinavian Journal of Medicine and Science in Sports*, 21: 351–8.

Hardman, A. E. and Stensel, D. J. (2009) *Physical Activity and Health: The evidence explained*. London: Routledge.

Hartley, P. H. S. and Llewellyn, G. F. (1939) 'The longevity of oarsmen', *British Medical Journal*, 1(4082): 657–62.

Hoar, S. D. (2007) 'Arousal, anxiety, and sport performance', in P. R. E. Crocker (ed.) *Sport psychology: A Canadian perspective*, Toronto: Prentice Hall, 102–28.

Hyman, M. H., Dang, D. L. and Liu, Y. (2012) 'Differences in obesity measures and selected comorbidities in former national football league professional athletes', *Journal of Occupational and Environmental Medicine*, 54: 816–19.

Kamphuis, C. B., Van Lenthe, F. J., Giskes, K., Huisman, M., Brug, J. and Mackenbach, J. P. (2008) 'Socioeconomic status, environmental and individual factors, and sports participation', *Medicine and Science in Sports and Exercise*, 40: 71–81.

King, P. and Gagné, M. (2012, July) 'A league at the crossroads', *Sports Illustrated*, 117(4): 50–7.

Kowalski, K. C. (2007) 'Stress and coping in sport', in P. R. E. Crocker (ed.) *Sport Psychology: A Canadian perspective*, Toronto: Prentice Hall, 129–54.

Kujala, U. M., Kvist, M. and Heinonen, O. (1985) 'Osgood-Schlatter's disease in adolescent athletes. Retrospective study of incidence and duration', *American Journal of Sports Medicine*, 13: 236–41.

Kujala, U. M., Marti, P., Kaprio, J., Hernelahti, M., Tikkanen, H. and Sarna, S. (2003a) 'Occurrence of chronic disease in former top-level athletes', *Sports Medicine*, 33: 553–61.

Kuss, O., Kluttig, A. and Greiser, K. H. (2011) 'Longevity of soccer players: An investigation of all German internationals from 1908 to 2006', *Scandinavian Journal of Medicine and Science in Sports*, 21: 260–5.

McCann, S. J. H. (2001) 'The precocity-longevity hypothesis: Earlier peaks in career achievement predict shorter lives', *Personality and Social Psychology Bulletin*, 27: 1429–39.

McCann, S. J. H. (2003) 'Younger achievement age predicts shorter life for governors: Testing the precocity-longevity hypothesis with artifact controls', *Personality and Social Psychology Bulletin*, 29: 164–9.

Menotti, A., Amici, E., Gambelli, G. C., Milazzotto, F., Bellotti, P., Capocaccia, R. and Giuli, B. (1990) 'Life expectancy in Italian track and field athletes', *European Journal of Epidemiology*, 6: 257–60.

Nicholas, S. J., Nicholas, J. A., Nicholas, C., Diecchio, J. R. and McHugh, M. P. (2007) 'The health status of retired American football players', *The American Journal of Sports Medicine*, 35: 1674–9.

Pärssinen, M., Kujala, U., Vartiainen, E., Sarna, S. and Seppälä, T. (2000) 'Increased premature mortality of competitive powerlifters suspected to have used anabolic agents', *International Journal of Sports Medicine*, 21: 225–7.

Pate, R. R., Trost, S. G., Levin, S. and Dowda, M., (2000) 'Sports participation and health-related behaviors among US youth', *Archives of Pediatrics and Adolescent Medicine*, 154: 904–11.

Piano, M. R., Benowitz, N. L., Fitzgerald, G. A., Corbridge, S., Heath, J., Hahn, E., Pechacek, T. F. and Howard, G. (2010) 'Impact of smokeless tobacco products on cardiovascular disease: Implications for policy, prevention, and treatment: A policy statement from the American Heart Association', *Circulation*, 122: 1520–44.

Räty, H. P., Kujala, U. M., Videman, T., Impivaara, O., Battié, M. C. and Sarna, S. (1997) 'Lifetime musculoskeletal symptoms and injuries among former elite male athletes', *International Journal of Sports Medicine*, 18: 625–32.

Redwood, J., Wattie, N., Ardern, C. I., Lemez, S. and Baker, J. (2013) *An Exploratory Examination of Mortality in Ex-elite Rugby Union Players*. Manuscript under review.

Reynolds, R. and Day, S. (2012) 'Life expectancy and comparative mortality of major league baseball players, 1900-1999', WebmedCentral, *Sport Medicine*, 3(5): WMC003380.

Saint Onge, J. M., Rogers, R. G. and Krueger, P. M. (2008) 'Major league baseball players' life expectancies', *Social Science Quarterly*, 89: 817–30.

Sapolsky, R. M. (2004) *Why Zebras Don't Get Ulcers*, 3rd edn, New York: Holt Paperbacks.

Sarna, S., Sahi, T., Koskenvuo, M. and Kaprio, J. (1993) 'Increased life expectancy of world class male athletes', *Medicine and Science in Sports and Exercise*, 237–44.

Simonton, D. K. (1988) 'Age and outstanding achievement: What do we know after a century of research?', *Psychological Bulletin*, 104: 251–67.

Simonton, D. K. (2003) 'Qualitative and quantitative analyses of historical data', *Annual Review of Psychology*, 54: 617–40.

Sundgot-Borgen, J. and Torstveit, M. K. (2004) 'Prevalence of eating disorders in elite athletes is higher than in the general population', *Clinical Journal of Sports Medicine*, 14: 25–32.

Taioli, E. (2007) 'All causes mortality in male professional soccer players', *European Journal of Public Health*, 17: 600–4.

Taylor, J. and Ogilvie, B. (2001) 'Career transition among elite athletes: Is there life after sports?', in J.M. Williams (ed.) *Applied Sport Psychology: Personal growth to peak performance*, Toronto: Mayfield, 480–96.

Teramoto, M. and Bungum, T. J. (2010) 'Mortality and longevity of elite athletes', *Journal of Science and Medicine in Sport*, 13: 410–16.

Thun, M. J., Carter, B. D., Feskanich, D., Freedman, N. D., Prentice, R., Lopez, A. D., *et al.* (2013) '50-year trends in smoking-related mortality in the United States', *The New England Journal of Medicine*, 368: 351–64.

Tucker, A. M., Vogel, R. A., Lincoln, A. E., Dunn, R. E., Ahrensfield, D. C., Allen, T. W. *et al.* (2009) 'Prevalence of cardiovascular disease risk factors among National Football League players', *Journal of the American Medical Association*, 301: 2111–19.

Tveit, M., Rosengren, B. E., Nilsson, J. A. and Karlsson, M. K. (2012) 'Former male elite athletes have a higher prevalence of osteoarthritis and arthroplasty in the hip and knee than expected', *The American Journal of Sports Medicine*, 40: 527–33.

Wiese-Bjornstal, D. M. (2004) 'From skinned knees and Pee Wees to menisci and Masters: Developmental sport injury psychology', in M. R. Weiss (ed.) *Developmental Sport and Exercise Psychology: A lifespan perspective*, Morgantown: Fitness Information Technology, 525–68.

Williams, J. M., Rotella, R. J. and Scherzer, C. B. (2001) 'Injury risk and rehabilitation: Psychological considerations', in J. M. Williams (ed.) *Applied Sport Psychology: Personal growth to peak performance*, Toronto: Mayfield, 456–79.

Willis, D., Popovech, M., Gany, F. and Zelihoff, J. (2012) 'Toxicology of smokeless tobacco: Implications for immune, reproductive, and cardiovascular systems', *Journal of Toxicology and Environmental Health*, 15: 317–31.

Woodward, J. R. (2004) 'Professional football scouts: An investigation of racial stacking', *Sociology of Sport Journal*, 21: 356–75.

Zwiers, R., Zantvoord, F. W. A., Engelaer, F. M., Bodegom, D. V., Ouderaa, F. J. G. V. D. and Westendorp, R. G. J. (2012) 'Mortality in former Olympic athletes: Retrospective cohort analysis', *British Medical Journal*, 345: 19–27.

9 An early grave or the fountain of youth

Sport and the malleability of chronological age

James Gillett, Alison Ross and Amanda Switzer

Controversies in the field of sport are circulated and perpetuated through stories and narratives played out on the field, that are then taken up in conversation and broadcast through increasingly diverse media formats and outlets. Currently, on the competitive sport scene, there are two dominant story lines that are tied closely to malleability of chronological age for athletes at different stages of the lifecourse. The first warns of the dangers and destructive potential of competitive sport. This alarm is sounded predominately about brain injuries among youth who are involved in high-contact sport (Stern *et al.*, 2009). Yet, it echoes beyond brain injuries to include the negative health effects of bullying, competition stress, eating disorders and hazing rituals that are linked to sport involvement among younger athletes (Holm-Denoma *et al.*, 2009). Dangerous outcomes of sport are often described using the language of epidemics and calls are made to medical science, new technologies and the restructuring of sport as potential solutions (Benson *et al.*, 2009; Finch *et al.*, 2011).

The other predominate controversy story line, ironically, is the transformative capacity of sport. Participation in competitive sport, especially, is portrayed as the means by which people can overcome personal and social challenges and constraints. The 'power of sport' narrative is diverse, ranging from individuals overcoming the limitations of old age, critical illness (Blech, 2009; Matheson, 2011), or as a means of increasingly their health and well-being (Blech, 2009; Gill *et al.*, 2013), contributing to youth and social development, and even advancing international development initiatives (Baker *et al*, 2010; Darnell, 2010). Often implied, and occasionally made explicit, is the severe underlying concern of the reluctance among the body politic to take advantage of sport and physical activity. This chapter explores the intersection between narratives of transformation and destruction in sport and the untying of age from a set, fixed chronological structure or linear logic. As a social structure, chronological age (i.e., how many years a person is alive since birth) has been conventionally tied to capacity. In other words, as you get chronologically older your physical capacity diminishes. While this may be true in some cases, in the context of competitive sport this relationship can be disrupted. Our analysis examines two counter-posing cases of this type of disruption: the first looks at concerns about premature aging and the resulting illness among chronologically younger athletes with brain injuries resulting from participation in high-impact sport; and the second, the transformative and restorative power of sport in enabling chronologically older athletes. In other words, is sport a fountain of youth or an early grave?

Aging, sport and time

The existing literature on aging and sport includes extensive research on sports participation at different life course stages (Jose *et al.*, 2011). This research largely examines the nature of this sporting involvement in different age cohorts and the recurrent patterns of participation that emerge (Baker *et al.*, 2010). A smaller subset of this literature specifically examines these patterns in the older population, and only examines this group insofar as to understand the benefits derived from sport and to understand sport participation at the Masters level (Wicker *et al.*, 2009). More relevant to the topic at hand are the even fewer studies that focus on the negotiation of age through sports participation (Hirvensalo and Lintunen, 2011). This section reviews current literature on age and sport and explores how our research can extend current knowledge of aging and sport.

Research on social and personal development points to the positive influence of child and youth involvement in sport. Sport participation contributes to childhood development and promotes qualities that encourage one to contribute meaningfully to society (Taylor *et al.*, 1985). However, patterns of involvement are shaped by social relations like gender and social class. Male children, for instance, are more likely to engage in sporting activities (Fairclough *et al.*, 2009), especially male children from high socioeconomic status backgrounds (Fairclough *et al.*, 2009; Hirvensalo and Lintunen, 2011; White and McTeer, 2012). It has additionally been found that children are more likely to maintain levels of sports participation if the relationships with their teammates and their parents remain positive (Ullrich-French and Smith, 2009). Ultimately, at this stage of the lifecourse, sport participation is understood to serve essential functions in terms of physical, social and emotional development (Baker *et al.*, 2010).

Research on youth sport participation recognizes its vital developmental function (Jose *et al.*, 2011; Taylor *et al.*, 1985). However, in the literature on children and youth, there are socioeconomic structures that create inequities in access to sport, though this is less evident for youth who have access to sport at the high school level (White and McTeer, 2012). Additional studies point to gender differences in sports involvement during the transition for youth to adulthood, with males more likely to continue if their fathers are active, and females more likely to continue if they perceive themselves to be athletically competent (Jose *et al.*, 2011).

Socioeconomic status and gender remain prominent themes in sports participation through to adulthood (Hirvensalo and Lintunen, 2011). However, at this life stage, a polarization between two groups appears: the physically active versus the physically inactive (Hirvensalo and Lintunen, 2011). Wicker *et al.* (2009) examined the influence of sport infrastructure on sport participation in different age cohorts and their findings suggest that people in middle age access sporting facilities most easily. This access is largely attributed to their more stable and independent lifestyle and the flexible and extended hours of many fitness facilities (Wicker *et al.*, 2009). Additional research on the meaning of sport for adults finds that sport involvement in adulthood serves a psychosocial function in addition to a physiological function (Baker *et al.*, 2010). Specifically, Masters athletes experience psychosocial benefits, including continued motivation for physical activity, the ability to negotiate the aging process, and opportunities to challenge ageist stereotypes (Baker *et al.*, 2010).

A small subset of the current aging and sport literature has explored sport in the later lifecourse stages. The limited research on this group has focused nearly exclusively on the benefits of sports for older people and has made efforts to understand sports participation at the Masters level. For instance, it has been widely accepted that sport participation in old age holds extensive physiological benefits (McPherson, 1984). Additionally, the continued theme of socioeconomic status and gender persists through to old age, with childhood sports involvement more likely to be maintained across the life course for males and for those of higher socioeconomic status (Hirvensalo and Lintunen, 2011). Therefore, it appears that wealthier men are more likely to benefit from the psychosocial benefits of athletics in old age and are more likely to successfully negotiate the aging process. Older adults are commonly encouraged to participate in more age appropriate sport activities that are seen to be more suitable to the limitations that accompany the aging process (Grant, 2001). Research does recognize older adults' participation in Master's sport but, in such cases, the focus tends to be on individuals who have competed since their youth and are considered veterans of their sport (Grant, 2001; Kluge *et al.*, 2010; Tulle, 2008).

The aging and sport literature focusing on the negotiation of age through sports participation is more limited, but most relevant to the relationship between participation in sport and aging. This research includes Dionigi *et al.*'s (2013) investigation of the meaning attached to sport participation for older adults. Using semi-structured interviews with Masters athletes, they conducted an in depth exploration of the dialogue surrounding aging and sport. Older athletes, they found, use sport to avoid old age, to challenge the natural processes of aging, to alter definitions of the self as an older person, and to adapt and accept the ever-changing physiological self. Ultimately, sport participation in old age was found to effectively modify the popularized negative narratives of aging. Baker *et al.* (2010) describe similar negotiations of the aging process via sport. They argue that, although much of the current research on aging athletes has focused on physiological benefits, the psychosocial benefits are equally significant. Baker *et al.* (2010) call for more empirical studies that test sport participation's potential to enhance the quality of the aging experience and explore the potential for negative outcomes that are similarly found in youth sport participation.

Current research largely overlooks the flexibility of age within sport and sporting contexts. The examination of sport participation within the context of age cohorts reinforces the rigidity of chronology, which largely ignores external environmental forces that function to manipulate chronological age. For example, collision sports (football, ice hockey) have been associated with the onset of dementia-like conditions, specifically Alzheimer's disease, much earlier than the general population (Guskiewicz *et al.*, 2005). In such cases, one's chronological age is accelerated in association with the type of sport one engaged in. In contrast, some sports have been argued to defy chronological age, extending life expectancy and enhancing quality of life of participants. Specifically, cycling has been found to successfully extend one's life while simultaneously enhancing quality in terms of physiological, social and emotional well-being (Wallack and Katovsky, 2005). Extending and building on this research we now turn to a closer examination of the malleability of chronological age, acknowledging that the dynamic relationship that exists between time, age and sport is vital to comprehensively understanding the landscape of sport studies.

Sport and the malleability of age

In this section, we turn to an empirical investigation of two case studies demonstrating the contrasting relationship between age and participation in sport. The first investigates representations of premature aging among competitive athletes in high impact sports, while the second looks at the portrayal of reverse aging that is seen to result from involvement in sport among older adults. Data were collected from media representations of celebrated athletes or athletes who have gained notoriety through their sport or life circumstances. Each case study describes recurrent themes and points of divergence across the profiles of athletes who have been portrayed as reversing or reducing their age through sport.

Premature aging

The destructive capacity of sport is a central concern in the media, recently. In contact/high impact sports such as hockey, football and boxing, competitors are subject to conditions that put them at greater risk for injury (McIntosh and McCrory, 2005). For professional athletes, these sports are typically the athlete's primary occupation and source of income, yet these workplace injuries frequently require athletes to recede, often reluctantly, from the sport for extended periods of therapy or rehabilitation (Podlog and Eklund, 2006). What follows is an analysis of media portrayals of athletes involved in football and hockey. While not a competitive sport as conventionally defined, ballet is also included as an example of how dance as sport performance (a category which would also include gymnastics) similarly takes its physical toll on participants and transforms chronological age. We examine the background of the athlete, their experiences with injury/illness and aging and the repercussions of this premature aging for the athlete. Athlete profiles are a lens through which to analyse discourses about the destructive capacity of sport and the implications of this for how individuals are seen to be older than their chronological age.

The benefits of sports participation are immense and include but are not limited to increased physical and emotional health and feelings of community belonging (Baker *et al.*, 2010). However, in certain sports, these benefits must be weighed against extreme risks. The very nature of football, for example, puts its participants at increased risk for traumatic injury, specifically to the brain and spinal cord, as compared to the wider general population (McIntosh and McCrory, 2005). The following case study profiles former professional football player Ted Johnson and the detrimental physical effects of his sporting career.

Ted Johnson is a renowned football player, having won three Super Bowl Championships with the New England Patriots. Following a celebrated career as a linebacker at the University of Colorado, Johnson was drafted in the second round to the New England Patriots in the 1995 National Football League (NFL) Draft (Sanchez, 2009). Throughout his football career, Johnson experienced six formally reported concussions but, in accounting for all those unreported, the football star estimated that he likely suffered nearly 100 concussions (*New York Daily News*, 2009). As a result of these multiple head traumas, Johnson retired from the NFL in 2005 at age 33 (Schwartz, 2007) and has since been at the center of extensive media coverage of head injuries in contact sport, which has gained increasing attention due to chronic traumatic encephalopathy (CTE) – a degenerative brain disease resulting from repetitive trauma to the head (Gavett *et al.*, 2011).

In this widespread media coverage, Johnson is positioned as aged and is frequently compared to his youthful and more vital previous self. This juxtaposition of vitality and deterioration proves to be a common media tool in describing Johnson as prematurely aged. A notable example of this approach comes from *Denver Magazine*, in which Sanchez (2009) described 'pre-injury' Johnson as "a concrete block of a kid: 6-foot-4 and 240 pounds of pure linebacker who had the unique talent of dispatching offensive linemen 70 pounds heavier and then brutally nailing running backs". However, post-injury, the same media outlet described Johnson as appearing "sick, glassy-eyed, empty" (Sanchez, 2009). This media collocation effectively demonstrates Johnson's premature decent into age – an outcome of his lifelong dedication and professional status in contact sport.

To further position Johnson as prematurely old, the media commonly cites conditions that are popularly understood to be concerns of the older population as uniquely experienced by a chronologically younger person. Most notably, the cognitive deterioration associated with multiple head traumas is central to the media's representations of Johnson, specifically memory loss. Such portrayals include claims that "his memory was shot" (Sanchez, 2009); that he was going "crazy" with memory loss, and is unable to remember people's names, where he parked his car, appointments, and so forth. *Denver Magazine* (Sanchez, 2009) reports on Johnson's own interpretation of such experiences, quoting him as stating, "Bro, I feel like I'm going crazy". The *Boston Globe* (2007) also described further "incidents of memory loss and confusion". Such cognitive decline is widely considered to be an inevitable and undesirable element of the aging process, one that Ted Johnson experienced earlier than his peers of the same age cohort who did not participate extensively in contact sport.

Additional negative stereotypes of the aging process include the descent into senility and social reclusion (Thornton, 2002). For Ted Johnson, multiple head traumas in his professional career led to the premature emergence of such challenges. Specifically, *Denver Magazine* (Sanchez, 2009) reported that Johnson experienced such concerns, particularly "worries about dying young, about not knowing his kids' faces as he grew older, of living alone, drugged and depressed". His increasing social disengagement is presented by the *Boston Globe* (2007), reporting that "some mornings he literally cannot pull himself out of bed. When the crippling malaise overtakes him, he lies in a darkened room, unwilling to communicate with his closest family members".

Numerous media representations of Ted Johnson have effectively accelerated his process of aging, positioning him as physiologically older than his chronological self. However, he is not the only football player who has prematurely aged as a result of participation in contact sport. For example, Kevin Everett was forced into retirement at the age of 25 due to a traumatic spinal injury (Pincus, 2012). Although he has regained the ability to walk, he will never play football again and will endure a lifetime of residual side effects. Furthermore, he is at increased risk for stroke and infection (ESPN, 2007). Other football players who have shown signs of prematurely aging include Fred McNeill (Laskas, 2011) and Junior Seau (Fainaru-Wade and Avila, 2013). In fact, in 2013, ESPN (Fainaru-Wade and Avila, 2013) reported that studies from the University of California Los Angeles found that 34 living former NFL players have been diagnosed with CTE (Stern *et al*., 2009; Yi *et al*., 2013).

Similar to football, hockey is a contact sport that puts its participants at increased risk for injury. A culture of fighting and aggression has enhanced this risk even further, consequently accelerating the aging process for many hockey players (Pappas *et al*., 2004). The following case study profiles Reg Fleming and the detrimental effects of his professional participation in hockey. Playing for 13 seasons (1959–1971) on six teams in the National Hockey League (NHL), Reg Fleming endured many injuries to his head (*Globe and Mail*, 2009). The majority of his hockey career was spent in the 1960s, the period before helmets were a required piece of equipment (*Globe and Mail*, 2009). As a result of inadequate protection and the fundamentally violent nature of the sport, Fleming is reported to have had experienced approximately 20 concussions over the course of his career (*Globe and Mail*, 2009). Following his death at age 73, Fleming was found to be suffering from CTE (ESPN, 2009), the first hockey player to be diagnosed with the condition (*Globe and Mail*, 2009).

As was the case with Ted Johnson, the media portrayed Reg Fleming as physiologically older than his chronological age. The *Globe and Mail* (2009) reports Chris Fleming's (Reg Fleming's son) recollection of his father's struggles as a result of multiple head traumas, including a "severe lack of concentration, memory impairment and, ultimately, full dementia". This same report describes additional detrimental consequences of CTE from sports, quoting Chris Fleming's claim that:

[the CTE] had something to do with his strokes… It had to do with other parts of his body shutting down. It had to do with the Parkinson's disease that he got as well. It's a shame because we all love the sport, but there are repercussions from it.

(Globe and Mail, 2009)

In the *Globe and Mail*'s (2009) report on Fleming, it is explained that CTE is typically misdiagnosed while the person is alive and that is it only after one's death that a formal diagnosis can be made. As a result, the symptoms are often used in the misdiagnosis of other conditions, most notably psychiatric disorders such as bipolar disorder (if the symptoms are emotional in nature) or Alzheimer's disease (if the symptoms are cognitive in nature) (*Globe and Mail*, 2009). The media portrays Fleming as having aged at an accelerated rate by describing his experience with conditions typically reserved exclusively for an older population. While Fleming died at the age of 73 (falling short of the average life expectancy of 79 years for Canadian males), the media reports his challenges throughout middle age with problems surrounding concentration, memory impairment, dementia, strokes and Parkinson's disease (ESPN, 2009). These 'conditions of age' are portrayed by the media to be the result of Fleming's extensive involvement in hockey, placing him at increased risk for brain injury, ultimately enhancing his capacity for premature aging.

Premature aging is a frequent occurrence in hockey that has affected many athletes in addition to Reg Fleming. For example, Bob Probert of the Detroit Red Wings and Chicago Blackhawks was known as a 'fighter'. In his 40s, he presented with mental decline including difficulties with short-term memory, attention and a short temper. Following his death at age 45, his brain showed classic signs of CTE (TSN, 2011). Other hockey players to be inflicted by this degenerative brain disease include Rick Martin (*Globe and Mail*, 2011) and Rick Rypien (Kelly, 2011). Ultimately, extensive involvement in the violent elements of hockey enhances the capacity for accelerated aging in comparison to the general population. The media effectively represents this process in its reports on individual athlete experiences.

In addition to contact sport, performance sport like forms of dance and gymnastics also takes a degenerative toll on the bodies of its participants. Although the media has not extensively covered an individual dancer in comparison to hockey and football stars, there does seem to be a general acceptance that professional and competitive involvement in ballet accelerates the body's deterioration process (Wainwright and Turner, 2006). For example, research has been conducted to explore the physical manifestations of ballet. The *Journal of Sports Medicine* published research comparing former professional ballet dancers to pair-matched controls. In comparison to the control group, former ballet dancers had a clinically significant increase in hallux valgus deformity (commonly referred to as bunions) and arthrosis of the ankle and smaller joints of the foot, likely caused by small repetitive trauma (Niek van Dijk *et al.*, 1995). The BBC News (1999) also reported on the degenerative effect of competitive and professional ballet, reporting that 'en-pointe' move (dancing on tiptoe) puts dancers at increased risk for developing arthritis in the ankle. This arthritis has been found to develop in dancers as young as 11 years old. Arthritis is commonly understood to be a condition of age but its classification as an overuse injury puts dancers at risk for accelerated aging.

Similarly, *Dance Magazine* (2013) includes ballet dancer Michael Blake's personal reflection upon his experience with dance. Blake explains that at age 40, he was told he needed hip replacement surgery and had to quit ballet. Blake reflects on his diagnosis, writing that, "one day I was a healthy 39 year-old dancer; the next day I was a crippled 40 year-old" (*Dance Magazine*, 2013). This drastic push into old age can be understood as his direct consequence of his extensive participation in ballet.

The above case studies of football, hockey, and ballet demonstrate how athletes' chronological age can be warped by involvement in sports of a certain nature. Contact sports such as hockey and football increase the risk of brain injury and other musculoskeletal injury (McIntosh and McCrory, 2005). Similarly, sport involving intense repetitive traumas, such as ballet, increases the risk of overuse injuries such as arthritis, which typically accompany processes of aging (BBC News, 1999). The following section examines the other side of the coin: the capacity for sports of a different nature to effectively reverse the effects of aging.

Reversed aging

Media attention is also drawn to the regenerative power of sport. Athletes at an older age are becoming more involved in competitive sports like swimming, triathlon, marathons and track and field. Cardio-endurance sports of this kind are seen to be available for older adults in their efforts, largely though not exclusively in a leisure context, to sustain and participate in an active meaningful life (Baker *et al.*, 2010). This section explores media representations of marathon running and track and field to prolong the aging process. Athlete profiles are presented in each sport, providing a descriptive framework by which athletes are presented by the media as defying the typical experiences of growing old.

At 82 years old, Ed Whitlock has set multiple records, including being the oldest person to run a marathon in less than 3 hours and the fastest person over age 80 to complete a 10 kilometre run (Douglas, 2013). Whitlock rediscovered his love for running in his forties (Ewing, 2012a, 2012b), and now plans to run as long as his body allows him to (Inside Halton, 2013). Whitlock credits his good genes for his "age-defying" athletic abilities and has been looked to as inspiration for those wishing to maintain meaningful activity across the life course (Ewing, 2012b). In media representations, Whitlock is consistently described in relation to his age. His many accomplishments are made increasingly more impressive by references to his age and the typical activities of others of the same cohort. For instance, when discussing Whitlock's future athletic plans, Inside Halton (2013) notes that "at the age of 82, few people are plotting the future of their athletic career". Ewing (2012b) makes cognitive comparison between Whitlock and his same-aged peers, writing that "he's still with it, he's still sharp. He's not acquiescing to the norm". By comparing Whitlock's lifestyle to that of the average 82 year old, his chronological age becomes warped, presenting him as physiologically younger than his chronological self.

Portrayals of Whitlock tend to be quite explicit in references to age, as such meaningful athletic engagement at such an advanced age is widely considered to be miraculous. These age references include claims that Whitlock is "turning back the aging odometer" (Ewing, 2012a), "a genetic marvel" (Ewing, 2012b) and "age-defying" (Inside Halton, 2013). The *Toronto Star* (Ewing, 2012b) even suggests that "he's redefining how we understand how aging affects the body". To further emphasize Whitlock's age-defying capacities, multiple media outlets have used the image of Whitlock running through a cemetery (Ewing, 2012a). Although this is reported to be Whitlock's favourite place to run (due to proximity to his house), this image effectively symbolizes the 'looming death' that Whitlock is evading through his cardiorespiratory sporting participation. Such discourses of Whitlock demonstrate his ability to 'defy the aging odds'. Whitlock's sporting participation has manipulated his physiological age, allowing for the maintenance of youthful vitality much later in life than the broader aging population.

Fauja Singh, age 102, ran his first marathon at age 89 (Fainaru-Wade and Avila, 2013). Following the death of his wife, he took up marathon running to evoke new meaning and purpose in his life (Fainaru-Wade and Avila, 2013). Beyond the physiological benefits of marathon running, Singh runs for spiritual purposes, stating that running soothes his soul. Through this holistic approach to caring for himself, Singh is another example of an older athlete whose involvement in sport has warped his chronological age. Similar to Whitlock, Fauja Singh is compared in the media to the broader older population as a means of accentuating his unique capabilities. For example, CNN (Morley, 2013) reported that "at an age when most pensioners are winding down their lives, Fauja Singh began a new one" and the Toronto Waterfront Marathon (2011) acknowledged that "Singh is hardly a typical British old age pensioner". In addition to comparisons to his same aged counterparts, Singh is presented as youthful in comparisons to younger athletes. CNN (Morley, 2013) employed this type of comparison in their report that "his left leg had the bone density of a 35-year-old and his right leg that of a 25-year-old". In making such statements, the media judges Singh's physical self against the ideal youthful body and ultimately praises him for having maintained such capabilities.

Recent reports claim that "age has caught up with Singh" and he will be retiring from marathon running (Turnbull, 2013). Singh rejects the negative connotation of the word "retire" and asserts that he will remain physically active as long as his body allows (Turnbull, 2013). The *Daily Times* quotes Singh's concerns regarding the matter of retirement: "I fear that when I stop running, people will no longer love me. At the moment, everyone loves me. I hope nobody will forget or ignore me. When you become old, you become like a child and you want the attention" (*The Daily Times*, 2013).

This fear of being forgotten speaks to the broader concern surrounding the aging process: that if one does not remain meaningfully engaged, one becomes a burden to society – a person of less worth. Involvement in cardiorespiratory sport functions to avoid this ageist label and maintain an external perception of value.

Ninety-four year old Olga Kotelko is a track and field star, a world record holder and an Olympic torch bearer (CTV News, 2010). Although Olga did not take up sport until later in life (at age 77), her accomplishments speak volumes. With a "remarkable retention for muscle mass" and a reliance on complementary and alternative therapies, Kotelko has won over 650 medals and has set 23 world records (CBC, 2011). Similar to Ed Whitlock and Fauja Singh, Kotelko is portrayed in the media as an exception to the aging rule. This representation is often accomplished through comparisons to her same aged peers, with claims that Kotelko is "more active than people half her age" (CTV News, 2010). Comparisons of this nature successfully emphasize Kotelko's exceptional quali- ties, suggesting that she has somehow rebelled against aging expectations and has consequently made herself physiologically younger.

Kotelko's unique abilities have functioned as a catalyst for intensive research into the 'reversal of the aging clock'. The CBC (2011) notes how athletes such as Kotelko have initiated such research, claiming that "unlocking the secrets of Olga's athletic prowess and remarkable longevity could mean future treatments for a host of age-related diseases, including dementia". Such statements suggest that sporting participation not only manipulates one's physiological self, but also one's cognitive self – both elements that are thought to inevitably deteriorate with age. In other words, athletes such as Kotelko are not only 'young in body', they are also 'young at mind'. Research into interventions suggested by Kotelko is portrayed by the CBC (2011) as innovative because "until 20 years ago, most researchers thought turning back the aging clock was impossible. Aging may be inevitable but more and more scientists believe how we age can be changed". Olga Kotelko has been at the center of extensive media hype surrounding the reversal of the aging clock. Her participation in cardiorespiratory sporting activ- ities has made her the media's 'poster-girl' for age defiance, inspiring new research initiatives.

This analysis of media representations reveals the process by which older athletes of cardiorespiratory sports are represented as reversing their age, giving the impression that their physiological aging is slower in comparison to their chronological aging. Ed Whitlock, Fauja Singh and Olga Kotelko are just a few examples of older athletes who are taken up as evidence in the media that they are younger than their actual chronological age, because of their involvement in sport. This trend around which older adults are stretching chronological age shows up in other instances. Min Bahadur Sherchan (the oldest person to climb Mount Everest) (*Guardian*, 2013), Don Pellman (96 year old track and field) (*Huffington Post*, 2012) and brothers John and Brad Tatum (competitive swim- mers in their early nineties) (Buerger, 2011) are similarly seen to be extending the typical aging process.

Conclusion

This chapter has explored the intersection between narratives of transformation and degeneration in sport and the untying of age from a set, fixed chronological structure or logic. We used counter-posing case studies to show how the meanings of age are disrupted through the physical ramifications of involvement in sport. This analysis indicates that our conventional understanding of what is possible at different stages of the life course is changing. Age is becoming more flexible and malleable in the landscape of competitive sport.

Story lines about the capacity of competitive sport amplify the private troubles of citizens and announce them more broadly as issues of common concern (cf., Ingham, 1985). When raised to the level of public debate, the controversies in sport are implicated within broader debates about a range of social issues and injustices. An interesting side effect of this public debate is an emergent critique of taken for granted assumptions not only about the structure of competitive sport but about the institutional structures that shape the lives of athletes. This critique is taken up often in demonstrating the fluid nature of what were once considered fixed – at times natural – structures such as gender (Kamberidou *et al.*, 2009; Hardy, 2013), race (Yep, 2012) and disability (Devlieger, 2011). The fluidity of late modern societies is a predominant motif in the writings of sociologists such as Bauman (2013), who contend that we are currently in an era in which institutional structures are becoming increasingly open, flexible, fluid and open to critique. The source of this unhinging is contested among theorists where some suggest, as examples, capitalism (Hall and Thelen, 2009), communication (Wilkins, 2000) or democracy (Inglehart and Welzel, 2005). Regardless, this quality of late modernity – that social structures are contested and no longer held sacred and anchored in a single authoritative truth – is central to social scientific inquiry. Just as gender, race, class and sexuality are increasingly being unhinged from their once structured, taken for granted status, we are seeing a similar process with regards to chronological age in the context of sport.

The implications of this unhinging of age and physical capacity are wide ranging. They demonstrate the limitations of competitive sport in placing younger athletes at physical harm and how older athletes are challenging the limits to participation widely held in our society due to expectations linked to the life-course and chronological age. Beyond that, as age is questioned in our society, it points to the increasing legitimacy of claims that performance-enhancing drugs in sport can serve as a means of reversing the aging process.

References

Baker, J., Fraser-Thomas, J., Dionigi, R.A. and Horton, S. (2010) 'Sport participation and positive development in older persons', *European Review of Aging and Physical Activity*, 7: 3–12.

Bauman, Z. (2013) *Liquid Times: Living in an age of uncertainty*, Polity.

BBC News (1999) 'Ballet move causes arthritis', *BBC News*. Online at: http://news.bbc.co.uk/2/hi/health/544604.stm (accessed 18 March 2014).

Benson, B.W., Hamilton, G.M., Meeuwisse, W.H., McCrory, P. and Dvorak, J. (2009) 'Is protective equipment useful in preventing concussion? A systematic review of the literature', *British Journal of Sports Medicine*, 43(1): i56–i67.

Blech, J. (2009) *Healing Through Exercise: Scientifically proven ways to prevent and overcome illness and lengthen your life*, Boston: Da Capo Press.

Boston Globe (2007) 'I don't want anyone to end up like me', *Boston Globe*. Online at: www.boston.com/sports/articles/2007/02/02/i_dont_want_anyone_to_end_up_like_me /?page=full (accessed 15 June 2014).

Buerger, M. (2011) 'Documentary highlights D.C. brothers, other athletes in Senior Games', *The Washington Post*. Online at: http://articles.washingtonpost.com/2011-06-23/local/35235675_1_senior-games-tatums-athletes (accessed 18 March 2014).

CBC (2011) 'Olga the Magnificent'. Online at: www.cbc.ca/thesundayedition/documentaries/2011/12/04/olga-the-magnificent/ (accessed 18 March 2014).

Conn, J. (2013) 'The Runner', ESPN. Online at: http://espn.go.com/espn/story/_/page/Fauja-Singh/fauja-singh-runner (accessed 9 April 2014).

CTV News (2010) '90-year-old torch bearer not slowing down'. Online at: http://bc.ctvnews.ca/90-year-old-torch-bearer-not-slowing-down-1.482771 (accessed 18 March 2014).

Daily Times (2013) 'Marathon runner, 101, sad over retirement', *Daily Times*. Online at: http://archives.dailytimes.com.pk/sport/22-Feb-2013/athletics-marathon-runner-101-sad-over-retirement (accessed 15 June 2014).

Dance Magazine (2007) 'First You Cry', *Dance Magazine*. Online at: www.dancemagazine.com/issues/January-2007/First-You-Cry (accessed 15 June 2014).

Darnell, S.C. (2010) 'Power, politics and "Sport for Development and Peace." Investigating the utility of sport for international development', *Sociology of Sport Journal*, 27(1): 54–7.

Devlieger, P. (2011) 'Can disability be fluid? Ethnography, sports and the making of "part of the game"', *Ethnographica Journal on Culture and Disability*, 1(1): 104–10.

Dionigi, R.A., Horton, S. and Baker, J. (2013) 'Negotiations of the ageing process: Older adults' stories of sports participation', *Sport, Education, and Society*, 18(3): 370–87.

Douglas, S. (2013) 'Age-group wonder Ed Whitlock running 10-K', *Runner's World*. Online at: www.runnersworld.com/elite-runners/age-group-wonder-edwhitlock-racing-10-k-june-2 (accessed 2 June 2013).

ESPN (2007) 'Surgeon: Everett has life-threatening spinal cord injury'. Online at: http://sports.espn.go.com/nfl/news/story?id=3012739 (accessed 18 March 2014).

ESPN (2009) 'Report: trauma affected player's brain'. Online at: http://sports.espn.go.com/nhl/news/story?id=4753874 (accessed 18 March 2014).

Ewing, L. (2012a) 'Cemetery provides backdrop for octogenarian's running career', *Globe and Mail*. Online at: www.theglobeandmail.com/sports/more-sports/cemetery-provides-backdrop-for-octogenarians-running-career/article4604276/ (accessed 18 March 2014).

Ewing, L. (2012b) 'Ed Whitlock, 81, running for the record books at Toronto Waterfront Marathon'. Online at: www.thestar.com/sports/2012/10/11/ed_whitlock_81_running_for_the_record_books_at_toronto_waterfront_marathon.html (accessed 18 March 18, 2014).

Fainaru-Wade, M. and Avila, J. (2013) 'Doctors: Junior Seau Brain had CTE', ESPN. Online at: http://espn.go.com/espn/otl/story/_/id/8830344/study-junior-seau-brain-shows-chronic-brain-damage-found-other-nfl-football-players (accessed 18 March 2014).

Fairclough, S.J., Boddy, L.M., Hackett, A.F. and Stratton, G. (2009) 'Associations between children's socioeconomic status, weight status, and sex, with screen-based sedentary behaviours and sport participation', *International Journal of Pediatric Obesity*, 4: 299–305.

Finch, C.F., Gabbe, B.J., Lloyd, D.G., Cook, J., Young, W., Nicholson, M., Seward, H., Donaldson, A. and Doyle, T.L.A. (2011) 'Towards a national sports safety strategy: addressing facilitators and barriers towards safety guideline uptake', *Injury Prevention*, 17(3): 1–10.

Gavett, B.E., Stern, R.A. and McKee, A.C. (2011) 'Chronic traumatic encephalopathy: a potential late effect of sport-related concussive and subconcussive head trauma', *Clinics in Sports Medicine*, 30(1): 179.

Globe and Mail (2009) 'Requiem for Reg Fleming', *Globe and Mail*. Online at: www.theglobeandmail.com/commentary/editorials/requiem-for-reg-fleming/article4296384/ (accessed 18 March 2014).

Globe and Mail (2011) 'Former Sabres Star Rick Martin had Brain Disease', *Globe and Mail*. Online at: www.theglobeandmail.com/sports/hockey/former-sabres-star-rick-martin-had-brain-disease/article556072/ (accessed 18 March 2014).

Gill, D.K., Hammond, C.C., Reifsteck, E.J., Jehu, C.M., Williams, R.A., Adams, M.M., Lange, E.H., Becofsky, K., Rodriguez, E. and Shang, Y.T. (2013) 'Physical activity and quality of life', *Journal of Preventative Medicine and Public Health*, 46(1): S28–S34.

Grant, B. (2001) '"You're never too old": Beliefs about physical activity and playing sport in later life', *Aging and Society*, 21: 777–98.

Guardian (2013) 'Nepalese man, 81, abandons attempt to become oldest to climb Everest', *The Gaurdian*. Online at: www.theguardian.com/world/2013/may/29/nepalese-man-abandons-attempt-everest (accessed 18 March 2014).

Guskiewicz, K., Marshall, S., Bailes, J., McCrea, M. Cantu, R., Randolph, C. and Jordan, B. (2005) 'Association between recurrent concussion and late-life cognitive impairment in retired professional football players', *Neurosurgery*, 57(4): 719–26.

Hall, P.A. and Thelen, K. (2009) 'Institutional change in varieties of capitalism', *Socio Economic Review*, 7(1): 7–34.

Hardy, E. (2013) 'The female apologetic within Canadian women's rugby: Exploring level of competition, racial identity and sexual orientation', unpublished thesis, University of Manitoba.

Hirvensalo, M. and Lintunen, T. (2011) 'Life-course perspective for physical activity and sports Participation', *European Review of Aging and Physical Activity*, 8: 13–22.

Holm-Denoma, J.M., Scaringi, V., Gordon, K.H., Van Orden, K.A. and Joiner, T.E. (2009) 'Eating disorder symptoms among undergraduate varsity athletes, club athletes, independent exercisers, and nonexercisers', *International Journal of Eating Disorders*, 42(1): 47–53.

Huffington Post (2012) '7 Senior Fitness All-Stars Who Stay Competitive'. Online at: www.huffingtonpost.com/2012/01/07/senior-athletes-masters-athletes-track-_n_1187679.html (accessed 18 March 2014).

Ingham, A. G. (1985) 'From public issue to personal trouble: Well-being and the fiscal crisis of the state', *Sociology of Sport Journal*, 2(1): 43–55.

Inglehart, R. and Welzel, C. (2005) *Modernization, Cultural Change, and Democracy: The Human Development Sequence*, Cambridge: Cambridge University Press.

Inside Halton (2013) 'Whitlock refuses to let knees slow him down'. Online at: www.insidehalton.com/sports-story/3067849-whitlock-refuses-to-let-knees-slow-him-down/ (accessed 18 March 2014).

Jose, K.A., Blizzard, L., Dwyer, T., McKercher, C. and Venn, A. (2011) 'Childhood and adolescent predictors of leisure time physical activity during the transition for adolescence to adulthood. A population based cohort study', *International Journal of Behavioural Nutrition and Physical Activity*, 8(54): 1–9.

Kamberidou, I., Tsopani, D., Dallas, G. and Patsantaras, N. (2009) 'A question of identity and equality in sports: Men's participation in men's rhythmic gymnastics', in Madeleine Arnot and Mairtin Mac An Ghaill (eds) *Routledge Falmer Reader in Gender and Education*, New York: Routledge, 220–37.

Kelly, N. (2011) 'Rick Rypien and the modern concussion epidemic', *The Vancouver Observer*. Online at: www.vancouverobserver.com/loveofthegame/2011/08/17/rick-rypien-and-modern-concussion-epidemic (accessed 18 March 2014).

Kluge, M., Grant, B., Friend, L. and Glick, L. (2010) 'Seeing is believing: Telling the "inside" story of a beginning masters athlete through film', *Qualitative Research in Sport and Exercise*, 2(2): 282–92.

Laskas, J.M. (2011) 'The people v. football', *GQ*. Online at: www.gq.com/news-politics/big-issues/201102/jeanne-marie-laskas-nfl-concussions-fred-mcneill (accessed 18 March 2014).

Maki, A. (2009) 'Former NHLer had condition linked to concussions at time of death', *The Globe and Mail*. Online at: www.theglobeandmail.com/life/health-and-fitness/health/conditions/former-nhler-had-condition-linked-to-concussions-at-time-of-death/article597014/ (accessed 18 March 2014).

Matheson, G.O., Klügl, M., Dvorak, J., Engebretsen, L., Meeuwisse, W.H., Schwellnus, M., Blair, S.N., van Mechelen, W., Derman, W., Börjesson, M., Bendiksen, F. and Weiler, R. (2011) 'Responsibility of sport and exercise medicine in preventing and managing chronic disease: Applying our knowledge and skill is overdue', *British Journal of Sports Medicine*, 45(16): 1272–82.

McIntosh, A. S. and McCrory, P. (2005) 'Preventing head and neck injury', *British Journal of Sports Medicine*, 39(6): 314–18.

McPherson, Barry. (1984) 'Sport participation across the life cycle: A review of the literature and suggestions for future research', *Sociology of Sport Journal*, 1(3): 213–30.

Morley, G. (2013) 'World's oldest marathon man, 102, can't imagine life without running shoes'. Online at: http://edition.cnn.com/2013/05/09/sport/fauja-singh-marathon-oldest (accessed 18 March 2014).

New York Daily News (2009) 'Once a patriot, now a victim: Ted Johnson tried to KO demons', *New York Daily News*. Online at: www.nydailynews.com/sports/football/patriot-victim-ted-johnson-ko-demons-article-1.420793 (accessed 18 March 2014).

Niek van Dijk, L., Poortman, S. and Marti, R.K. (1995) 'Degenerative joint disease in female ballet dancers', *American Journal of Sports Medicine*, 23(3): 295–300.

Pappas, N.T., McKenry, P.C. and Catlett, B.S. (2004) 'Athlete aggression on the rink and off the ice: Athlete violence and aggression in hockey and interpersonal relationships', *Men and Masculinities*, 6(3): 291–312.

Pincus, D. (2012) '9/09/2007 – Kevin Everett suffers paralysis', *SN Nation*. Online at: www.sbnation.com/2012/8/9/1228326/9-09-2007-kevin-everett-suffers-paralysis (accessed 18 March 2014).

Podlog, L. and Eklund, R.C. (2006) 'A longitudinal investigation of competitive athletes' return to sport following serious injury', *Journal of Applied Sport Psychology*, 18(1): 44–68.

Sanchez, R. (2009) 'This is Ted Johnson's brain', *The Denver Magazine*. Online at: www.5280.com/magazine/2009/08/ted-johnsons-brain?page=0,4 (accessed 18 March 2014).

Schwartz, A. (2007) 'NFL: Concussions are game's dark side', *International Herald Tribune*. Online at: www.nytimes.com/2007/02/02/sports/02iht-nfl.4444608.html? pagewanted=all&_r=2& (accessed 18 March 2014).

Schwartz, D. (2011) 'Are NHL enforcers' addictions, depression a result of on-ice brain trauma?', *CBC News*. Online at: www.cbc.ca/news/canada/story/2011/09/02/f-robert-cantu.html (accessed 9 April 2014).

Stern, R.A., Riley, D.O., Daneshvar, D.H., Nowinski, C.J., Cantu, R.C. and McKee, A.C. (2009) 'Long-term consequences of repetitive brain trauma: Chronic traumatic encephalopathy', *Physical Medicine and Rehabilitation*, 3(10): S460–S467.

Taylor, C.B., Sallis, J.F. and Needle, R. (1985) 'The relation of physical activity and exercise to mental health', *Pub Health Rep*, 100: 195–202.

Thornton, J.E. (2002) 'Myths of aging or ageist stereotypes', *Educational Gerontology*, 28(4): 301–12.

Toronto Waterfront Marathon (2011) '"Fauja Singh One Hundred Years Young," by Paul Gains', *Toronto Waterfront Marathon Blog*. Online at: www.torontowaterfrontmarathon.com/blog/2011/09/fauja-singh-one-hundred-years-young-by-paul-gains/ (accessed 18 March 2014).

TSN (2011) 'Researchers find CTE in Probert's brain tissue'. Online at: www.tsn.ca/nhl/story/?id=356264 (accessed 18 March 2014).

Tulle, E. (2008) 'The ageing body and the ontology of ageing: Athletic competence in later life', *Body and Society*, 14(3): 1–19.

Turnbull, S. (2013) 'Age catches up with Fauja Singh', *The Independent*. Online at: www.independent.co.uk/sport/general/athletics/age-catches-up-with-fauja-singh-8508316.html (accessed 18 March 2014).

Ullrich-French, S. and Smith, A.L. (2009) 'Social and motivational predictors of continued youth sport participation', *Psychology of Sport and Exercise*, 10: 87–95.

Wainwright, S.P. and Turner, B.S. (2006) '"Just crumbling to bits?" An exploration of the body, ageing, injury and career in classical ballet dancers', *Sociology*, 40(2): 237–55.

Wallack, R.M. and Katovsky, B. (2005) *Bike for Life: How to ride to 100*, Boston: Da Capo Press.

Warburton, D.E., Nicol, C.W. and Bredin, S.S. (2006) 'Health benefits of physical activity: The Evidence', *Canadian Medical Association Journal*, 174(6): 801–9.

White, P. and McTee, W. (2012) 'Socioeconomic status and sport participation at different developmental stages during childhood and youth: Multivariate analyses using Canadian national survey data', *Sociology of Sport Journal*, 29: 186–209.

Wicker, P., Breuer, C. and Pawlowski, T. (2009) 'Promoting sport for all to age-specific target groups: The impact of sport infrastructure', *European Sport Management Quarterly*, 9(2): 103–18.

Wilkins, K.G. (2000) *Redeveloping Communication for Social Change: Theory, practice, and power*, New York: Rowman & Littlefield.

Yep, K.S. (2012) 'Peddling sport: liberal multiculturalism and the racial triangulation of blackness, Chineseness and Native American-ness in professional basketball', *Ethnic and Racial Studies*, 35(6): 971–87.

Yi, J., Padalino, D.J., Chin, L.S., Montenegro, P. and Cantu, R. C. (2013) 'Chronic traumatic Encephalopathy', *Current sports medicine reports*, 12(1): 28–32.

Section III

From self to society

Select topics on the elite sport–health question

10 'To thine own self be true'

Sports work, mental illness and the problem of authenticity

Martin Roderick and Ben Gibbons

I felt myself fighting for breath and for a single moment's peace. "God. Make it stop. Please" Should I call someone? You're joking. What, let someone see me like this? I can't let anyone see me like this, going half out of my mind. What would I tell them? What could I say to them? What could I say to them to make them understand what was happening to me when I didn't know what the hell was going on myself?

The fear filled up every part of me.

(Trescothick, 2009: 201)

In February 2006, England international cricketer, Marcus Trescothick, returned unexpectedly from England's winter tour of India. Extraordinary media speculation about his early return ensued, yet the on-looking cricket world knew nothing of his physical and psychological suffering. Diagnosed with depression, and prescribed anti-depressant medication, Trescothick subsequently set about regaining his health, restoring his reputation and, once again, his place as opening batsman for the England international cricket team. Even so, while speculation about his return diminished, questions about this unprecedented incident never disappeared. In November 2006, Trescothick, now feeling more secure, flew to Australia as a member of the 2006 Ashes Tour yet, just a few days prior to the opening Ashes Test, he once again walked out on his teammates and returned to his family in England. In their press release on the matter, the English Cricket Board cited a recurrence of a 'stress-related illness'. Trescothick found himself the target of the English press once more. Writing in the *Daily Mail* (20 November 2006), journalist Jeff Powell made the following remarks:

The Ashes are about to be reignited Down Under and England's opening batsman is back in Blighty but, as yet, Marcus Trescothick's doctors have not made public an exact diagnosis of his condition ... Now this will come as a seismic shock to the millions who would willingly trade five years of life expectancy for the honour of playing for their country ... don't we realise that these icons are just simple folk like ourselves who deserve our sympathy, not our scorn, when they crack under the pressure? No we do not. Not when they eagerly reap the rewards of representing the country.

(Powell, 2006)

In 2008, Trescothick declared publicly the fact that he was suffering from mental illness in his acclaimed autobiography, *Coming Back to Me*,[1] a book that describes in exhaustive detail firstly the commingling of the pressures of his private life and his 'work place' – professional cricket – and, secondly, his experience of the physical and mental pains and silent distress that characterize depression. Sufferers related intimately with the emotion-laden descriptions he offered of his private, torturous episodes. His account detailed also his shame and embarrassment; to use his words, "what the hell did I have to be depressed about?" (Trescothick, 2009: 247). Issues of presentation of self are key for all sufferers of stigmatized illnesses like depression (Goffman, 1961), but Trescothick's account describes relations that reach beyond everyday encounters that most endure to the watching cricket audiences who sit in stadia and pour over media outlets.

Trescothick's case is valuable for this introductory essay on sports work and mental illness since, unlike most other studies (and autobiographies) of the downfall of professional athletes that largely offer tales of loss and 'adjustment' trauma *post* career (Frith, 2001), Trescothick describes compellingly the ongoing, *mid-career* effects of a life as a sports worker and goes some way to problematize the illusion that professional sport is a labor of love. His narrative highlights the relentless self-identity constraints and performance scrutiny that characterize sports work, integral to which are his experiences of 'achieved' celebrity; in other words, what it means to be well-known and recognizable for your work. He draws attention also to the human cost of his work, including the inexorable entangling of his private and public lives, circumstances that raise the issue for him of job-related burnout (Hochschild, 1983).

Trescothick's account illustrates aptly the ideological-based conjecture of fans and journalists who formulate explanations for the motives and behavior of professional athletes; fans are shocked when athletes-cum-celebrities admit to mental health 'issues' and journalists – like Powell quoted above – struggle to rationalize the *depressive* and *suicidal* actions of professionals whose lives are assumed to offer possibilities for self-realization (Kaye, 2012; Powell, 2006). Thus, sport provides a fascinating lens on such labelled, stigmatized groups in social life precisely because of the assumptions that are made about contemporary sporting figures. Since the publication of *Coming Back to Me* in 2009, the title of which focuses fittingly on Trescothick's private identity-crisis, there have been several other sports workers who have talked publicly about issues connected with their physical and mental states of health. Accounts of this kind are no longer the preserve of retired athletes who struggle with the loss of a former, often celebrated self-identity. Emerging from their silence, a number are now reporting illnesses such as forms of addiction, depression and practices of self-harm as on-going issues throughout periods of their sporting careers. For example, there have been several professional athletes who have been interviewed for television documentaries about experiences of depression (Flintoff, 2012) or disclosed details to national newspapers (Cochrane, 2012). Athletes' (including players') unions such as the Professional Footballers' Association, have issued official advice to members on how to deal with personal 'welfare' concerns,[2] and there has been some exposure to newly established welfare 'retreats' for sports men and women specifically who experience various problems connected to addiction, among other mental health conditions. While there is now some formal recognition of these welfare issues, to date very few academics have attempted to explain the prevalence of mental health illnesses among high-level athletes. An issue for all social scientists attempting to comprehend this social problem is the complex confusion of mental health issues, the pressures of the excesses of professional sport and dangerous sporting practices; a multifaceted set of social processes that require much further academic attention.

In the light of the notes offered in relation to this opening case, the objects of this chapter are twofold: 1) to explore the connections between the conditions of work for professional athletes and mental illness; and 2) to propose an initial explanation for the 'apparent' prevalence of mental illness problems among professional athletes in contemporary sport. Representations of professional athletes on the matter of mental illness have been obtained from a range of media sites, from journalism, popular writing and academic texts since 2006. These do not constitute a systematic documentary or content analysis; even so, many articles and biographies have been considered. These representations are not intended to stand as a representative sample, nor would we claim that this is the *only* way in which athletes are represented. Even so, the data gathered here help shed light on how athletes experience mental health issues and how well existing explanatory concepts of stress and the working environment explain the experiences and outcomes for this subset of sports workers. As part of a wider project on professional sport and mental health, which is in its early stages, seven semi-structured, qualitative interviews have been conducted. Data segments from these interviews that are illustrative of key ideas have been included in this chapter where relevant to do so.

Conditions of work in sport

In discussing in interview with an ageing Premier League football player his successes as an international and multiple cup winner, the high-tech and (observably) impressive facilities at his club, and the material rewards and celebrity status he has acquired, he said, reflecting on his career, "the better it looked, the worse it felt". While statements that capture the spirit or essential beauty of sport – for example, the *flow* of executing skill to an audience – dominate media and fan-based accounts of sport (Hornby, 1992), on-going academic research on high-level athletes nevertheless has consistently revealed that the structures of professional sport are such as to (all-but) inevitably rebound on individual athletes in the form of social, emotional and psychological problems (Hoberman, 1992; Nesti, 2010). Empirical studies of sports work refer often to cynically minded professional athletes – mostly team players – who slowly come to recognize and accommodate over time the notion that they are 'pieces of meat', 'commodities', 'just another number' and 'not worth anything to anyone' (Robidoux, 2001; Roderick, 2006; Wacquant, 2001). Yet such unambiguous narratives of alienation are rarely articulated beyond a narrow group of academics and their research, and are nearly absent from serious media-led debate. Mental health illnesses – like depression – have been least often utilized to describe the nature of the dark side of sports work, specifically because the prevailing logic of this work purports that fulfilment and authentic self-realization are attainable and the logical outcome of success.

Writing in *The Lancet* (2005: 36, emphasis added), Kerry Mummery makes the following point: "athletes may be more predisposed than the general population to depression, because of the physical and psychological demands placed on them by the *sporting environment*. Stress, for example, is associated with depression and is inherent in the life of the athlete". Mummery's thoughtful essay does not offer empirical evidence to support this argument, but he conveys the well-appreciated idea that people tend not to dispute the nature of the connections between the work 'environment' characteristic of professional sport, the stress associated with performance and the impact this may have on individual athletes. Few academics have taken seriously the dramatic consequences of these 'biopsychosocial' relations (Douglas, 2009; Nesti, 2010). Even so, in discussing issues bound up with the conditions of his work, an experienced footballer made the following point:

> It's just the pressure cooker environment...it's difficult physically, and mentally, and emotionally...it's tough and you can see why unsupported issues may develop into some kinds of clinical issues, you know? Different personalities are predisposed to these I'd imagine...but it's just the rollercoaster of football. You win and everything is fantastic; a great team, great players. You lose and the whole world caves in and that goes on every three days, fifty times a year, for ten years and it literally is a rollercoaster and some that don't have the skills to separate out, you know, who get caught up in the rollercoaster, you know that constant up and down...it's not healthy I think.

The upshot and (moral) outcomes of 'careers' in professional sport for athletes who repeatedly come through the ebb and flow of identity-arresting employment contingencies *can include* a questionable sense of dignity at work; a diminished sense of respect for colleagues; the development of wholly individualistic frames of reference; the devaluing of work responsibilities; and cynical and uncommitted relationships with managerial and leadership figures (Roderick, 2006; Wacquant, 1995).

In addition to (auto)biographies (Kirwin, 2010; McKenzie, 2012; Reng, 2011; Thorpe, 2005), research on athletes' careers illuminates their attempts to maintain some sense of existential poise (agency) when it comes to managing their on-going careers in professional sport (Douglas, 2009). The constant battle with identity issues, dignity at work issues and their struggles to retain – perhaps reclaim – some comprehension of authenticity in terms of their self-identities at work (and how these are blurred by the public nature of their jobs), weathers athletes' psychological and physical resilience. Professional sport is assumed to be a labor of love undertaken by high wage earners (now often celebrities) who single-mindedly commit body and soul to achieve valorized goals. It is a career associated with privilege, recognition and glamour, but the public nature of this body-centered 'performance' trade bleeds into their lives and professional athletes frequently report on their loss of control of their everyday realities (Thorpe, 2012). In this respect, former tennis champion, Andre Agassi (2009: 168) makes the following point: "Fame is a force. It's unstoppable. You shut your windows to fame and it slides under the door". Following various transitional experiences, rather than their selves being unalterably shaped by coach and managerial rhetoric, the consequent development of distrust helps athletes to keep workplace norms at a distance such that they are no longer internalized (Roderick, 2013). One outcome of the impact of these social processes is that, in time, athletes dis-identify with values tied to team and work culture, and exhibit high levels of cynicism to managerial powers in order to repossess a sense of self-truth and overcome tensions between who they feel *they really are* and who *they need to be 'at work'* (Roderick, 2013). Even so, athletes struggle to develop any sense of who they are (and what they have become) because all their work stems from others' (legitimate) claims to control, survey, observe and correct their working bodies (Shogun, 1999). These structural conditions paradoxically collude to constrain their ability to remain true (authentic) to themselves – that is, to locate their inner voice. A current professional footballer articulated the following point in interview:

> It's the survival of the fittest. The ones who flourish are the ones who survive. My argument would be, imagine what those players could be with added support, you know, how good they could be not just performance wise, but in becoming authentic with themselves and the positives that that has.

Yet the conditions, and natural logic, of sports work imply a lack of control over athletes' immediate circumstances such that they focus on what they are, rather than who they might become.

The constant stress of the demands of sports work to which Mummery (2005) makes reference – including specifically to be successful and to behave in accordance with normative sub-cultural values – can exhaust the psyche of the athlete, a context that leads them concurrently to lose a sense of adequate future perspective and produce the conditions for the internalization of depression. In summarizing current sociological understandings of professional athletes, we can say that many are celebrated, sensationalized, mortified, dehumanized and commodified. They are subject to constant observation, scrutiny and correction in relation to their working bodies, their talent and performances (Manley, 2012). They are susceptible to changing technological and medical (scientific) innovation and development (Miah, 2013). All these processes are rationalized and justified as fundamental features of the logic of work, a logic that espouses the twin ideas that athletes must always strive to win and be successful, and that they must love their work and treat it as a privilege; they must realize, and not squander, their 'God given' talents. The effects of the power of this discourse – one that has no meaningful rival – are to camouflage often chronic underlying (mental) health issues and stifle athletes' genuine motives for seeking help.

Depression among athletes

Since the 1980s, there has been a substantial rise in incidence of mental illness (Rodgers and Pilgrim, 2010). Controversies abound concerning the burgeoning mental and emotional disorders of late modernity (Horzitz and Wakefield, 2007); newly classified illnesses feature a broad range of reactions to stress, loss and grief (Kokanovic *et al.*, 2013). Indicators of this apparent rise in depression's status as a major social trend include: the widespread perception that depression is increasing rapidly in the community; the escalation in the number of people being treated for depression; the rise in prescriptions for anti-depressants; and the explosion of academic and media attention on psychiatric problems (Rodgers and Pilgrim, 2010). Diagnostic guidelines are mostly based on a medical model of care and often present anti-depressants as the treatment of choice (McPherson and Armstrong, 2006). Yet for all this, physicians' accounts of diagnosing depression – and all the conditions often subsumed under this expanding label – indicate that they experience a tension between the biomedical discourse of depression that warrants a clinical label, and in which they are trained, and the recognition that the social contexts of patients' lives contribute essentially to their experience of emotional distress (Thomas-MacLean and Stoppard, 2004). Kokanovic *et al.* (2013) indicate that some physicians feel powerless when dealing with patients they have diagnosed as depressed because they see the origin of patients' suffering as social and therefore beyond the medical domain.

Studies of lay accounts of mental health suggest that individuals typically navigate between the social and biomedical explanatory frameworks in making sense of their experiences of emotional anguish (Kokanovic *et al.*, 2013). Likewise, professional athletes seem most regularly to locate their experiences of mental illness within the broader context of their social and personal lives, attributing distress primarily to adverse life events rather than medical causes. For example, in articulating his personal story to a counsellor, Marcus Trescothick (2009: 249) notes:

> I tried to explain as best I could about the ghastly day-merging-into-day grind of international cricket and how the enjoyment and even the joy I had always felt about playing the game . . . had all but disappeared and how I felt I might never get it back.

Other professional athletes who have similarly experienced mental illness have discussed the conditions that underscore an apparent disregard for their emotions and their management, and which appear simultaneously to (re)shape athletes' sentiments towards their work. Former English professional footballer, Leon McKenzie (2012: 27), made the following point:

I know the world of professional football is a cut-throat business and players are often treated like commodities to be bought and sold on a whim, but at the end of the day we are human beings with feelings. We cry, we get upset, we get scared.

The social origins of psychiatric illness thus weigh heavy in athletes-as-sufferers' narratives of their experiences of depression. Although there has not been an obvious shift towards categorical symptom-based biological diagnosis in those medical encounters described, in consultation with medical professionals, several athletes have indicated that they have initially been prescribed anti-depressants.[3] This method of diagnosis typically makes invisible the social forces at work among this occupational community of professional athletes and falls back on treatment and prevention strategies that target the individual; thus highlighting the limitations of employing a medical paradigm to solve what are perceived as entrenched social and personal issues. So while the biological model prevails – a situation that has led to an emphasis on clinical diagnosis and prescription drug treatment – the case of professional athletes illuminates the complexity of all manner of biopsychosocial effects of a life pursuing sport-as-work.

In serious discussions of the links between athletes and mental illness, journalists and academics have referred almost exclusively to the stress of athletic performances and the conditions of work to comprehend what is going on in their sporting lives (Hodgson, 2006; Murphy, 2009; Roxby, 2011). In many respects – for example, in the case of media reactions to Trescothick – an overly simplistic cause and effect has been established that overstates athletes' sporting environments and under-theorizes the structures of self-identity and how these are impacted by living a (public) life valorized by fans of sport. Yet even though this form of employment – like those in the creative or entertainment industries – might well fall under that category of work that people *just cannot help doing*, there are some distinctive post-modern occupational stressors to which athletes now make regular mention; in this respect we are thinking of the escalating effects of social media developments. Although the pressured nature of performances has been prioritized in sport science and medicalized accounts, including to some degree the (career) uncertainty of injury and athletes' fear of failure and loss (Mummery, 2005), less explanatory effort has been focused on comprehending the consequences of the commodification of human feelings (Hochschild, 1983) in the context of professional sport and the effects this has on social spaces in their private and public lives; what might be termed the on-going effects of 'well known-ness' (Boorstin, 1992). A former international cricketer described a typical incident that he had to deal with as a *recognizable* sporting figure:

The weirdest thing is when you go somewhere . . . I came back off an [international] tour, and I was having dinner with my first wife at a restaurant . . . and some bloke just pulled up a chair and sat at the table. He said I just wanna talk to you about the tour. I said, I don't know who you are . . . I'm having a private meal with my wife . . . you wouldn't expect a stranger to come and sit at your table when you're having dinner with your missus... I just said I don't give a f***, get lost... I hadn't gone there as a cricketer, and I wasn't f****** there for his pleasure, I was there for my own.

Many athletes gain public profiles and sometimes achieve a level of celebrity status. Accordingly, the balance between the public and private spaces of their lives changes and, as indicated, dramatically for some. All athletes who aspire to make sport their work come sooner or later to appreciate the ineluctable prominence of this 'unusual' work. A former, English county cricketer remarked poignantly:

> In sports we are pushing all the time to be quicker, stronger, technically better... your employers are expecting improvement every single year. I don't think in a normal job... the employer is putting you under that stress on a day-to-day basis and if he was I think you might get a few people crumbling. I think within a sporting environment it's more accepted that this is what you are doing... you're up on a pedestal to be knocked off every single day you're performing because you are visible because you are in the public eye... in the normal working environment that isn't the case.

In describing the major categories of job demands typical of sport – the deprivations, rewards and environment – little mention is ever made of the emotional facets of surrounding work contexts. Psychology studies of sport are focused more often on performance stress(ors) (Mellalieu *et al.*, 2009), and to date there has been an overabundance of (theoretical) speculation accompanied by a severe lack of (empirical) verification. In other words, individuals writing about the careers of athletes have not prioritized the personal, felt-identity struggles between the kind of athlete-as-worker the employer expects them to be, which might require them to *fake* a preferred workplace self, and the requirement to produce a certain emotional climate that can stir-up emotional dissonance and impair a sense of authenticity.

Sport work, mental illness and authenticity

Performances in professional sport are, like entertainment work, intangible, consisting of (emotive) experiences that are produced and consumed simultaneously. There are intensely social aspects of athletes' roles as a direct outcome of the public nature of their employment, which of course attracts media attention. Hence, sports work involves often regular and concentrated episodes of emotional labor (Hochschild, 1983; Lee Sinden, 2012). Although there is a suggestion that sports work performed by professional athletes may make them especially vulnerable to forms of anxiety and mental distress (Nesti, 2010), this final section examines the extent to which the experience of a lack of authenticity related to their work, as an effect of this emotional labor, serves as a mediator between such employment and (sometimes severe) psychological disquiet. Although classic sociological research has identified a range of workers' *psychological* responses to interactive service jobs – which have similarities with sports work – and the emotional labor they entail, for example occupational burnout (Hochschild, 1983), little is known about the relationship between specific facets of performance work in elite sport and the mechanisms through which such conditions may influence mental health.

Hochschild (1983) found that performing emotional labor requires some workers to suppress unfitting emotions and, in others, to heighten or essentially transform the emotions they are experiencing. The concept of emotional labor attracts interest to the efforts involved in controlling and regulating feeling, and its display, in ways that are consistent with occupational (sub-cultural) guidelines. Athletes who have admitted to suffering from depression, both in academic interview and in the media, have implied that they have not always been forthcoming about their illness during their careers – in part because of their fear of repercussions – and, therefore, have needed to 'work at' their presentation of self; admitting to fear openly runs counter to the display of 'heart' expected of *true* athletes. An experienced professional footballer, for example, said in interview: "I just put up a shield, a persona that people would say, I was of some sort of confidence ya know, all of a sudden a mask, another persona . . . not letting people see the other side". Similarly a former international cricketer recalled: "It's almost like my life was made up of acting and when I got home and I shut the doors. Then I was myself". He went on to explain that in time he reached a point where he "couldn't act anymore". In his autobiography, former International cricketer, Graham Thorpe (2005: 10), drew attention implicitly to the stress of emotional labor as follows:

> You can't just walk off the field when you're playing for your club or country, let alone England, but that's what I wanted to do. Hide . . . Sometimes you just have to put on a face, even though you're feeling awful and your self-esteem in on the floor.

Finally, interviewed for the *Daily Telegraph*, former English professional footballer, Darren Eadie, said: "I'd go out, be a footballer, put on this facade, be bubbly, and then get home and completely collapse . . . There are players going into training now, laughing and joking, getting home and thinking 'thank God that's all over'" (Winter, 2012).

Athletes develop and mature (often at relatively young ages) into a supposedly 'meritocratic' world dominated by very specific ideological values, a schemata that prioritizes winning, achievement, dedication, hard work, commitment and delayed gratification (Warriner, 2012). The danger is though, that the dynamics of relationships and meanings among members of sports 'teams' trap athletes continuously in a position where they feel the need to be at opposite poles of this value schemata at the same time: for example, as a squad member in a football team a player may need to demonstrate submission to the wider goals and good of the team (over other individual desires), but feel demeaned by the role they are asked to play (i.e., substitute) in the production of the performance. Many

professional athletes are thus repeatedly and unendingly developing strategies –
rationalizing ways – to enable them to reconcile such competing values; a situation that may demand the performance of determined and spirited emotion work.
Australian Olympic swimmer, Ian Thorpe (2012: 7), noted in this regard: "I felt
like my career had been taken over by others…I felt like a performing seal in a
zoo". The trigger for mental illness may come when, time after time, what is
absolutely unacceptable to an athlete's sense of dignity at work is simultaneously
understood as unavoidably necessary for career survival.

Thus, mental illness cannot be explained by recourse to a simple cause and
effect calculation; that is, understood solely in terms of the unintended consequence of performance stress. Over the years and always in relation with others,
a professional athlete's social self can be shaped and structured in such a way that
it eventually comes to be ensnared in an insoluble, anguished dilemma. British
Olympic Champion, Kelly Holmes, offered telling details of self-harm practices
she subjected herself to and, in attempting to rationalize her behavior, she noted:
"you are looking in the mirror and you don't really see yourself" (Holmes, 2012).
English International cricketer, Andrew Flintoff (2012), drew attention to the
complex problem of in-authenticity and the depression he experienced in the
following way: "I was always seen as this character who was unflappable,
however, you do go back to your room every night and whatever people think
about who you are, I think at times it can be very different". He went on to say,
"I don't want to have to pretend to be something I'm not. Nor do I want to play
up to what everyone wants from me. I think now it's just time for me to be
myself". Flintoff argues therefore that the questions professional athletes should
ask themselves are: 'Who am I and what am I?'. The upshot for athletes is that,
for many, and in particular those suffering mental illness, the authentic emotions
they once harbored towards their work become ever more distant – at times, lost
or forgotten – and they struggle to recognize the person they have turned out to
be. They no longer connect with an inner self – externalizing their motives for
continual action – and lose all sense of meaning in terms of the work role they
feel constrained to perform, yet for which, paradoxically, they can oftentimes
receive public acclaim. Sports workers who no longer recognize what constitutes
for them an authentic sense of self are susceptible to mental health illnesses such
as depression.

Contemporary professional sport has undergone a period of technological and
cultural transformation in which, at an individual level, athletes have come
increasingly to be 'other-directed' (Riesman, 2001) in an industry where mass and
social media are now forceful manipulators of reality. In this 'hyper real' world,
high-profile athletes must learn how to present and manage their social selves
efficiently (Cowen, 2002). It is in such social conditions that they have offered
detailed reflections on the existence of a 'real me' that survives separately from
the social persona they feel is required at work; a context that in time may lead to
self-estrangement. In other words, many athletes, in particular those in the early
'hedonistic' stages of their careers, can be taken in by their own 'performances'
at work. As Goffman (1959: 80–81) noted:

the performer comes to be his [sic] own audience; he comes to be performer and observer of the same show... In everyday terms, there will be things he knows, or has known, that he will not be able to tell himself. This intricate manoeuvre of self-delusion constantly occurs.

This occupational psychosis may endure and athletes may be unaware of how 'authentic' they are feeling at any given moment; yet an athlete's customary workplace personality may be called into question when career contingencies like demotion, injury, failure and coach succession arise. At that stage some athletes strain to rediscover a sense of the authentic and to re-engage with their 'real' social self – 'coming back to me' was how Trescothick captured this sentiment – yet some are so fragmented by their daily lives that they struggle to recapture the morally grounded centre of identity that represents their unfeigned selves (Erickson and Wharton, 1997). An issue for academics interested in the ties between mental illness and professional sports work is that in attempting to theorize about 'what is going on' in the darker spaces of their lives, any humanistic methodological approach must allow for inconsistency within the self "without an accompanying abandonment of the potential for authenticity" (Erickson, 1995: 122). Thus, it should be anticipated that athletes may feel exploited and demoralized by employers, yet still recognize the value of their singular contribution to the production process; a *value* that finds meaningful expression only in relation to athletes' self-referential understanding of their selves.

Concluding points

We look at professional sportspeople... [and] make the assumption that because you're successful and earning lots of money, because you are acclaimed by society, you are going to be living in an emotional nirvana. You're going to be happy, you're going to be philosophically certain and everything is going well for you. That is a myth.

(Syed, 2012)

Sport offers overwhelming evidence that when athletes break down it is as a result of a complex mix of social and psychological circumstances – consistent feelings of failure, loss, shame, humiliation, exclusion and discrimination are all played out around issues of career freedom, dependence and uncertainty. Whilst eschewing dominant psychological comprehensions of athletic identity – that overstate the single-mindedness of an athlete's outlook and impoverishes their sense of agency – we want readers ultimately to appreciate how immensely complicated the structuring of each athletes' social self is; how many factors are involved (in their own and significant others' daily lives in sport); and how many opportunities, pitfalls and traps await their corporeal efforts. These are hazardous situations they all want to avoid, but cannot. The conditions of sports work add to this multi-faceted psychosocial environment and can be summarized by reference to the dehumanized search for success (Hoberman, 1992), the constant, unavoidable surveillance of performance and workplace behavior (Shogun, 1999) and their 'docility' (Manley, 2012). The all-encompassing nature of sports work on athletes' sense of self breeds a lack of autonomy and freedom of expression. A key socio-logical problem however for all who have an interest in this 'unusual work' is overcoming the value-laden idea that it is hard to understand such well-being issues for athletes 'gifted' with talent, who stereotypically live celebrated and privileged careers. As journalist, Piers Morgan said to Andrew Flintoff (2012):

> I don't honestly think most sports journalists... really cared that much about the sensitivities of highly paid athletes... to actually claim to be depressed as you're having to stay in a five-star hotel while you're playing cricket for England to me seemed ridiculous.

Attempts to control the emotions of workers reach into the very core of an individual's sense of self (Petersen, 2011). Due to the contradictions embedded in the constraint that athletes-as-workers produce 'authentic' performances, the loss of control over their work may be particularly harmful to individual well-being. Employer regulation may indeed create problems of identity and authenticity for athletes and for their audiences. As Hochschild (1983) described it, the more features of one's self-identity that an organization puts up for sale, the harder it becomes to recognize which aspects of self are truly one's own. Like identities, one's sense of authenticity is grounded in self meanings that saturate the key assumptions that athletes make about who they are (Erickson, 1995). Athletes' feelings for their work and their emotional reactions are governed by, sometimes silenced, and rarely expressed to critical audiences; 'true' feelings towards the production of their performances are kept in check and, accordingly, athletes can feel emotionally isolated. It is understood that there are permitted and forbidden stories about their work that they are compelled either to share or silence; opportunities to be free to voice aspects of personhood are severely limited. A sense of authentic self-realization at work is therefore hard to achieve for professional athletes in part as an outcome of the ever-increasing social spaces where they are 'on guard', a situation that raises the question of where in their lives they can shed the fear of exposure and publicity and be 'themselves'.

Notes

1   Trescothick's autobiography won wide acclaim and was awarded the William Hill Sports Book of the Year prize in 2008.
2   In 2011, the Professional Footballers' Association issued the *Footballers' Guidebook* to all current and former professional players. It looks at all kinds of stress-inducing circumstances faced by players.
3   Systematic evidence to corroborate this statement has not been obtained, but several elite athletes have discussed in print their use of anti-depressants. See for example *The Secret Footballer* (2012).

References

Agassi, A. (2009) *Open: An Autobiography*, New York: Harper Collins.

Boorstin, D.J. (1992) *The Image: A guide to pseudo-events in America*, New York: Vintage Books.

Cochrane, K. (2012) 'Kira Cochrane meets Victoria Pendleton', *The Guardian*, 10 September.

Cowen, T. (2002) *What Price Fame?*, Cambridge, MA: Harvard University Press.

Douglas, K. (2009) 'Storying my self: negotiating a relational identity in professional sport', *Qualitative Research in Sport and Exercise*, 1(2): 176–90.

Erickson, R.J. (1995) 'The importance of authenticity for self and society', *Symbolic Interaction*, 18(2): 121–44.

Erickson, R.J. and Wharton, A.S. (1997) 'Inauthenticity and depression assessing the consequences of interactive service work', *Work and Occupations*, 24(2): 188–213.

Flintoff, A. (2012) *Hidden Side of Sport*, TV interview, BBC1, January 2012.

Frith, D. (2001) *Silence of the Heart: Cricket suicides*, Edinburgh: Mainstream Publishing.

Goffman, E. (1959) *The Presentation of Self in Everyday Life*, New York: Doubleday Anchor Books.

Goffman, E. (1961) *Asylums*, Harmondsworth: Penguin.

Hoberman, J. (1992) *Mortal Engines: The science of performance and the dehumanization of sport*, New York: The Free Press.

Hochschild, A. R. (1983) *The Managed Heart: Commercialization of human feeling*, Berkeley, CA: University of California Press.

Hodgson, M. (2006) 'Pressure on the pros: Why do so many of our top athletes suffer from stress?', *The Independent*, 19 November.

Holmes, K. (2012) *Sports Life Stories*, TV interview, ITV4, April 2013.

Hornby, N. (1992) *Fever Pitch: A fan's life*, London: Victor Gollancz.

Horwitz, A.V. and Wakefield, J.C. (2007) *The Loss of Sadness*, New York: Oxford University Press.

Kay, O. (2012) 'A year on from Speed's death and sport still has its demons to fight', *The Times*, 27 November.

Kirwin, J. (2010) *All Blacks Don't Cry: A story of hope*, Rosedale, North Shore: Penguin Books.

Kokanovic, R., Bendelow, G. and Philip, B. (2013) 'Depression: The ambivalence of diagnosis', *Sociology of Health and Illness*, 35(3): 377–90.

Lee Sinden, J. (2012) 'The sociology of emotion in elite sport: Examining the role of normalization and technologies', *International Review for the Sociology of Sport*, 48(5): 613–28.

Manley, A.T. (2012) 'Surveillance, disciplinary power and the social construction of "professionalism": A sociological investigation into the culture of elite sports academies', unpublished Ph.D. thesis, Durham University.

McKenzie, L. (2012) *My Fight with Life*, Peterborough, Cambridgeshire: MacAnthony Media.

McPherson, S. and Armstrong, D. (2006) 'Social determinant of diagnostic labels in depression', *Social Science and Medicine*, 62: 50–68.

Miah, A. (2013) *Genetically Modified Athletes: Biomedical ethics, gene doping and sport*, London: Routledge.

Mellalieu, S.D., Neil, R., Hanton, S. and Fletcher, D. (2009) 'Competition stress in sport performers: Stressors experienced in the competition environment', *Journal of Sports Sciences*, 27(7): 729–44.

Mummery, K. (2005) 'Essay: Depression in sport', *The Lancet*, 366: S36–S37.

Murphy, C. (2009) 'The pressures of professional play', BBC News Health [online], 11 November. Online at: http://news.bbc.co.uk/2/hi/health/8354979.stm (accessed 18 March 2014).

Nesti, M. (2010) *Psychology in Football: Working with elite and professional players*, London: Routledge.

Petersen, A. (2011) 'Authentic self-realization and depression', *International Sociology*, 26(1): 5–24.

Powell, J. (2006) 'How modern-day sport maladies let the side down', *The Daily Mail*, 20 November.

Reng, R. (2011) *A Life Too Short: The tragedy of Robert Enke*, London: Yellow Jersey Press.

Riesman, D. (2001) *The Lonely Crowd: A study of the changing American character*, Yale University Press.

Robidoux, M.A., (2001) *Men at Play: A working understanding of professional hockey*, Montreal and Kingston: McGill-Queen's University Press.

Roderick, M.J. (2006) 'A very precarious 'profession': Uncertainty in the working lives of professional footballers', *Work, Employment and Society* 20(2): 245–65.

Roderick, M.J. (2013) 'From identification to dis-identification: Case studies of job loss in professional football', *Qualitative Research in Sport, Exercise and Health* 6(2): 143–60.

Rogers, A. and Pilgrim, D. (2010) *A Sociology of Mental Health and Illness*, Berkshire: McGraw-Hill International.

Roxby, P. (2011) 'Why are sports stars so prone to depression?', BBC News Health [online], 26 March. Online at: www.bbc.co.uk/news/health-12860916 (accessed 18 March 2014).

Shogun, D. (1999) *The Making of High-Performance Athletes: Discipline, diversity, and ethics*, Toronto: University of Toronto Press.

Syed, M. (2012) *Hidden side of sport*, TV interview, BBC1, January 2012.

The Secret Footballer, (2012) *I Am the Secret Footballer: Lifting the lid on the beautiful game*, London: Guardian Books.

Thomas-MacLean, R. and Stoppard, J.M. (2004) 'Physicians' constructions of depression: inside/outside the boundaries of medicalization', *Health*, 8(3): 275–93.

Thorpe, G. (2005) *Rising From the Ashes: The autobiography*, London: Collins Willow.

Thorpe, I. (2012) *This Is Me: The autobiography*, London: Simon and Schuster.

Trescothick, M. (2009) *Coming Back to Me: The autobiography*, London: HarperSport.

Wacquant, L.J.D. (1995) 'The pugilistic point of view: How boxers think and feel about their trade', *Theory and Society*, 24(4): 489–535.

Wacquant, L.J.D. (2001) 'Whores, slaves and stallions: Language of exploitation and accommodation among boxers', *Body and Society*, 7(2–3): 181–94.

Warriner, D. (2012) 'Depression in sport', *BMJ Group* [online], 20 January. Online at: http://blogs.bmj.com/bmj/2012/01/20/david-warriner-depression-in-sport/ (accessed 18 March 2014).

Winter, H. (2012) 'Former Norwich player Darren Eadie wants to tackle depression with a retreat for players', *The Daily Telegraph*, 21 August.

11 Pushing[1] towards excellence

Is Paralympic sport a healthy pursuit?

P. David Howe

> My shoulder is killing me! That is the end of my season. It has been really playing up and I am in a great deal of pain. The doctor says I need an oper-ation – there is so much wear-and-tear in there that we will not know how serious it is until the doc gets in with the scope. If it is really bad – it may be the end of the road for me as a (wheelchair) racer.

This quote was taken from an in-depth interview that I had with a high-perform-ance wheelchair racer in regards to why he had just pulled out of his remaining events at the 1996 Paralympic Games in Atlanta, USA. The athlete in question was a fierce competitor and did go on to represent his country at another Paralympic Games. In competing at the highest level, pain and injury took its toll on his body. When I last saw him, at a reunion of Paralympians held during the London 2012 Paralympic Games, his comment to me was rather poignant: 'Look at me, I am now truly disabled'. This great athlete, who once had a champion's physique, was now confined to an electric wheelchair because his shoulders were no longer able to push a manual wheelchair. This story is a stark reminder of the delicate balance between health and illness in Paralympic sport.

There has, over the last 25 years, been an ever-increasing rhetoric surrounding the broad field of adapted physical activity (APA) regarding the positive impact that sports participation can have upon the health of people with impairments. This chapter highlights ethnographic research on the Paralympic sport of track and field athletics in an attempt to unpack the relationships between the dualisms of health/illness and pain/injury and to get a more nuanced understanding of how the embodied practice of high-performance sport impacts upon on the lives of impaired individuals who are traditionally seen as inactive. The history of the Paralympic Movement is, to many, a tale of triumph over adversity about giving impaired bodies, traditionally seen as ill within society, an opportunity to show the world what they can do (Scruton, 1998). Beyond this celebration, high-performance sport can also be seen as an environment where, due to the risk of injury, there could be negative consequences for the long-term well-being of the Paralympic Movement (Howe, 2006, 2008). Since high-performance impaired bodies are often seen as antithetical to the traditional image of dependency that surrounds this population, the increasing level of injury for Paralympic athletes may be taken as a sign that their bodies, yet again, are not suitable for sporting purposes.

The importance of being physically active for athletes with impairments has been highlighted by much research that goes on in the field of APA (Rimmer *et al.*, 2004; Tweedy, 2002). The Paralympic Games are the most high profile of disability sports events with a history that is inextricably linked to the conceptual understanding of disability as a medical problem that is transformed (on the surface at least) into a high-performance sporting spectacle over a relatively short period of time (Tweedy and Howe, 2011). The most recent Summer Paralympic Games in London, England, in 2012 attracted 164 nations and over 4300 athletes competing in a variety of sports. Some events have the same rules as mainstream sport, some with adapted rules and yet others that have been specifically developed to highlight the abilities of impairment specific groups. Since their conception, the Paralympic Games have gone from being a pastime enjoyed by the performers to a spectacle that has attracted increasing amounts of media attention (Howe, 2008). The changes that have occurred in the world of Paralympic sport have both a positive and negative effect on elite sporting performers with impairments.

In this chapter, I am concerned with the negative consequences of achieving the high-performance fitness levels upon the health and well-being of athletes. The difficulty, of course, is that our conceptualization of health, as well as that of pain, exists at the intersection between biological and social worlds (Bendelow and Williams, 1995). In order to unpack this in the cultural environment surrounding the Paralympic sport, ethnographic data from the sport of track and field athletics that illuminate the tension between intense physical activity, such as the training and competing in high performance sport, and a healthy individual are highlighted below. These ethnographic data collected at a series of major International Paralympic Committee (IPC) events suggest that elite sporting performers with impairment are not particularly distinctive with respect to the way in which they deal with pain and injury. The types of injury, and the responses to the same, vary as much between athletes with impairment as they do within the mainstream elite sporting population. However, the culture of Paralympic sport does mean that sporting ill-health brought on by pain and injury can have a significant impact on the Paralympic Movement.

In order to make sense of the Paralympic movement in the past, I have drawn upon Bourdieu's theory of practice (see Howe, 2008; Howe and Jones, 2006; Kitchin and Howe, 2012). For the purposes of this chapter, however, it is enough to highlight that the Paralympic Movement has developed a distinctive sporting culture that, at times, shares understanding with mainstream able-bodied high-performance sport. This chapter therefore begins with a brief examination of the distinctive cultural context of the Paralympic Movement followed by a discussion of how pain and injury are managed in Paralympic athletics. The chapter then turns to the nature of 'Paralympic' injury before examining the 'pain of injury' in Paralympic sport as it draws to a close.

The cultural context of Paralympic athletics

Today, the IPC's Paralympic Games are arguably the most important event in the Paralympic calendar in part due to the reasonable amount of media attention they receive. Attention that the Paralympic Games receives in the national mainstream media is significant considering there is little, if any, attention paid to Paralympic sport in the two years between the summer and winter versions of the Games. Media attention is not, however, anywhere near the same scale as that of the Olympic Games. The data collected for this chapter were obtained through the ethnographic method of participant observation collected over a period of a quarter century of involvement in the Paralympic Movement, first as an athlete and then as a coach and journalist. An understanding of pain and injury and its implications upon the health and well-being of Paralympic track and field athletes come from first-hand experience (I ruptured my Achilles tendon three time during my athletic career), but also from research that I engaged in during my doctoral studies (see Howe, 2001, 2004). In addition, I draw upon my experiences as an administrator who was able to observe the urgent consequences of injury upon participation levels at key events throughout the build-up the Paralympics.

The physical action of a participant within the Paralympic Movement (see Howe and Jones, 2006) is strategic and, the better the physical action, the more embodied cultural capital or physical capital a participant possesses (Shilling, 2003; Wacquant, 1995). For example, the qualities that are associated with high-performance track and field athlete bodies, such as the ability to push themselves through pain, leads to kudos within the culture of the Paralympic Movement. The physical act of being at the Paralympics requires the athlete to perform at certain times of the year and particular events as organised by the IPC and their affiliates, the National Paralympic Committees (NPCs).

As an athlete, I was confronted with pain and injury in the sporting context from time to time as part of the training regime that I undertook to become an elite middle-distance runner. My impairment, muscle atrophy in the right hemisphere of my body, known as cerebral palsy, made me eligible for Paralympic sport in a category of my physical equals and thus, in some respects, makes this a personal research endeavor (Camilleri, 1999). Many of the athletes whom I competed against (either impaired by cerebral palsy on the right or left side) also fell victim to pain and injury and these events shaped the discourse and, therefore, the world that we occupied at these events. This world was not, however, limited to those with whom I directly competed but included other eligible Paralympians with whom I socialized and trained in the lead up to and during major championships. In a sense, this work was conducted in an environment similar to the 'sportnet' articulated by Nixon (1992, 1993a, 1993b, 1996).

At the Paralympic Games and other disabled sporting events, such as sport-specific world championships, a taxonomy is used to divide participants not only by sex but also by degrees of 'ability' (Tweedy, 2002). The categorization of bodies or 'classification' as it is known within the Paralympic Movement is at the heart of what makes this sporting culture distinctive (Howe and Jones, 2006).

Classification is simply a structure for competition within Paralympic sport where participants are categorized not only by sex (and at times weight) but also by the body's functional ability. This is the backbone of a classification system that has been inherited by the IPC from International Organisations for Sport for the Disabled (IOSDs), four of whom were the founding members of the IPC. These federations, Cerebral Palsy – International Sport and Recreation Association (CP-ISRA), International Stoke Mandeville Wheelchair Sports Federation (ISMWSF), International Blind Sports Federation (IBSA) and International Sports Organisation for the disabled (ISOD) had all independently developed their own classification system, which they felt provided equitable competitive opportunities for their constituent members. Today, these federations use their own classification systems based upon a tried and tested medical taxonomy at their own regional and international championships.[2] In 1989, when the IPC was established, these federations were at the frontline offering expertise. Many of the first officials of the new organization had held posts within these founding federations. One of the legacies of this heritage therefore is a complex classification system that, to many in the IPC, is seen as cumbersome and, as a result, could negatively impact the marketability of the games (Steadward, 1996).

With eight classes for athletes with cerebral palsy, three classes for the visually impaired, nine classes for the amputee and four wheelchair classes for both track and field events, as well one class for those athletes with intellectual impairment, the logistics of organizing the athletics program at Paralympic sporting events are complex. It is the complexity of classification that has made it difficult for the IPC in the past to attract the media attention that it desired. According to Steadward, 'the potential benefits of decreasing classes by using a functional integrated classification system is that it may simplify the integration into the rest of the sports world' (1996: 36). Since Steadward made this statement, there has been a streamlining of the Paralympic Athletics program and there has been increased media attention. With so many classes of eligibility for participation in the Paralympics, the IPC implemented a rule that stated an event must have at least six competitors from at least four nations and have at least ten athletes on the previous year's ranking list to make it viable within the Paralympic program. In terms of mainstream sport, this does not seem as though it should impact upon the viability of events. However, in terms of Paralympic sport, within some impairment classifications, this means certain types of bodies will be removed from the Paralympic athletic program.

The complete cancellation of events or, in some cases, the moving of competitors 'up' to the next least impaired class have an impact on future programs. Competitors who get moved to a lesser impaired class are not competing on a level playing field and have limited chance of sporting success. This negatively impacts upon their selection by their NPC. In an environment where medal tallies increasingly matter, an athlete whose event is removed from the program is unlikely to be selected by their NPC for an event that they will not perform relatively as well in. If all NPCs act in this way, a particular class 'disappears' from a sport. It then becomes difficult (if not impossible) to get the event included on future programs because of the apparent 'disinterest' by those in the classification grouping.

In an attempt to stop the cancellation of events, the medical classification used in the sport of athletics is being phased out in favor of an integrated functional classification system that allows athletes with varying impairments to compete against each other because they have the same sport-specific function (Tweedy, 2002). This may lead to performance banding that eliminates much of the unexpected thrill of sport. The irony concerning the use of the integrated functional classification system is that such a system, which is not medically based, is contrary to the systems used within mainstream sport where the model 'higher, faster, stronger' is determined by a classification system based around the biological parameters of age, sex and weight. The use of the integrated functional classification system does reduce the 'unexpected' cancellation of events that has often occurred in the past because it means that there should be more athletes in each event. Of course, the numbers are considerably lower than those of equivalent mainstream able-bodied high-performances contests. Even using the integrated functional system classification is still complex and it divides a small high-performance sporting population into even smaller parcels to enact a 'level playing field'. Simply put, there are fewer Paralympic bodies vying for selection to Paralympic teams.

While no one wishes to get injured in pursuit of sporting excellence, there is an inherent increased pressure on Paralympians to remain healthy. In essence while pain and injury clearly manifest themselves in similar ways in Paralympic sport as they do in mainstream high-performance sporting contexts, there is a twist. The complex classification system that governs Paralympic sport, as well as the need for technological innovation in terms of mobility apparatus such as racing wheelchairs and prosthetic limbs, for some, are the hallmark of the Paralympic Movement today. Yet, multiple classifications mean that if injury randomly hits a number of competitors in the same class, this could lead to the cancellation of an event at the Paralympic Games. With such a small number of competitors in some classes, the IPC might take event cancellation as a sign of a lack of interest on the part of the athletes even though this is seldom the case. A closer link must be established between the registration of injury and the IPC in order that events that have low numbers of competitors (and these are often the events featuring the severely impaired or women) are given every opportunity to take place in the Paralympic Games.

Managing injury in Paralympic athletics

Cancellation of events due to lack of numbers as a result of injury to competitor is a logistical problem for the IPC. The alleviation of pain and the elimination of injury has been a concern for all nations with large Paralympic programs that send teams to the Paralympic Games since at least 1988 in Seoul, Korea (Ferrara and Peterson, 2000). Adoption of sports medicine by nations who provide these services to Olympians already is clearly not a big step. Nations with strong NPCs are often at the forefront of pushing for social justice, both inside sport and in society more generally, for marginalized populations, including the impaired. Norway, for example, has an integrated high-performance sport system where the National Olympic and Paralympic committees are one and the same. Such countries provide sports medicine to all elite athletes in order to ensure that more athletes go into competition in the best shape possible. From here sports medicine provision at the Paralympic Games is a relatively easy step as NOCs and NPCs can work in harmony. For example, the vast majority of treatment room equipment is exactly the same for Olympic and Paralympic sports so the clinic materials only have to be transported once to the Olympic/Paralympic venues. For smaller nations, less developed in international sporting terms, a central Olympic/Paralympic Village medical clinic has been a feature since 1988. That said, the need for sports medicine is not just limited to equipment; the fact that national teams' treatment staff are seldom paid for trips away and have to take unpaid leave from their busy clinic environments means that the quality of service or level of expertise is variable.

The physical availability of sports medicine facilities at major events on the Paralympic calendar does, however, provide its own difficulties. This is on two distinct levels. Firstly, many athletes may not have access to affordable high-quality sports medicine treatment throughout the year so they may quite literally come limping into major championship events with minor injuries or, in some cases, a catalogue of them. One reason for this may be a lack of finance in their nation that effectively blocks access to sports medicine except during major events. The cost of providing high-quality care can be extremely expensive and is often only covered for performers with star potential in nations like Canada and Britain that invest in Paralympic success. If the Paralympic athlete is not recognized as having medal potential, such services outside major competition may not be available to that individual. Within Paralympic sport, an athlete from most western countries needs to be ranked in the top four in the world to receive funding from their NPC; athletes at this level are clearly medal contenders. Mainstream able-bodied athletes in the sport of track and field athletics ranked inside the world's top 50 often receive funding. Therefore, athletes are better supported in mainstream able-bodied sport, with the logic being that the contest to be the world's best is more difficult. In reality, this ablest logic dictates that disabled populations are less important in society (Campbell, 2009) and hides an injustice. Supporting less-competitive mainstream athletes is wrong because, while the talent pools are less deep in Paralympic athletics, the number of athletes with a bonafide chance of winning a medal is actually the same. The lack of sports medicine infrastructure for some Paralympians exacerbates this injustice.

What is needed is a more comprehensive system of monitoring potential Paralympians between major competitions and, elsewhere, I have discussed the importance of keeping records of the diachronic nature of injury in order to assess the impact of injury on participation rates at major Paralympic events (Howe, 2006). One problem is that the Paralympic schedule is nowhere near as full as that of mainstream athletics – with many athletes only having one or two key competitions a year. With an often sparse competition schedule, a potential Paralympian who gets injured in out-of-competition training, which is the most likely scenario, is unlikely to be noticed as missing from action unless the NPC has a well-developed sport medicine infrastructure. Absence from a competition or two may be perceived as a lack of interest in the sport or a statement that the athlete has permanently retired. This is particularly problematic for athletes in countries with little sports medicine infrastructure as compared to athletes who are lucky enough to be from developed Paralympic nations, such as Canada or the UK, and who often have access to sport medicine support. Another problem rests with collecting this information through ethnographic means as injured athletes are seldom at events where participant observation takes place. The collection of data is often sporadic or snapshot by its very nature because the world best impaired athletes congregate, at most, once a year at major events, when a discourse of trials and tribulations related to their successful attendance at the event can best be documented.[3] Discussions of the chronology of pain and injury that athletes have survived to get to the year's major event are key to understanding the importance of these concepts to the culture of Paralympic sport.

Distinction of 'Paralympic' injury

In the world of Paralympic athletics, injury can occur on a number of fronts. On one hand, an individual's impairment may lead to biomechanical and or physiological deficiencies that, as a result of everyday life, may lead to injury. On the other, it may be simply the nature of the training an elite disabled sporting participant undertakes in preparation for competition in their sport of choice. What is clear is that either form of injury runs counter to the traditional notions of health; pushing the body to the point where injury occurs goes counter to the conventional definition of health. Being healthy for high-performance sport is not the same as being healthy for life. Health in the 'everyday' world means avoiding illness, including pain and injury. High-performance sport, however, requires athletes to be in a healthy state of fitness. As one informant suggested: 'Being fit is like being on a tightrope between health and illness but, as a person with impairment, I am never seen as completely healthy – perhaps it is [because of] my prosthesis that people often treat me as if I am ill'.

This suggests there is a distinctive tension between the concept of health and an impaired body. Following the medical model of disability developed by Oliver (1990), people with impairments can be seen to be disabled by society. One of the ways this occurs is to limit opportunities for those with impairments to engage in physical activity. APA programs have been continually developing across the globe at an ever increasing rate over the last 25 years but seldom are impaired populations consulted about their provision. It is unsurprising therefore that there is often a poor uptake of APA programs as they are introduced for and not with input from impaired populations (Silva and Howe, 2012). This lack of involvement could be one of the reasons people with impairments are less healthy than the general population. Paralympic athletes have been more fortunate than most in that they have been able to gain access to sporting provision at an elite level; however, the nature of Paralympic sport may mean that these athletes have been 'fast-tracked' in a push to win more medals. In fact, NPCs specifically target events where there are a small number of competitors internationally since these events are often easier to win (Howe, 2008). The downside of this approach is that the athletes recruited often lack an understanding of elite sporting culture to deal with the rigorous training that their body must go through. This fast track may circumvent the proper development of a healthy philosophy regarding high-performance sporting culture.

Obviously injury does not just befall those who are not properly indoctrinated into the culture of elite sport. One of the fiddles of this type of research is not knowing when a healthy body is going to become an ill one. This being said, impairment-specific injuries can take any number of forms. For an individual with an amputation, particularly part or all of a leg, difficulties may arise with regards to swelling. The area around the amputation, often referred to as the stump, is often prone to swelling particularly during the healing process. As the skin toughens in the area of the stump the individual will be able to engage in increasingly greater levels of physical activity but it takes time and a process of trial and error to fit the prosthetic limb so that it does not irritate the stump. Observations from my research suggest, however, that many elite sporting participants with lower limb amputations suffer regular bouts of swelling after some rigorous training sessions. This is particularly evident when athletes are fast-tracked into the Paralympic system; a common practice in Canada and the UK, with injured soldiers being introduced to and participating in athletics through such military initiatives as *Soldier On* or *Battle Back*. Because of the fast-track system, the wounds of amputation may not have had time to properly heal before rigorous training commences. This may lead to increased rates of injury but, even for the seasoned amputee, the stresses placed on the body because of biomechanical inefficacies may lead to other forms of over-use injuries.

With the shift from pastime to spectacle that has occurred in Paralympic sport, there has also been increased research and development directed toward improving the technology used by impaired sporting participants (Howe, 2004, 2008). For example, to alleviate some of the pain and swelling associated with an amputees' stump, prosthetic limb manufacturers have started to use gel padded covers for stumps that are widely regarded as superior to the more traditional bandage wraps. These gel covers allow for less friction in the manmade ball-and-socket fittings of high-performance prosthetic limbs and, as a result, are less likely to cause painful swelling. This technological advancement also impacts upon wheelchair user: over-use injuries associated with wheelchair use occur less often but because the Paralympic athletes are able to train harder in their new chairs, when injuries do occur they often can be more serious. The technology allows these re-embodied athletes to perform feats that are equal or better than high-performance able-bodied athletes (Howe, 2011). However, the cost of being able to push your body harder, in training and competition because of the improved technology, is that when it breaks down through injury it is often more serious both physically and culturally (Howe, 2004, 2006). This means it takes longer for the athlete to return to a healthy state of fitness.

The 'pain of injury' in Paralympic athletics

The persistent cost of sport-related injury, both from a curative and preventative perspective, continues to grow. While countries with developed NPCs fund the training of their elite Paralympic athletes, which also includes access to high-quality sports medicine, the system is not as comprehensive as that which is developed for mainstream high-performance able-bodied athletes nor for those athletes with impairment moving up the competitive sport ladder. In other words, the system caters for performers who have already achieved elite status and little is done for athletes with the potential to make the grade.

There are a small number of Paralympic potential athletes in some classes. If some athletes are forced to leave their sport through the onset of chronic injury before they can achieve elite status this places the future of the Paralympic movement in a degree of jeopardy. A serious injury to a handful of potential Paralympians can mean the cancellation of some events, as suggested earlier in this chapter. While it seems realistic to cancel international events with small numbers, the elimination of one competitive opportunity that may be a result of injury may lead to more serious consequences for the careers of the athletes involved in the event. The cancellation of an event means that it will be six to eight years before the event is back on the program. Some time ago it was suggested that, as a result of this situation and the importance of pain and injury outlined above, there was a need for an International Injury Register for Potential Paralympians (IIRPP) (Howe, 2006); to date this has not been developed. This call for an IIRPP was misguided because it fails to take into consideration the competitive nature of international sport. NPCs can be very secretive about their preparations for the Paralympic Games. Exposing their preparations in relation to sport science and medicine could be counterproductive to achieving the best results at the Paralympic Games and negatively impact upon the funding the NPC receives from their government. Mindful of this, I still believe that NPCs need to keep track of injuries of all Paralympic potential athletes. Athletes do retire and/or turn their back on the sport they once loved for many reasons but, because numbers are relatively small, it is important that NPCs are aware of the injury and career status of athletes so that they can determine how many healthy athletes are available for competition.

My research suggests that injuries are on the increase within high-performance sport for the disabled and, with only a limited number of high-profile sporting events every quadrennial, injury for these athletes can have significant implications to the future of their sport. Financially the sponsorship and government assistance programs that are part of these athletes' livelihood in countries, like Canada and the United Kingdom, are often performatively linked to success at sports-specific IPC events or the Paralympic Games and as such missing one of these events through injury can place added stress on an athlete. If similar misfortune befalls several athletes in the same classification, particularly in the more severely impaired classes, then their event could be cancelled.

Paralympic culture is not simply defined by the 'ability' of a performer, but whether their impairment fits within the rules dictated by the IPC regarding the classification of bodies eligible for the Paralympic Games. As a result, there is a need to closely document the injuries that befall potential Paralympians. What seems to be of fundamental importance is how the 'imperfect' sporting body in its injured state can have an impact on the structure of Paralympic sporting practice that ultimately may lead to the disempowering of some of these athletes. Even the most celebrated of Paralympic athletes can be disempowered (see Gerschick and Miller, 1995) if they do not take center stage at a major international event because of chronic injury.

The absence from the Paralympic stage of particular qualified groups of impaired bodies because of low numbers is the distinctive dimension of pain and injury as the antithesis of health on which this chapter focuses. This highlights the importance of the body in Paralympic sport as the site of resistance to ablest norms and values regarding the number of competitors required for a successful contest on the one hand and, on the other, the location where discipline and conformative physical action is celebrated and rewarded with the achievement of sporting success. When pain and injury 'capture' an elite sporting performer with impairment, health becomes a distant memory. Therefore the consequences of pain and injury sustained in the pursuit of Paralympic success may be far reaching. Because of the importance of the Paralympic movement as a successful flagship within the field of APA, it raises significant questions related to health, and well-being may become increasingly important for those who advocate participation over performance.

Notes

1   The act of moving a racing wheelchair forward at pace is referred to as 'pushing'.
2   Follow the links from the IPC website (www.paralympic.org) to get details of the individual federations' classification systems.
3   In the age of Skype and other forms of electronic communication, it is possible to continue real-time discussions from the far corners of the world and some data are collected in this manner.

References

Bendelow, G. and Williams, S. J. (1995) 'Transcending the dualism: Towards a sociology of pain', *Sociology of Health and Illness*, 17: 139–65.

Campbell, F. K. (2009) *Contours of Ableism: The Production of Disability and Abledness*, New York: Palgrave MacMillian.

Camilleri, J. M. (1999) 'Disability: A personal odyssey', *Disability and Society*, 14(6): 845–53.

Ferrara, M. S. and Peterson, C. (2000) 'Injuries to athletes with disabilities: Identifying Injury Patterns', *Sports Medicine*, 30(2): 137–43.

Gerschick, T. J. and Miller, A. S. (1995) 'Coming to terms: Masculinity and physical disability', in D. Sabo and F. Gordon (eds) *Men's Health and Illness: Gender, Power, and the Body*, London: Sage Publications, 183–204.

Howe, P. D. (2001) 'An ethnography of pain and injury in professional Rugby Union: The case of Pontypridd RFC', in *International Review of Sport Sociology*, 35(3): 289–303.

Howe, P. D. (2004) *Sport, Pain and Professionalism: Ethnographies of Injury and Risk*, London: Routledge.

Howe, P. D. (2006) 'The role of injury in the organization of Paralympic sport', in S. Loland, Skirstad, and I. Waddington (eds) *Pain and Injury in Sport: Social and Ethical Analysis*, London: Routledge, 211–25.

Howe, P. D. (2008) *The Cultural Politics of the Paralympic Movement: Through the Anthropological Lens*, London: Routledge.

Howe, P. D. (2011) 'Cyborg and supercrip: The Paralympics technology and the (dis) empowerment of disabled athletes', *Sociology*, 45(5): 868–82.

Howe, P. D. (2012) 'Children of a lesser god: Paralympics and high-performance sport', in J. Sugden and A. Tomlinson (eds) *Watching the Olympics: Politics, power and representation*, London: Routledge.

Howe, P. D. and Jones, C. (2006) 'Classification of disabled athletes: (Dis)empowering the Paralympic practice community', *Sociology of Sport Journal*, 23: 29–46.

Kitchin, P. J. and Howe, P. D. (2012) 'How can the social theory of Pierre Bourdieu assist sport management research?' *Sport Management Review* 16(2): 123–34.

Nixon, H. L. (1992) 'A social network analysis of influences on athletes to play with pain and injuries', *Journal of Sport and Social Issues*, 16: 127–35.

Nixon, H. L. (1993a) 'Accepting the risks of pain and injury in sport: Mediated cultural influences on playing hurt', *Sociology of Sport Journal*, 10: 183–96.

Nixon, H. L. (1993b) 'Social network analysis of sport: Emphasizing social structure in sport sociology', *Sociology of Sport Journal*, 10: 315–21.

Nixon, H. L. (1996) 'The relationship of friendship networks, sports experiences, and gender to express pain thresholds', *Sociology of Sport Journal*, 13: 78–86.

Oliver, M. (1990) *The Politics of Disablement*, London: Macmillan.

Rimmer, J. H., Riley, B., Wang, E., Rauworth, A. and Jurkowski, J. (2004) 'Physical activity participation among persons with disabilities: Barriers and facilitators', *American Journal of Preventive Medicine*, 26(5): 420–5.

Scruton, J. (1998) *Stoke Mandeville: Road to the Paralympics*, Cambridge: Peterhouse Press.

Shilling, C. (2003) *The Body and Social Theory*, 2nd edn, Sage: London.

Silva, C. F. and Howe, P. D. (2012) 'Difference, adapted physical activity and human development: Potential contribution of capabilities approach', *Adapted Physical Activity Quarterly*, 29(1): 25–43.

Steadward, R. D. (1996) 'Integration and sport in the Paralympic movement', *Sport Science Review*, 5(1): 26–41.

Tweedy, S. M. (2002) 'Taxonomic theory and the ICF: Disability athletics classification', *Adapted Physical Activity Quarterly*, 19: 220–37.

Tweedy, S. and Howe, P. D. (2011) 'History of the Paralympic Movement', in Y. Vanlandewijck, and W. Thompson (eds) *The Paralympic Athlete*, Lausanne: IOC Press, 3–30.

Wacquant, L. (1995) 'Pugs at work: Bodily capital and bodily labour among professional boxers', *Body and Society*, 1(1): 65–93.

12 Re-imagining the urban citizen

Leveraging physical cultural legacies

*Amanda De Lisio, Inge Derom and
Robert VanWynsberghe*

Living in Vancouver, in the midst of all the 2010 Olympic-hype, we were intuitively drawn to the human and financial investment dedicated to projecting an image of active and healthy citizenship to the watching world. The combination of our personal and professional interests and expertise in human action and social change led us to theoretically and empirically examine the impact of this high-profile sport event on local identities. In approaching our research at the time, we were aware that the sport mega-event literature had discussed the extent to which hosting an internationally recognized event alters not only the material or built environment of local communities (e.g., with the construction of new infrastructure) but also the immaterial or ideological notion of citizenship (e.g., with the establishment of new social, economic policies and political agenda) for those living in the area (Burbank *et al.*, 2002; Harvey, 1989). We recognized that the short-term ornamentation of former local communities has had permanent effects for both host cities and the bodies embroiled in the mix – processes that become difficult to reverse once written into legislation and rendered in stone, steel, glass and cemented into the urban consciousness. Given our engagement with this literature, we retreated to classical urban theories often echoed within more contemporary studies and, in particular, were inspired by the ideas put forth by Robert Park nearly a century ago (see, for example, Park 1929, 1967 and Park *et al.*, 1984). In his analysis of human nature and social life under the modern city condition, Park argued that more than a physical thing or artificial construction, cities are a state of mind. To Park, in making cities, inhabitants inevitably (re)made themselves: That is, the relation to sentience, the technologies deemed necessary, and the aesthetic tendencies valued are (re)made in our construction of urban life. In engaging with his work, we started to consider opportunities to empirically observe the ways in which the urban environment mediates certain ideologies in relation to citizenship. And, more pointedly, the ideologies related to citizenship and health.

The accelerated processes of urban reform, undertaken in the staging of a sport mega-event, combined with our location within a host context, offered an opportune moment to evaluate the processes involved in the (re)construction of local identities. Situating our work within the sport mega-event literature, we want to be clear that our focus here is less on the (re)building of the material environment and more so directed at the presence (or not) of an effort to create an ideological interruption to citizenship/local identities for those living within host communities, coordinated under an Olympic-oriented political agenda. In connection with the theme of the book, we use the 2010 Winter Olympics as a case to demonstrate the use of elite, high-performance sport, celebrated in the hype of international sporting competition, as a chance to fashion sport and physical activity (or health, more broadly) legacies associated to the Games. As we discuss in greater detail below, health and wellness social legacies have universal appeal, articulating a preferred future of a more physically active, healthy citizen and although we do not intend to critique this aim, we do intend to illustrate that these citizen-dependent imaginaries are constructed from within, and work to maintain, a broader socio-political and economic agenda. The purpose for which is to illustrate the extent to which the effort to create or establish legacies for host communities is a political process – one that does not (often) reflect the necessities of those most in need.

Event leveraging: Keeping the liberal in neoliberalism

The sport event literature has differentiated between event impact and event leverage. Chalip (2004, 2006) and Smith (2012) have both been influential in illuminating this conceptual difference. For the sake of this chapter, impact studies are defined as those, which are invested in the evaluation of the immediate fallout associated to the event. These studies differ from leverage studies, which are more longitudinal in nature and focus on the organizational processes and strategies that are associated to the planning as well as the long-term legacies related to the event (Chalip, 2004, 2006; Smith, 2010). "It is no longer suitable merely to host an event in the hope that desired outcomes will be achieved", Chalip notes, "it is necessary to form and implement strategies and tactics that capitalize fully on the opportunities each event affords" (2004: 245). The strategy for building up long-term benefits or legacies involves identifying event structures – infrastructure, knowledge, image, emotions, networks and/or culture – that will satisfy the long-term needs of the host region (Gratton and Preuss, 2008; Preuss, 2007).

Recent studies have increased scepticism and critique with respect to mega-event hosting (see, for example, Gaffney, 2010; Jennings and Sambrook, 2000; Lenskyj, 2002; Shaw, 2008). The promise of future legacies (and their attendant leveraging strategies) has often been used to rationalize the enormous human and financial investment dedicated to hosting an internationally recognized sport mega-event. Chalip (2004) introduced the concept of 'event leveraging' to denote activities undertaken around the event to maximize long-term benefits. O'Brien (2007) later built on his work and described the event as merely seed capital, arguing that it was the responsibility of host communities to use this capital to realize sustainable legacies. At first, 'event leveraging' referred to processes and strategies, which fuelled future economic growth. As Green (2001) argued, a sport event could no longer be just about providing a forum for athletic competition; it also had to be viewed as a catalyst for future economic development. Paraphrasing from the work of Chalip (2004), it was believed that a mega-event was able to create additional revenue streams for host communities via two somewhat related processes: first, from a consumer perspective (i.e., from attendees to local businesses) and second, from international media exposure. Combined, these two processes were/are thought to increase immediate revenue through tourism and/or (international, national or local) private and public contracting/collaboration. Long-term economic gain was also purportedly maximized through heightened media coverage, advertising and reporting on the host and thought to attract more growth-inducing resources than those accumulated during the actual sport event itself (Chalip 2004).

Despite the privileging of economic legacies, local communities started to demand more socially oriented legacies from events that necessitate such a massive public investment. Waitt (2008) has referred to the mega-event phenomenon as constructing "geographies of hype" and has argued that "social implications of hosting a festival are considered as equally important for political authorities during an era of diverging life opportunities and rising trends of depression and anxiety" (Waitt, 2008: 515). As Gold and Gold (2008) illustrate, the unproblematic approach of coupling a (sport) mega-event with a cosmopolitan (corporate) agenda started to complicate disparities emanating from the political spectrum. With the Olympic Movement ascending upon the 'developing' world, starting in 1968 with the Mexico City Games, local civic opposition protested the public expenditure on a two-week festival in lieu of much needed socio-economic interventions. Forced to navigate the burden of representation, the Mexican Organizing Committee assembled a place-promotion campaign that leveraged the perceived national strength of the country, through various cultural festivities and public discourse, while, simultaneously, working to reconfigure (and erase) its weaknesses (Zolov, 2004). Learning from the political uproar that was Mexico '68, host cities further emphasized the establishment of social legacies to appease people living within local communities while also distracting from the mega-cost affiliated to the event itself.

Sport and health legacies

In the past, host cities have frequently focused on public health policies and sporting opportunites to garner lasting social legacies. In the context of the 1996 Olympic Games, the Georgia State Health Agency started to plan for event-related health legacies immediately after Atlanta won the bid in 1990. One eventual action taken was the creation of a health promotion brochure that was mailed with ticket information to those who participated in the Olympic ticket lottery. Information covered in the brochure included physical fitness, injury prevention, health care and insurance and tobacco use (Meehan *et al.*, 1998). In the case of the 2004 Summer Olympics in Athens, several national health promotion strategies were attached to an Olympic agenda. For example, shortly after the 2004 bid announcement, several anti-tobacco policies were enacted and an advertising campaign with a particular slant on tobacco use was publicized across host communities. Atlanta and Athens focused on the dissemination of health information (e.g., brochures, media campaigns) while London, host of the 2012 Summer Olympics, focused on the creation of local physical activity programming and services (Mahtani *et al.*, 2013). As Girginov and Hills (2008) note, London worked to promote sustainable health legacies with an emphasis on mass participation in sport, exercise and physical activity. In hosting the 2012 Olympic event, political parties in power promised "to bring together a unique combination of government resources and commitment from the sporting community and participants to create a truly world-class sporting nation" (DCMS, 2007: 7). In honouring this commitment, Sport England implemented 'Places to Play', a £135-million initiative (funded by the National Lottery) that provided additional funding for grassroots organizations to upgrade sport facilities, train volunteers and create opportunities for people to be more active (http://archive.sportengland.org/). We realize that this is a rather basic summation of lengthy leveraging processes, however, we wanted to merely make the point that it is common practice for a sport mega-event to be paired with a sport and/or physical activity agenda.

The assumption underpinning these legacies is that with increased access to elite athletic competition and facilities, host communities will be inspired to partake in physical activities and lead a healthier life (Hindson *et al.*, 1994; Hogan and Norton, 2000; McCartney *et al.*, 2010; Shipway, 2007; Veal, 2003; Veal *et al.*, 2012). Unpacking this belief, several studies have helped illustrate that health legacies "should not be considered as an automatic 'trickle down' – rather, they need to be planned for, organized, and funded in the same way as the mega-sport events" (Mitchell *et al.*, 2012: 17). In relation to planning specific health legacies, the event must be carefully aligned to a particular physical activity or sport intervention (Potwarka and McCarville, 2008) that is coordinated, strategic and intended to outlast the Games. Such an intervention will be part and parcel of a broader, more long-term political agenda – one that will subsist long after the event itself (Coalter, 2004; Weed *et al.*, 2009, 2012). The creation of one such health initiative (described below), in the context of 2010 Olympic planning, offered a case to examine processes involved in the (re)construction of local identities and citizenry. Nevertheless, before we detail this effort, we want to illustrate the manner in which Vancouver (in conjunction with the province of British Columbia) reflected the shift in legacy rhetoric – from economically oriented to more socially oriented leveraging strategies – discussed above.

Event leveraging within British Columbia

Dating back to 1986, the World Exposition was hoped to create a 'publicity bonanza' that would draw international fame, attract tourism and secure future economic development to Vancouver and the surrounding area (Dawson, 2006: 14). In hosting the Expo, political parties in power maximized the economic potential of the event by marketing downtown real estate opportunities to foreign investors (VanWynsberghe *et al.*, 2012). The former railway land on the north shore of False Creek was one such site sold by the province to Concord Pacific Development Ltd whose majority shareholder was (and is) Hong Kong business-man Li Ka-Shing, one of the wealthiest people in the world (Surborg *et al.*, 2008). False Creek is a small inlet in the city that separates the downtown core from the rest of the city. Millions were spent on the redevelopment project – including the cost needed to lobby the City of Vancouver to have the north shore of False Creek re-designated from industrial and office-zoned land. The success of this effort paved the way for the condominium development that dominates the Vancouver skyline (and image) even today. Unlike the legacies of the 1986 World Exposition, in staging the 2010 Games, political parties in power focused on the establishment of social legacies, which sought to brand local communities as the healthiest Olympic/Paralympic host in the world.

With this focus in mind, it is important to note the health status of the metro-politan host (and the province, as an extension) in the pre-Olympic era. As a city, Vancouver has been celebrated for maintaining the second lowest rate of physical inactivity, the third lowest rate of obesity, the lowest rate of smoking and the second lowest rate of heavy drinking when compared to other large urban areas in Canada (Gilmore, 2004). By extension, the province of British Columbia continues to be ranked well above the national average with respect to the propor-tion of the population considered active or moderately active. Further, in relation to smoking and exposure to second-hand smoke as well as overweight and obesity, British Columbia is again below the national average (Statistics Canada, 2012).

Despite these data, in the midst of building Olympic infrastructure, health performance (as related to smoking, physical activity, obesity and drinking) was purported to be at risk. As the former British Columbia Minister of Education, Shirley Bond, announced in a press release, "one in four of our children are now overweight or obese. For their future, and for the future of our province, this must change" (Shirley Bond, Minister of Education, September 2007). Municipal documentation also reinforced this threat:

> Conversely, the lack of physical activity has significant personal and finan-cial costs to the individual and society. Obesity levels amongst our youth are becoming alarmingly high and have more than doubled between 1975 and 1990. A majority of adult Canadians are not active enough to benefit their health and adult obesity rates have increased by more than 2.5 times in the past decades. Among the four chronic diseases that result in 2/3 of deaths in Canada – diabetes, cardiovascular disease, cancer, respiratory disease – all share common preventable risk factors including physical inactivity.
>
> (Vancouver Board of Parks and Recreation, 2006: 4)

In responding to the impending risk, in June 2000, once Vancouver/Whistler won the endorsement of the Canadian Olympic Committee over Calgary and Quebec City, the provincial government partnered with the Vancouver Bid Corporation to create sport legacies for the province. This partnership would mark the inception of 2010 LegaciesNow, a non-profit organization with the intention to create sustainable Olympic legacies. The first mandate of the organization was to support sport development in the province and create opportunities for local athletes to participate on the Olympic and Paralympic stage. This sport-oriented mandate would later expand to include arts and culture, volunteerism, literacy and accessibility for people with disabilities; however, the expansion did not occur until 2010 LegaciesNow became an independent not-for-profit organization that was in need of further support from the private sector.

The provincial commitment to health was further demonstrated in February 2003, with the announcement the British Columbia Healthy Living Alliance (BCHLA), a non-government health organization. The BCHLA was announced as an umbrella organization, representative of several non-government agencies in the health sector, whose goal was to promote collaborative action and avoid overlap between interests/responsibilities of not-for-profit agencies within the health sector. Members of the BCHLA include: the British Columbia Lung Association; the Canadian Cancer Society; the Heart and Stroke Foundation; Dietitians of Canada; the Canadian Diabetes Association; the British Columbia Pediatric Society; the Public Health Association of British Columbia; the British Columbia Recreation and Parks Association; and the Union of British Columbia Municipalities. On 3 July 2003, British Columbia (more specifically, the cities of Vancouver and Whistler) won the 2010 Olympic bid. The Public Health Agency of Canada (2009: 11) stated that the announcement "opened a clear window of opportunity to move population health promotion onto the political agenda" in the province. On 8 February 2005, Premier Gordon Campbell declared in the Speech from the Throne that one of the five "great goals for the golden decade ahead" was for British Columbia "to lead the way in North America in healthy living and physical fitness" (Campbell, 2005: 9). The effort made by the BCHLA and 2010 LegaciesNow contributed towards achieving this Great Goal although better cohesion between agencies (non-government, private and not-for-profit) and government ministries was required to fully achieve its aims.

On 23 March 2005, ActNow BC was launched in British Columbia, a public initiative that was designed to coordinate cross-ministerial, intersectoral action and facilitate future health strategies for the province. ActNow BC became a "whole-of-government health promotion initiative designed to reduce the incidence of chronic illness through individual behavioral changes" (Anderson *et al.*, 2010: v). The impetus for action was straightforward: "without new actions to promote health, the BC Ministry of Health would require an estimated 72 per cent of the total government budget by 2017 to address all health needs" (Anderson *et al.*, 2010: 7). To this end, ActNow BC developed a plan for 2010 with the overall objective of "making the province the healthiest jurisdiction to ever host an Olympic event" (BCHLA, 2005: 28). In doing so, ActNow BC aimed to achieve each of these targets:

1   To increase by 20 per cent the proportion of the British Columbia population (aged 12+ years) that is physically active or moderately active during leisure time from the 2003 statistic of 58.1 per cent to 69.7 per cent.

2   To increase by 20 per cent the proportion of the British Columbia population (aged 12+ years) that eats the daily recommended amount of fruits and vegetables from the 2003 statistic of 40.1 per cent to 48.1 per cent.

3   To reduce by 10 per cent the proportion of the British Columbia population (aged 15+ years) that uses tobacco, from the 2003 statistic of 16 per cent to 14.4 per cent.

4   To reduce by 20 per cent the proportion of the British Columbia population (aged 18+ years) that is currently classified as overweight or obese from the 2003 statistic of 42.3 per cent to 33.8 per cent.

5   To increase by 50 per cent the number of women who receive counseling about alcohol use during pregnancy, and employ focused strategies for the prevention of fetal alcohol spectrum disorder (FASD) in all regional health authorities.

(Ministry of Health, Press Release, 23 March 2006)

As an organization, ActNow BC promoted cohesion through two distinctive funding strategies (see Table 12.1). First, it provided a one-time endowment given to the British Columbia Healthy Living Alliance and 2010 LegaciesNow, which was the largest transfer of financial support (CAN$30 million) from the provincial government to a non-government, health promotion organization in history (Geneau *et al.*, 2009). Second, in order to leverage cooperation across government ministries, ActNow BC established an incentive fund in the amount of $15 million payable over a three-year period. The $15 million incentive fund supported strategies proposed by other ministries that aligned with their health campaign. Owing to the affiliation between ActNow BC and the Ministry of Health at the time – before it was designated as its own ministry with the Olympics in June 2009 – administration of the incentive fund was given to the Ministry of Health. As such, all ministries were invited to submit an application to the Ministry of Health for review.

Between 2005 and 2008, the incentive fund supported approximately 30 different strategies from ten ministries (Geneau *et al.*, 2009). Some of the initiatives included an oral health program created by the Ministry of Community Services, a Fetal Alcohol Spectrum Disorders (FASD) awareness campaign established by

Table 12.1 Breakdown of the financial investment made by ActNow BC

Organization	Investment (CAN$)	Year
Union of BC Municipalities	5 million	2005
British Columbia Ministry of Health (through ActNow BC)	15 million/3-year period	2005–2008
British Columbia Healthy Living Alliance	25.2 million	2006
2010 LegaciesNow	4.8 million	2006

Source: Public Health Agency of Canada, 2009

the Ministry of Child and Family Development, and an Elementary School Milk Program created by the Ministry of Agriculture and Land. The Ministry of Education also received financial support from ActNow BC in implementing a number of school health policies. Three of these policies were announced in September 2007. An example of one such health policy was the establishment of Daily Physical Activity (DPA) – a school-based health policy that made it compulsory for all children in the province (kindergarten to Grade 12) to participate in and record moderate to vigorous physical activities (150 minutes/week) in order to graduate.

Despite the progress made by each initiative supported through the ActNow BC incentive fund, shortly after the 2010 Olympic/Paralympic closing ceremonies, much of the financial aid was exhausted. On 11 June 2010, Minister McNeil was appointed Minister of Citizen Services, the former Minister of State for the Olympics and ActNow BC. No one was appointed to fill her position. In May 2011, the Ministry of Health refashioned ActNow BC into Healthy Families BC, an online resource for health and wellness information. Healthy Families BC is the provincial health promotion plan "dedicated to helping British Columbians make healthier choices" in relation to "four key areas: proper nutrition, healthy lifestyles, resources for parents, and fostering healthy communities" (www.healthyfamiliesbc.ca/home/about-us).

Extrapolating from the British Columbian case, we intended to demonstrate that the naming of legacies (and their associated leveraging strategies) is a highly political process, necessitating the socio-political construction of crises. If those involved in the leveraging of 2010 Winter Olympics consulted with local communities or considered the Inner-City Inclusivity Commitment Statement (ICICS), as one example of an expression of local voice, more (or different) legacies would have been molded to meet the realities of local communities most in need of health legacies. Created by the Vancouver Bid Corporation in 2002, the ICICS sought "participation and equity for all British Columbians, including low and moderate-income people" in the Winter Games (Vancouver Bid Corporation, 2002). Organized around the development of an 'inclusive' approach to planning for the Olympic Games, the ICICS sought to "create a strong foundation for sustainable socio-economic development in Vancouver's inner-city neighbourhoods, particularly in the Downtown Eastside, Downtown South and Mount Pleasant" (Vancouver Bid Corporation, 2002: 1).

Reference to the ICICS is meant to illustrate that even while 2010 host communities worked to democratically express their anxieties about the Games, authorities charged with creating social legacies failed to heed their advice. As a result, the autocratic formulation of legacies neglected those most in need of the resources made available in the staging of a sport mega-event. In leveraging physical activity, those responsible for creating 2010 Olympic legacies neglected the less celebrated local communities. As Cornelissen (2010) has illustrated:

Whether hosted by developing or developed countries, sport mega-events involve the representation, branding and imagineering of cities or nations for local and international consumption under the legitimation of transnational competitiveness. This involves the manipulation of material conditions and is dependent on processes of symbolic construction. In this, the meanings, values and affiliations that are attached by political actors to places in order to distinguish them can be viewed as the product of narrative assemblage. Whose narratives predominate and by which causes they prevail are generally the results of compound processes of social and political negotiation and intense if often concealed contesting.

(Cornelissen, 2010: 3013)

We argue, following the work of Cornelissen (2010), that in deconstructing the leveraging strategies observed in the context of Vancouver 2010, it was evident that political parties in power were interested in creating the most favorable impression of certain select communities while ignoring the less glamorous social realities experienced across the host region. The (re)construction of local identities thus focused on the (always-already) celebrated citizen while failing to embrace the diversities and complexities of the metropolitan center or the province as a whole. In examining ActNow BC, we observed the manner in which social legacies offered a decoy to the extravagances dedicated to a one-off event by prepackaging reconciliation in anti-corporate, liberal promises. In this neoliberal moment, social legacies offer justification to the (increasing) extravagances host cities dedicate to an event by prepackaging their (much needed) reconciliation in anti-corporate, liberal promises.

Concluding remarks

It is clear that social leveraging strategies do more to project a particular media-friendly image of citizenship to the (watching) world rather than adequately address the realities of those living within host communities. Social leveraging strategies continually fail to create the impact initially intended and often misrepresent the needs of local communities. Following Smith (2013), legacies (and the broader leveraging rhetoric) are part and parcel of a convenient justification, used to pacify the uneven distribution of event-related resource material. Given the autocratic form in which legacies are continually constructed and enforced, we are more inclined to encourage host communities to re-appropriate the resources and opportunities made available in the staging of an event. We realize now in reflecting on ActNow BC and the entire 2010 process that, if nothing else, this effort compelled discussion (like that observed in the development of the ICICS) and more potently, had local communities (like those with decision-making power) imagining their own preferred future. Encouraging host communities to question the kind of imaginaries celebrated (or legacies deemed worthy) could be the most effective social outcome an event can generate. In a sense, we realize that this could be construed as an entrepreneurial refashioning of local communities but, in working within radically (neo)liberal processes, we want to be realistic about the terms in which local citizens have to contend. If there is room for host communities to socially benefit, at this time, we see the strategies (like the event itself) to be more entrepreneurial in nature – one that has host communities realizing their own health imaginaries with the aid (not at the mercy) of those responsible for creating legacies. As Darnell (2012) has explained in his work on Rio 2016, the global mantra of Olympism (or ideologies surrounding the use of sport in development, more broadly) is in constant negotiation – resisted and reshaped – by local communities. More work is needed to better understand the manner in which local communities interpret, support and/or resist politically prescribed, autocratically imposed event-leveraging processes in order to effectively realize their own imaginaries.

References

Anderson, I., Anderson, I., Beak, C., O'Reilly, C. and Roberts, C. (2010) *Building on the Momentum of ActNow BC: A whole-of-government approach to population health*. Online at: www.academia.edu/330294/Building_on_the_Momentum_of_ActNow_BC (accessed 19 May 2013).

BCHLA (British Columbia Healthy Living Alliance) (2005) *The Winning Legacy: A Plan for Improving the Health of British Columbians by 2010*, Vancouver: BCHLA.

Burbank, M. J., Andranovich, G. and Heying, C. H. (2002) 'Mega-events, urban development, and public policy', *Review of Policy Research*, 19(3): 179–202.

Campbell, G. (2005) 'Speech from the Throne', 6th session, 37th parliament, 8 February. Online at: www.leg.bc.ca/37th6th/4-8-37-6.htm (accessed 18 March 2014).

Chalip, L. (2004) 'Beyond impact: a general model for sport event leverage' in B. W. Ritchie and D. Adair (eds) *Sport Tourism: Interrelationships, impacts and issues*, Clevedon, UK: Channel View Publications, 236–62.

Chalip, L. (2006) 'Towards social leverage of sport events', *Journal of Sport and Tourism*, 11(2): 109–27.

Coalter, F. (2004) 'London 2012 : A sustainable sporting legacy?', in A. Vigor and M. Mean (eds) *After the Goldrush: A sustainable Olympics for London*, London: Institute for Public Policy Research and Demos, 93–108.

Cornelissen, S. (2010) 'The geopolitics of global aspiration: Sport mega-events and emerging powers', *The International Journal of the History of Sport*, 27(16–18): 3008–25.

Darnell, S. C. (2012) 'Olympism in action, Olympic hosting and the politics of "Sport for Development and Peace": Investigating the development discourses of Rio 2016', *Sport in Society*, 15(6): 869–87.

Dawson, M. (2006) 'Acting global, thinking local: "liquid imperialism" and the multiple meanings of the 1954 British Empire and Commonwealth Games', *The International Journal of the History of Sport*, 23(1): 3–27.

DCMS (Department for Culture, Media and Sport) (2007) *Our Promise for 2012: How the UK will benefit from the Olympic and Paralympic Games*, London: DCMS.

Gaffney, C. (2010) 'Mega-events and socio-spatial dynamics in Rio de Janeiro, 1919–2016', *Journal of Latin American Geography*, 9(1): 7–29.

Geneau, R., Fraser, G., Legowski, B. and Stachenko, S. (2009) 'Mobilizing intersectoral action to promote health: The case of ActNow BC in British Columbia, Canada', Public Health Agency of Canada. Online at: www.bchealthyliving.ca/sites/all/files/ WHO_PHAC_ActNowBC_anbc_eng.pdf (accessed 18 March 2014).

Gilmore, J. (2004) *Health of Canadians Living in Census Metropolitan Areas*, Vancouver: Statistics Canada.

Girginov, V. and Hills, L. (2008) 'The 2012 London Olympic Games and participation in sport: Understanding the link', *The International Journal of the History of Sport*, 25(14): 2091–116.

Gold, J. R. and Gold, M. M. (2008) 'Olympic cities: Regeneration, city rebranding and changing Urban Agendas', *Geography Compass*, 2(1): 300–18.

Gratton, C. and Preuss, H. (2008) 'Maximizing Olympic impacts by building up legacies', *The International Journal of the History of Sport*, 25(14): 1922–38.

Green, B. C. (2001) 'Leveraging subculture and identity to promote sport events', *Sport Management Review*, 4: 1–19.

Harvey, D. (1989) *From Managerialism to Entrepreneurialism: The transformation in urban governance in late capitalism*, Stockholm: Stockholm University.

Hindson, A., Gidlow, B. and Peebles, C. (1994) 'The "trickle-down" effect of top-level sport: Myth or reality? A case-study of the Olympics', *Australian Journal of Leisure and Recreation*, 4(1): 16–31.

Hogan, K. and Norton, K. (2000) 'The price of Olympic gold', *Journal of Science in Medicine in Sport*, 3(2): 203–18.

Jennings, A. and Sambrook, C. (2000) *The Great Olympic Swindle: When the world wanted its games back*, New York: Simon and Schuster.

Lenskyj, H. (2002) *The Best Olympics ever?: Social impacts of Sydney 2000*, Albany, NY: SUNY Press.

McCartney, G., Thomas, S., Thomson, H., Scott, J., Hamilton, V., Hanlon, P. and Morrison, D. S. (2010) 'The health and socioeconomic impacts of major multi-sport events: Systematic review (1978–2008)', *British Medical Journal (BMJ)*, 340(c2369), doi:10.1136/bmj.c2369.

Mahtani, K. R., Protheroe, J., Slight, S. P., Demarzo, M. M. P., Blakeman, T., Barton, C. and Brijnath, B. (2013) 'Can the London 2012 Olympics "inspire a generation" to do more physical or sporting activities? An overview of systematic reviews', *British Medical Journal (BMJ) Open*, 3(e002058), doi:10.1136/bmjopen–2012–002058.

Meehan, P., Toomey, K. E., Drinnon, J., Cunningham, S., Anderson, N. and Baker, E. (1998) 'Public health response for the 1996 Olympic Games', *Journal of the American Medical Association (JAMA)*, 279(18): 1469–73.

Mitchell, M. S., Manson, H., Allison, K., Robertson, J., Donnelly, P. and Goodman, J. (2012) 'Leveraging legacies: Will the Toronto 2015 Pan Am Games really benefit public health?', *University of Toronto Medical Journal*, 90(2): 24–6.

O'Brien, D. (2007) 'Points of leverage: Maximizing host community benefit from a regional surfing festival', *European Sport Management Quarterly*, 7(2): 141–65.

O'Brien, D. and Chalip, L. (2008) 'Sport events and strategic leveraging: Pushing towards the triple bottom line', in A. G. Woodside and D. Martin (eds) *Tourism Management: Analysis, behavior, and strategy*, Cambridge, UK: CABI, 318–38.

Park, R. E. (1929) 'The city as a social laboratory', in T. V. Smith and L. D. White (eds) *Chicago: An Experiment in Social Science Research*, Chicago: University of Chicago Press, 1–19.

Park, R. E. (1967) *On Social Control and Collective Behavior*, Chicago, IL: University of Chicago Press.

Park, R. E., Burgess, E. W. and McKenzie, R. D. (eds) (1984) *The City*, Chicago, IL: University of Chicago Press.

Potwarka, L. and McCarville, R. (2008) 'Understanding the trickle-down effect of the Olympics on activity levels within host nations: An agenda for research and practice', *The 8th International Conference on Sports: Economic, Management, Marketing and Social Aspects*, Athens: Atiner Publishing.

Preuss, H. (2007) 'The conceptualisation and measurement of mega sport event legacies', *Journal of Sport and Tourism*, 12(3–4): 207–28.

Province of British Columbia (2005) *Legislative Assembly of British Columbia Speech from the Throne, 2005 Legislative Session: 6th Session, 37th Parliament*. 8 February. Online at: www.leg.bc.ca/37th6th/Throne_Speech_2005_6th_37th.pdf (accessed 18 February 2014).

Public Health Agency of Canada (2009) 'Mobilizing intersectoral action to promote health: the case of ActNow BC in British Columbia, Canada'. Online at: www.phac-aspc.gc.ca/publicat/2009/ActNowBC/pdf/anbc-eng.pdf (accessed 19 November 2012).

Shaw, C. A. (2008) *Five Ring Circus: Myths and realities of the Olympic games*, Gabriola Island, BC: New Society Publishers.

Shipway, R. (2007) 'Sustainable legacies for the 2012 Olympic Games', *The Journal of the Royal Society for the Promotion of Health*, 127(3): 119–24.

Smith, A. (2010) 'Leveraging benefits from major events: Maximising opportunities for peripheral urban areas', *Managing Leisure*, 15(3): 161–80.

Smith, A. (2012) *Events and Urban Regeneration: The strategic use of events to revitalise cities*, New York: Routledge.

Smith, A. (2013) 'Leveraging sport mega-events: new model or convenient justification?', *Journal of Policy Research in Tourism, Leisure and Events*, 6(1): 15–30.

Statistics Canada (2012) *2011 National Household Survey*, Geography division. Online at: www5.statcan.gc.ca/bsolc/olc-cel/olc-cel?catno=99-011-X2011007&lang=eng (accessed 10 June 2013).

Surborg, B., VanWynsberghe, R. and Wyly, E. (2008) 'Mapping the Olympic growth machine: Transnational urbanism and the growth machine diaspora', *City*, 12(3): 341–55.

Vancouver Bid Corporation (2002) *2010 Bid Book*, Vancouver: Bid Corporation.

Vancouver Board of Parks and Recreation. (2006) *Active Communities Initiative – Report to Vancouver City Council*. Online, Former City of Vancouver website. Available at: http://former.vancouver.ca/ctyclerk/cclerk/20060926/documents/a10.pdf (accessed 14 February 2014).

VanWynsberghe, R., Surborg, B. and Wyly, E. (2012) 'When the Games come to town: Neoliberalism, mega-events and social inclusion in the Vancouver 2010 Winter Olympic Games', *International Journal of Urban and Regional Research*, 37(6): 2074–93.

Veal, A. (2003) 'Tracking change: leisure participation and policy in Australia, 1985–2002', *Annals of Leisure Research*, 6(3): 245–77.

Veal, A. J., Toohey, K. and Frawley, S. (2012) 'The sport participation legacy of the Sydney 2000 Olympic Games and other international sporting events hosted in Australia', *Journal of Policy Research in Tourism, Leisure and Events*, 4(2): 155–84.

Waitt, G. (2008) 'Urban festivals: Geographies of hype, helplessness and hope', *Geography Compass*, 2(2): 513–37.

Weed, M., Coren, E. and Fiore, J. (2009) *A Systematic Review of the Evidence Base for Developing a Physical Activity and Health Legacy from the London 2012 Olympic and Paralympic Games*, Canterbury, UK: Centre for Sport, Physical Education and Activity Research.

Weed, M., Coren, E., Fiore, J., Wellard, I., Mansfield, L., Chatziefstathiou, D. and Dowse, S. (2012) 'Developing a physical activity legacy from the London 2012 Olympic and Paralympic Games: A policy-led systematic review', *Perspectives in Public Health*, 132(2): 75–80.

Žižek, S. (2009) *First as Tragedy, Then as Farce*, London: Verso.

Zolov, E. (2004) 'Showcasing the "Land of Tomorrow": Mexico and the 1968 Olympics', *The Americas*, 61(2): 159–88.

13 The Olympic Movement, sport and health

Louise Mansfield and Dominic Malcolm

The publicly acclaimed idea that sport, as physical activity, is good for one's health is prominent in both global health strategies and national physical activity policies. For instance, the World Health Organization emphasizes "the significance of physical activity on public health" and "the need for the development of global recommendations" on physical activity for "the prevention of non-communicable diseases (NCDs) and the general health of the population worldwide" (WHO, 2012: 7). The UK's Department of Health has embedded these ideas in public health campaigns such as *Start Active, Stay Active* (DOH, 2011). These policies stem from a range of scientific studies showing that physical activity, of a regular and moderate kind, is good for health, and the position statements of various specialist working groups recommend specific quantities and qualities of activity for reducing risk of disease and improving health in relation to cardiorespiratory function, muscular strength and endurance, flexibility and body composition (Bouchard *et al.*, 1990; DOH, 2004; Garber *et al.*, 2011; Pollock *et al.*, 1998).

Yet health matters are complex, with health a contested and relative concept. Inequalities in health exist on a global and local scale and in respect of such factors as levels of poverty, gender and sexuality, age, disability, ethnic grouping and social class (Bury and Gabe, 2004). Many people worldwide anticipate living relatively long lives with positive health experiences yet, at the same time and in a variety of contexts, people are faced with situations in which their health is diminished, at risk, or a problem requiring conscious effort (Albrecht *et al.*, 2000). The cultural specificity of health can be seen in the juxtaposition of western fears about the increasing prevalence of dementia with concerns about reducing infant mortality in the developing world. Because health is interpersonally relative, with the lifestyle of certain individuals deemed "unhealthy" (e.g., in relation to alcohol consumption) in comparison to that of others (e.g., those engaging in physical activity and healthy eating regimes), concepts of health and illness increasingly reflect competing moral views about "good/healthy" and "bad/unhealthy" lifestyles (Shilling, 1993; Turner, 2000).

Health should also be seen as historically specific and socially constructed via specific medical interventions. With the development of what has been termed "surveillance medicine" (Armstrong, 1995) – the mass screening of populations made possible by new technologies and expanded resources – medicine has moved from intervention to monitoring, from acute to chronic conditions, from disease to health and from the hospital back into the community (Nettleton, 2006). Health promotion is increasingly directed not simply at those who are sick, "but at all individuals at all levels of the population" (Lupton, 1995: 51). In the process, new notions of who is (un)healthy have come into existence, frequently mediated by estimations of health risk rather than the occurrence of symptoms. This is the context in which the current claims for an inactivity pandemic (Kohl *et al.*, 2012) should be seen. The American Medical Association (AMA)'s 2013 decision to (re-)classify obesity as a disease illustrates the historical specificity of illness, while the subsequent public and academic controversy underscores the contested nature of this antonym of health.

While we recognize historical variability in the link, sport has traditionally been seen as the most effective medium through which to promote increased physical activity (Atkinson, 1978; Hargreaves, 1986, 1994; Mangan and Park, 1992). However, given the complexities in understanding health that we have introduced above, there should be no surprise that the relationship between health and sport engagement is more complex than is expressed in current policies and governmental proclamations. Moreover, as knowledge, understanding, experiences and beliefs about health and the role of sport in health improvement are shaped by specific socio-cultural contexts and bio-psychological conditions, it is important to consider sport as both a historically dynamic and culturally variable global phenomenon. The Olympic Games, re-instituted in its modern form in 1896 and currently incorporating 204 member states, provides a useful illustrative vehicle for this analysis.

Consequently, this chapter critically examines the dynamics of what we might call the sport–health ideological nexus – the notion of a direct, immutable and unproblematic link between sport and health – in the context of the Olympic Movement; a concept we will explore later in the chapter.[1] Examining the sport–health nexus in this context enables us to explore three overlapping themes: 1) the links between medical science and elite athletes; 2) the links between sports medicine provision and wider public health; and 3) the relationship between elite sport and public health promotion designed to increase levels of physical activity. More specifically, we deconstruct the notion of sport, explore its boundaries with physical activity and identify tensions between sport's elite and mass manifestations. Subsequently we outline the development and peculiar structure of sports medicine; examine the medical provision at, and the healthcare needs generated by, staging an Olympic Games; and critically explore the legacy goal of increasing sports participation. Consequently we are able to demonstrate the broad extent of the contradictions in the ideology linking sport and health.

Health and sport

There is an extensive body of literature documenting the health benefits of physical activity. However the relationship between health and sport is complex and contested and marked by the dynamics of temporal and spatial change as well as by conceptualizations of what sport is. Sport can be defined as physical activity incorporating some degree of exertion, organizational structure (e.g., codified rules) and competition (usually against one or more persons). Consequently, sport involves varying and complex social relations in which bodily movements of one performer are produced and reproduced in relation to others. It is a different type of physical activity compared to play (characterized by spontaneous and flexible action) or exercise (involving rhythmic and regular movements of the body performed at intensity, frequency and timing more consciously controlled by participants). Importantly though, different forms of physical activity have different consequences for health. As Waddington points out:

> To suggest that a 30-minute gentle swim three times a week is good for one's health does not mean that running 70 miles a week as a means of preparing for running marathons is good for one's health in an equally simple or unproblematic way.
>
> (Waddington, 2000: 20)

Yet definitions of sport, exercise and play tend to be conflated, not only in popular consciousness but even in institutional promotions of physical activity. For instance, the aforementioned *Start Active, Stay Active* (DOH, 2011: 1) describes itself as "a new framework for the delivery of physical activity *aligned with sport*" (emphasis added).

The complexity of the sport–health nexus can be further explored through a distinction between two – often conflicting – organizational and value-orientated structures; those of elite sport and mass sport. The structure and ethos of elite sport is associated with the pursuit of performance-efficiency and competitive achievement. Mass sport is founded on a structure and belief system centering on widespread public participation, emphasizing an ethic of sport for all. The relationship between the two is marked by competition for influence and resources based on competing beliefs about the practice, place and status of sport in peoples' lives. While initially (in the UK at least) the two were institutionally conflated, in recent years there have been moves for each to operate under different organizational, management and funding systems. However, despite their increasing separation, the isolation of elite sports from mass participation has never been absolute. The social value of each is justified in relation to the other; elite sports success is said to inspire mass participation, while a broad participatory base is said to contribute to elite sports success. Furthermore, as Green and Houlihan (2005) note, there is a transfer of policy and an exchange of methods, experiences and ideas from the elite sport to mass participation contexts in terms of some (performance-related) goals such as talent development, the role of sport science in performance enhancement and the development of facilities.

The modern Olympic Games provide a vivid example of the complex relationships between elite sport and mass participation and the overlapping nature of the two. The Olympic Games can be considered an exemplar of the dominance of the global organization and practice of elite performance sport (Houlihan and

White, 2002). But the ideology, structure and character of the Olympic Games has always had social significance beyond sport and evoked a cultural impact wider than the temporal and spatial definition of the mega-event itself. Hence a distinction is frequently made between the Games themselves and a broader Olympic Movement, which incorporates all those (athletes, national Olympic committees, international sports federations) who commit to be guided by the Olympic Charter. The Charter, amongst other things, explicates the underpinning philosophy of the Olympic Movement – Olympism – as conceived by the founder of the modern Games, Baron Pierre de Coubertin. This was always a philosophy of social reform rooted in enlightenment politics, Greek philosophy, the nineteenth-century English education system, industrial capitalism and internationalization (Chatziefstahiou, 2007; Girginov, 2010). The mobilization of Olympism is historically variable, yet the Olympic Games themselves (i.e. the elite sporting competition) were always envisaged as a tool for social improvement through a broad set of ideals/values. Our intention in this chapter is to illustrate that there is a disconnect between the spirit of Olympism expressed in the Olympic Movement and Olympic Charter and the "win at all costs" ethos of the Olympic Games in relation to the sport–health nexus. Specifically, we show that: the social construction of medicine has generated particular characteristics of healthcare in the sports context; that taking part in Olympic sport entails considerable health costs for both participants and wider communities; and that attempts to promote the local, grassroots, development of sport for public health as a legacy of staging Olympic Games is highly problematic.

The social organization of sports medicine

Given the widespread acceptance of the sport–health nexus, and the place of the Olympic Games within the broader sporting landscape, it is perhaps somewhat ironic that the Olympic Movement has played a fundamental part in the development of the social institution that dominates the treatment of athlete health; namely sports medicine. The Grenoble Winter Games of 1928, for instance, provided the stimulus and meeting point for the establishment of Fédération Internationale de Médécine du Sport (FIMS).[2] However, over the course of the twentieth century, the orientations of sports medicine personnel have changed radically (Hoberman, 1992). Initially athletes were viewed simply as a source of interesting physiological data. Athletes were an extreme group through which medicine could learn more about the *normal* functioning of the human body and thus enhance public health. Athletes were seen as marvels of nature that needed no help or improvement and, initially, sports doctors did not seek to contribute to performance; indeed, often they sought to curb excessive activity on health grounds. Philippe Tissié, who Waddington (1996) describes as the most important sports physician from the turn of the century, did pioneering work on long-distance cyclists, exposing what he saw as the medical dangers of such exertions. Indeed Tissié publicly opposed de Coubertin's appeal to reintroduce the Olympic Games due to his concerns about the impact on the health of participants.

But while "sport served the ends of science" in the early twentieth century, the emphasis on the importance of performance in contemporary sport, and the increasing resources put at the disposal of sports administrators, has meant that, by the early 1990s, "physiology ha[d] been put in the service of sport" (Hoberman, 1992: 78). Again the Olympics provided a key stimulus through the growing international significance of sport in relation to the Cold War and the staging of the 1968 Olympic Games in Mexico City, in particular. At this point, western European concerns about the deleterious effects of altitude on (their) athletes' health coalesced with the emergence of drug testing and a growing awareness of international disparities in medical support. For example, it was following the Mexico City Games that Canadian sport officials became acutely aware of the relative deficiencies of their own medical provision, which in turn accelerated the development of Canadian sports medicine and sports science (Safai, 2007). These concerns were not, on their own, sufficient to secure full state support for sports medicine. Rather, in both Canada (Safai, 2007) and the UK (Carter, 2012) it wasn't until sports medicine made claims to contribute to the health of the wider population that the rationale for the formal establishment of medical specialism was deemed convincing. However, and in addition to key policing roles in relation to drugs, sex testing and disability classification, a notable trend during this century has been the growing involvement of an increasing number of diversely qualified healthcare professionals in the production of elite athletic performance.

The contemporary form of sports medicine is a striking example of the socially constructed character of healthcare and thus the illness/health dynamic. Indeed it could be argued that much of what passes as sports medicine is not actually medicine at all. Etymologically and historically, medicine has been defined by attempts to relieve human suffering and, according to Edwards and McNamee, "any practice which does not necessarily aim at relief of suffering cannot count as medicine" (2006: 105). But the mission statements of bodies like FIMS clearly illustrate that this is not the central goal of sports medicine. For instance, FIMS aims "to assist athletes in achieving optimal performance by maximising their genetic potential, health, nutrition, and high-quality medical care and training".[3]

While the problems of defining medicine in static and asocial terms are manifold, this definitional point alerts us to the relatively distinct structure of sports medicine. There are four interconnected features that have a tangible impact on the healthcare experiences of the Olympic athlete:

1   The performance orientation of sports medicine means that practitioners are judged according to athletes' competitive success. Consequently decisions are more fundamentally structured by the imminence of Olympic competition than the longer-term health of an individual. Resources are allocated to athletes according to medal potential rather than health needs (cf. Kotarba, 2001).

2   Sports medicine is client (or clients) oriented. Though highly dependent on particular networks of human interdependencies, sports clinicians are

relatively frequently required to be flexible in their prognoses and proscriptions, often choosing to comply with, rather than challenge, athletes' demands. Clinicians may need to be prepared to negotiate with their athlete patients to bend to the athletes' time-pressured concerns (Malcolm, 2006a), and to pursue competitive goals at the expense of health (Theberge, 2007).

3   Sports medicine is unusually influenced by lay knowledge. An essential characteristic of being an elite athlete is a continual and varied experimentation on the self in the pursuit of sporting achievement. Of course, all people reflect on the impact of medical interventions on how they feel and make changes as they see fit (often in discussion with doctors), but athletes do this more continuously, more holistically, and evaluate the outcomes (i.e. their performance) more systematically. Furthermore, their health knowledge is produced and exchanged in peer groups that experience the same kinds of injuries and share a relatively long-term chronic prognosis. Thus sport provides conditions that are conducive to the relatively effective mobilization of lay knowledge (Malcolm, 2006a).

4   Sports medicine entails a distinct division of labor. This may vary between national contexts, and across different sports, but sports medicine is fundamentally multidisciplinary both in terms of its organizational structures and everyday practice. Although status distinctions are largely upheld in the former (Safai, 2007), in the practice setting sports doctors express relatively heightened levels of professional deference to competing healthcare providers, such as chiropractors (Theberge, 2008), and particularly so while at major games when the significance of competitive success is at its most acute.

Consequently, sports medicine has been described as peculiar (Malcolm, 2006b). A more critical perspective suggests that the combination of these characteristics leads to relatively poor healthcare with medical "experts" bowing to the vagaries of obsessional athletes, unable to convey their honest opinion and gain patient compliance, and compromised into working alongside professions they consider to lack a valid evidence-base for their practice. Certainly evidence relating to appointment procedures (Malcolm and Scott, 2011; Waddington *et al.*, 2001) and medical ethics (Malcolm and Scott, 2013; Waddington and Roderick, 2002) supports that view. The emergence in North America, where relations with professional sport teams are so coveted that medical practices are prepared to *pay* in excess of US$1million per year for affiliation with a sport franchise, as opposed to receiving payment for healthcare provision, exemplifies this peculiarity (Dunn *et al.*, 2007). At the very least, the notion that sports medicine unequivocally fosters athlete health is highly problematic, a view augmented by our analysis of the scale of injury problems in sport presented in the next section.

Health, injury and Olympic sport participation

Paradoxically, given the ideological link between sport and health and sport and the Olympics, some of the most iconic images of Olympic competition involve injured athletes. For British sports fans, Derek Redmond's completion of his 400 meter semi-final race at the 1992 Barcelona Olympics epitomizes Olympism's celebration of human fortitude. Approximately half way through the race, Redmond suffered a hamstring injury and his father subsequently helped him to complete the lap. Americans more vividly remember Kerri Strug, the gymnast who damaged tendons during a vault at the Atlanta Olympic Games in 1996, but who vaulted again to secure the gold medal for the American team (the degree to which coach and peer pressure on Strug "coerced" her to do so is debated). Despite appearing unable to walk, she successfully completed the vault and was carried to the podium to receive her medal. Such imagery begins to expose the contradictions within ideas about the health promoting qualities of sport in the context of the Olympic Games.

Indeed, there is evidence that suggests that elite sport "entails a number of deeply embedded occupational hazards and health risks that are integral to the undertaking itself" (Beamish and Ritchie, 2006: 123). As an indication of this, and explicitly because of a commitment to reduce injury prevalence and improve athlete health, the IOC has introduced quantitative injury surveillance studies. The first audit, conducted at the 2008 Beijing Games (Junge *et al.*, 2009), collated reports from National Olympic Committee (NOC) physicians and medical stations at individual events and in the Olympic village. The results indicated an incidence of 96.1 injuries per 1000 athletes. There was also considerable variation between sports with, for example, 31.5 per cent of footballers receiving medical attention for a complaint arising from playing/training during the Olympiad, compared to just 0.8 per cent of sailors. A subsequent survey at the 2010 Vancouver Winter Games reported an injury incidence rate of 111.8 per 1000 athletes, again with wide variations between sports (from 35 per cent of cross snowboarders to 1 per cent of biathletes), in addition to one death in the luge (Engebretsen *et al.*, 2010). This survey, however, also examined the frequency of illness amongst athletes: 7.2 per cent of athletes sought medical treatment for an illness during the games, most in relation to the respiratory system and as a consequence of infection.

Intuitively one would not normally expect "healthy" people to seek medical treatment so frequently but, statistically, how does the incidence of injury in elite sport compare to that of other occupations? Hawkins and Fuller (1999) note that epidemiological studies in professional football in the UK show that there are an estimated 710 injuries per 100,000 working hours. This compares unfavorably to UK government statistics, which indicate that there is an average of 0.36 workplace injuries for every 100,000 working hours and even to relatively dangerous occupations such as mining and quarrying where there are 1.3 injuries per 100,000 working hours. Thus, the occupational injury rates in professional football are 2000 times greater than the UK average, and as much as 500 times greater than the occupations traditionally thought to be high risk. While it is surprising that an activity publicly acclaimed to be "healthy" leads to injury, the extent to which elite sport is *more* dangerous than all other occupations is striking.

Moreover, there is good reason to think that the data on sports injury rates considerably under-report the full extent of the phenomenon amongst this population. For instance, the authors of the Beijing study (Junge *et al.*, 2009) note that the real incidence is likely to be higher due to some non-cooperation from smaller NOCs (which have small medical staffs) and the incompletion of forms from some venues on some days. Data produced by the International Skiing Federation (ISF) reviewing injuries throughout the 2010 season identified additional injuries during the Vancouver Games' period inflating the initial findings by 31 per cent. Furthermore, both surveys exclude treatment of chronic and on-going conditions. These are likely to be significant. As an indication, attention has been drawn to the unusually high frequency of asthma amongst elite athletes, with some 20 per cent of the US team at the Atlanta Games in 1996 declaring the condition and almost 21 per cent of Team Great Britain testing positive for asthma prior to the Athens Games of 2004 (compared with just 8 per cent of the British population as a whole) (Arie, 2012).

Most importantly, however, these surveys fail to capture the social construction of concepts like illness and health. For instance, the definition of "injury" used in these studies is limiting, relating only to conditions presented for medical examination. We have no data exploring the frequency with which athletes decide to present their ailments to medical caregivers, but population studies show that the decision to consult is multifaceted, linked not just to severity of symptoms but also to interpersonal crises, restrictions to work or social activities and the responses of family and friends, which are required to legitimate the assumption of what Talcott Parsons called the "sick role" (Nettleton, 2006). Furthermore, the methodological concerns with the Beijing study evoke the notions of global health inequalities and social construction of illness through medical interventions discussed in the introduction. Specifically in relation to sport, studies have shown that athletes avoid consulting with medical staff if they feel that doing so would threaten their participation in competition (Malcolm, 2009). Given the significance attached to lay medical knowledge in sport and the propensity towards self-treatment (Howe, 2004) and ethnopharmacology (Atkinson, 2007), there are grounds for thinking that elite athletes are relatively independent in their healthcare regimes.

Despite these subcultural influences the provision of medical support at Olympic Games is extensive, further leading us to question the logic of the sport–health nexus. At the London 2012 Games, for example, three "polyclinics" were established at the main Olympic village, and the satellite villages for the sailing and rowing/canoeing. NOC team doctors could request physiotherapy and other musculoskeletal treatments, diagnostic imaging and laboratory tests from the British National Health Service (NHS). In contrast to the normal means-testing system for British citizens, certain pharmacies provided free prescriptions for Olympic athletes. Medical support was also made available at each of the training and competition venues. The scale of provision was dependent on the injury incidence of the sport concerned but generally included physiotherapy, sports massage, sports medicine, field of play recovery teams, athlete dedicated ambulance services and, in some cases, dental services. There were 11 designated Olympic hospitals (LOCOG, 2011) and 12 on-call consultants/scheduled clinics (including cardiology, dermatology, neurology and surgery). It was anticipated that a total of 3000 volunteers would be required (EMJ, 2008). All this was in addition to the medical provision that NOCs provide for their own teams and that deal with the vast majority of athlete injuries (Junge *et al.*, 2009). The US Olympic Committee (USOC), for instance, brought a reported 85 medical staff members to London to service 530 athletes.[4] It is difficult to support the sport–health ideological nexus in light of such provision.

Moreover, the previously noted problems of conceptually separating elite and mass sports resurface in relation to Olympic medical provision. This is because the medical services that local organizing committees provide are not solely devoted to athletes, but are made available to the wider "Olympic Family" (at London 2012 consisting of 25,000 people, including all athletes, commercial partners and official guests) and spectators. So, for instance, there were a reported 10,000 "medical encounters" at the venues and Olympic village during the Athens Games, only approximately half of which involved athletes (EMJ, 2008). Hospital, ambulance and dental services are provided to members of the "Olympic Family" who experience acute illnesses and injuries (but not for stable or pre-existing conditions). In London, the Olympic Family had its own desig-nated hospital (University College Hospital), a dedicated clinic for those travelling through Heathrow airport, and medical stations covering the "Olympic Family Hotels".

Such provision inevitably has an impact on the host community. As Paraschak (2012) has noted, albeit in relation to a much smaller multisport games than the Olympics, the staging of such an event is likely to lead to a prioritization of participant healthcare that is, at times, oppositional to the healthcare needs of non-participants and public health concerns more generally. Such separation and privileging mirrors the inequitable structure of sports medicine but is at odds with the philosophies of, for example, healthcare systems in Canada and the UK, where service access is dictated by need rather than social status. To compensate for such tensions, NHS London was given a reported £1.83 million to cover the impact of staging the Olympic Games.[5] However, this did not entirely allay fears that the games would have a negative impact on public medicine. For instance, the London Organizing Committee of the Olympic and Paralympic Games (LOCOG) was forced to deny allegations that members of the Olympic Family would receive preferential accident and emergency treatment, being fast-tracked to see senior clinicians in their designated hospital.[6]

Re-emphasizing our earlier comments on the complexity of health matters, we suggest that to provide a properly sociological analysis of the relationship between the Olympic Movement and health, we need to move away from the assumptions of biomedicine with its tendencies towards biological reductionism and the doctrine of specific aetiology; rather we should place the athlete's body within its social environment and identify medicine, and lay-medical interactions in particular, as fundamental to the construction of illness and injury. We need also to see that in practice there is no clear separation between elite sport and the public, and that the allocation of resources to the former will reinforce inequalities. Such inequalities might possibly be (partly) offset if the legacy goals of mega-event hosting are genuinely achieved, but as we explore in the final section, this too is also a highly problematic assertion.

Health and Olympic legacies: The case of London 2012

Combining the traditions of the Olympic Movement and health promotion, a central feature of the London 2012 Olympic legacy strategy was the commitment to boost levels of physical activity to improve the general health of the UK population. The politically and publicly oriented health legacy of the London 2012 Games was framed by a promise to harness the "power" of the Games to "inspire a generation" and a target to engage a million more people to do more physical activity as a mechanism and measure of improving the health of the nation (DCMS, 2007).

Girginov and Hills (2010) note that the concept of Olympic legacy crystallized in policy terms through changes to the Olympic Charter that were introduced in 2002. The Olympic Charter states that the IOC:

> takes measures to promote a positive legacy from the Olympic Games to the host city and the host country, including a reasonable control of the size and cost of the Olympic Games, and encourages the Organizing Committees of the Olympic Games (OCOGs), public authorities in the host country and the persons or organizations belonging to the Olympic Movement to act accordingly.
>
> (Olympic Charter, 2002: 12)

Since 2002, Girginov and Hills (2010) argue, the Olympic legacy has become centered upon the explicit identification and promotion of two key *positive* legacy strategies: 1) increased sport participation for a range of identified positive social and health outcomes; and 2) sustainable sport development. What, however, is the evidence to suggest that the former is achievable, rather than a continuation of the dominant Olympic sport–health ideological nexus already exposed as problematic?

In a worldwide systematic review of the evidence for developing a physical activity, sport and health legacy from the London 2012 Olympic and Paralympic Games, Weed et al. (2009) found that there was no evidence base upon which to claim an increase in participation from which positive health outcomes could be assumed and, moreover, identified that no previous Games administration employed strategies towards raising physical activity levels and/or sport participation. Two UK health impact assessments allude to the *potential* for increased interest and participation in sports and concomitantly the health benefits associated with hosting the Games (LHC and LDA, 2004; NEHPO, 2006). Sport programs that have been developed in association with acclaimed physical activity and health benefits of London 2012 include Change4Life sports clubs, which aim to harness the "inspirational" aspects of the Games to encourage the least active school children to take part in sport (Weed *et al.*, 2011). Moreover, the use of live sites or "big screens" has been advocated in leveraging a range of community and public health outcomes including providing health information, prompting healthful behaviors and promoting healthy lifestyles (Weed *et al.*, 2010). Still, evidence for the role of elite sport success in boosting participation remains inconclusive and the possibility that Olympic athletes might deter participation because of the perceived competence gap between elite performers and recreational participants has been identified (Hindson *et al.*, 1994). The assumption that the process by which major events engage non-participants in physical activity and sport is a "demonstration" or "trickle-down" effect whereby people are inspired by elite sport, sports events and sports franchises to do more sport is likely to be flawed (Weed *et al.*, 2009). Rather, there is a staged process of engagement with physical activity and/or sport through major events that depends on prior motivations, values, experiences and competence in sport and physical activity.

The question of the potential of the Olympic Games to leverage mass participation as a health legacy is, in part, informed by the impact of a "festival effect" in creating the positive perceptions that a significant event is taking place (Weed *et al.*, 2010). The sporting outcomes of any Olympic Games matter less to many people than the sense of community or "communitas" engendered by the feeling that something exciting is going on and being collectively experienced (Chalip, 2006). Celebration and camaraderie are important factors in creating the feeling of an event being bigger than, and beyond, sport and this aspect of the festival effect can be fostered by symbolism and iconography (Kennedy *et al.*, 2006). Positive imagery is significant in leveraging or optimizing intended event outcomes such as health at both global and local levels. Mega-events like the Olympic and Paralympic Games provide drama and festival on a global scale and engender a range of emotions or affects that are felt at a local level (Waitt, 2003). There is a perceptible emotional attachment created through sport mega-events and expressed in terms of civic pride, patriotism and an urge to be a part of something exciting, potentially through physical activity and other health-promoting activity participation (Weed *et al.*, 2010).

Even when Olympic sports do inspire people to participate in sport and physical activity, the relationship between sport and health is much more nuanced than universalized. Olympic sports could be said to operate as forms of corporeal control, offering sets of normalizing practices that serve to produce and reproduce an idealized healthy body in both form and function (Chatziefstahiou and Henry, 2013). Olympic athletes live their lives in a cult of bodily perfection, which is conflated into a representation rather than a reality of good health. As Girginov (2010: 1) explains, Olympism represents an "idealized vision of human being and a just society". Embedded in the ideological framework of Olympism was the "imagined perfectibility" of the human body and social relations (Seagrave and Chatziefstahiou 2008: 31). For de Coubertin, Olympic sports represented the aesthetic beauty of the human form; the foundation of progress towards excellence and perfection. Olympism gives an essential role for the body in human progress embracing the nineteenth-century British edict *mens sana in corpore sano*: physical beauty and health through a balanced mind and body (Seagreave and Chatziefstahiou, 2008). Olympism, then, produces and reproduces a moral imperative for corporeal regulation. Consequently the Olympic Movement closely resonates with the ideology that health is dependent on individual responsibility, self-control, self-discipline and abstention (Crawford, 1980). It is compatible with a public health agenda, of which physical activity promotion is a part, premised on (publicly displayed) individual/private responsibility to improve and/or preserve health (Lupton, 1995).

Crawford (1980) refers to the ideology of individual responsibility as "victim blaming" or a culture of "healthism" that stems from the competing moral views about "good/healthy" and "bad/unhealthy" lifestyles noted in the introduction to this chapter. Such an ideology serves to shift responsibility for health away from powerful groups who can and do impact upon peoples' health (Crawford, 1980). Responsibility for health is placed firmly in the hands of individuals who may or may not be able to significantly alter their health status. The ideology of healthism tends to blur many of the key issues associated with health, such as the role of government and other powerful agencies in: improving an inadequate health service; providing effective training and funding for health and exercise professionals; developing lines of communication between health providers; and improving measures of environmental pollution. A focus on individual responsibility for health does not adequately account for the impact that social processes like poverty, unemployment, pollution, poor education, lack of access to physical activities or healthcare have on peoples' health (Mansfield and Rich, 2013). Middle-class conceptions of health tend to provide narrow descriptions of "good" lifestyle choices and maintain the virtues of self-control, self-discipline and individual responsibility as the benchmark for appropriate values regarding bodies, health and morality.

The concept of Olympism reflects and reinforces a bodily morality focused on individual and social betterment. It is enshrined in the Olympic motto: *Citius, Altius, Fortius* (Faster, Higher, Stronger). Yet there are tensions between the ideal narratives of bodily perfection of elite athleticism and health. In addition to the frequency of injury and the extent of Olympic medical care that belie the idea that this pinnacle of sporting performance relates unproblematically to notions of health, Olympic Games sponsorship gives companies such as Coca Cola and McDonalds the opportunity to promote high-calorie, fat- and sugar-rich food and beverages to more than 200 countries worldwide, directly contradicting public health nutrition messages (Dickson and Schofield, 2005). Moreover, the staging of the Olympic Games can impact negatively on mass participation in sport and physical activity, which is antithetical to public health promotion of increasing physical activity. Some of the funding for the London 2012 Games, for example, came via an increase of funds from the UK National Lottery, which served to reduce funds for public sports developments at community and regional levels (Girginov and Hills, 2010). Beliefs that the Olympic Movement, through its promotion of sport, unequivocally contributes to the enhanced health of the human population are thus flawed.

Conclusion

Of all the Olympic events, none is more symbolic of the Games' history and more resonant with its social meaning than the marathon. The marathon stems from Ancient Greek legend and was created as a specific event for the reinvention of the modern Olympics in 1896. The world's major marathons – Berlin, Boston, Chicago, London, New York and Tokyo – are unrivalled in linking performance sport (with elite races for men, women and wheelchair athletes) and mass participation. Moreover, many use the experience as a vehicle for raising money for charities, the overwhelming majority of which are linked to medicine, healthcare and disability (indeed, of the 24 charities featured on the London 2013 website only one, the National Society for the Prevention of Cruelty to Children, fell outside this description).

While the marathon provides an apposite example of the intersection of the Olympic Movement, Olympic legacy, sport and health, it also provides one of the clearest illustrations of the contradictory nature of these ideologies. For instance, London Marathon race organizers suggest that participants should only compete with the agreement of their family physician or general practitioner. The marathon route itself is punctuated by more than 40 first aid stations, including cardiac units and resuscitation facilities. There are two field hospitals at the finish line and local "receiving hospitals" are pre-warned about the race and staffed by additional St John's ambulance liaison officers. In total, there are approximately 1000 St John's and 100 physiotherapist volunteers available on the day (Tunstall Pedoe, no date).

The full injury impact is hard to assess as "successful runners are euphoric, anxious to go home and usually convinced that they can handle the problem themselves" (Tunstall Pedoe, no date). However, there have been ten deaths since 1981.[7] Moreover, one survey indicated that of 36,396 registered entrants in 2007, over 10 per cent (3892) made contact with one of the 100 volunteer physiotherapists (Brown, no date). This figure, however, pales in comparison to the 92.4 per cent of runners who reported a specific health problem associated with a marathon race day in Auckland (Satterthwaite *et al.*, 1999).

The marathon thus encapsulates the complexities of the relationship between the Olympic Movement, (elite and mass) sports participation and the notion that such activities are necessarily beneficial for one's health. It also exposes many of the complexities of health that we raised in the introduction to this chapter. For instance, the growth in marathon running in recent years is clearly linked to what Lupton (1995) has called the imperative of health in contemporary society. Marathon running is also a distinctly class-based phenomenon and thus creates and perpetuates social inequalities.[8] As the medical charity dimension illustrates, it has become inextricably linked to notions of morally virtuous behaviors and lifestyles. Thus, the juxtaposition of the extensive medical support routinely supplied for a supposedly healthy activity reveals just how contested and contradictory the sport–health nexus is, and the logical inconsistency of linking sport, health and the Olympic Movement.

Notes

1   We recognize that the organization and structure of the Paralympic Games and the experiences of athletes with disabilities bring additional and important complexities in understanding the sport–health nexus but do not have sufficient space to address these here.
2   www.fims.org/en/general/history-and-purpose/ (accessed 6 July 2013).
3   www.fims.org/en/general/history-and-purpose/ (accessed 6 July 2013).
4   www.beaumont.edu/doctor-selected-us-olympic-medical-staff-summer-games-2012 (accessed 6 July 2013).
5   www.bbc.co.uk/news/health-18060121 (accessed 2 May 2013).
6   www.bbc.co.uk/news/health-18060121 (accessed 2 May 2013).
7   www.telegraph.co.uk/sport/othersports/athletics/london-marathon/9237808/Claire-Squires-runner-who-died-during-London-Marathon-suffered-from-heart-condition.html (accessed 2 May 2013).
8   See Smith (2000) or, more currently, www.runningguru.com/RunnerDemographics.asp (accessed 2 September 2013).

References

Albrecht, R., Fitzpatrick, S. and Scrimshaw, S. (eds) (2000) *Social Studies in Health and Medicine*, London: Sage.

Arie, S. (2012) 'What can we learn from asthma in elite athletes?', *British Medical Journal*, 344.

Armstrong, D. (1995) 'The rise of surveillance medicine', *Sociology of Health and Illness*, 17(3): 393–404.

Atkinson, M. (2007) 'Playing with fire: Masculinity and exercise supplements', *Sociology of Sport Journal*, 24: 165–86.

Atkinson, P. (1978) 'Fitness, feminism and schooling', in S. Delamont and L. Duffin (eds) *The Nineteenth Century Woman: Her cultural and physical world*, London: Croom Helm, 92–134.

Beamish, R. and Ritchie, I. (2000) *Fastest, Highest, Strongest: A critique of high performance sport*, London: Routledge.

Bouchard, C., Shephard, R., Stephens, T., Sutton, J. and McPherson, B. (1990) (eds) *Exercise Fitness and Health: A consensus of current knowledge*, Champaign, IL: HKP.

Brown, R. (no date) 'London Marathon Race Day'. Online at: http://images.parkrun.com/archived/formerwebsite/newsletter/parkrun_marathon_article.pdf (accessed 10 June 2014).

Bury, M. and Gabe, J. (eds) (2004) *The Sociology of Health and Illness: A reader*, London: Routledge.

Carter, N. (2012) 'From volunteerism to specialization: Sports medicine and the British Association of Sport and Medicine', in D. Malcolm and P. Safai (eds) *The Social Organization of Sports Medicine: Critical socio-cultural perspectives*, New York: Routledge, 54–76.

Chalip, L. (2006) 'Towards social leverage of sports events', *Journal of Sport and Tourism*, 11(2): 109–27.

Chatziefstahiou, D. and Henry I. (2013) *Discourses of Olympism: From the Sorbonne 1894 to London 2012*, New York: Palgrave MacMillan.

Crawford, R. (1980) 'Healthism and the medicalization of everyday life', *International Journal of Health Services*, 10(3): 365–89.

DCMS (Department of Culture, Media and Sport) (2007) *Our Promise for 2012: How the UK will benefit from the Olympic and Paralympic Games*, London: Crown Copyright.

Dickson, G. and Schofield, G. (2005) 'Globalisation and globesity: The impact of the 2008 Beijing Olympics on China', *International Journal of Sport Management and Marketing*, 1(1–2): 169–79.

DOH (Department of Health) (2004) *At Least Five a Week: Evidence on the impact of physical activity and its relationship to health*, London: Crown Copyright.

DOH (2011) *Start Active, Stay Active: A report on physical activity from the four home countries' chief medical officers*, London: Crown Copyright.

Dunn, W., George, M., Churchill, L. and Spindler, K. (2007) 'Ethics in sports medicine', *American Journal of Sports Medicine*, 35(5): 840–4.

Edwards, S. and McNamee, M. (2006) 'Why sports medicine is not medicine', *Health Care Analysis*, 14: 103–9.

EMJ (*Emergency Medicine Journal*) (2008) 'Medical services at the 2012 Olympic Games and Paralympic Games: An interview with Richard Budgett', *Emergency Medicine Journal*, May Supplement. Online at: http://emj.bmj.com/content/sippl/2008/04/22/22.5.DC1/may08/pdf (accessed 10 June 2014).

Engbretsen, L., Steffen, K. and Alonso, J.M. (2010) 'Sports injuries and illnesses during the Winter Olympic Games 2010', *British Journal of Sports Medicine*, 44: 772–80.

Garber, C., Blissner, B., Deschenes, M., Franklin, A., Lamonte, M., Lee, I., Nieman, D. and Swain, D. (2011) *ACSM Position Stand. Quantity and quality of exercise for developing and maintaining cardiorespiratory, musculoskeletal, and neuromotor fitness in apparently healthy adults: guidance for prescribing exercise*, USA: ACSM.

Girginov, V. (2010) 'Introduction', in V. Girginov (ed.) The *Olympics: A critical reader*, London: Routledge, 1–5.

Girginov, V. and Hills, L. (2010) 'A sustainable sports legacy: Creating a link between the London Olympics and sports participation', in Girginov (ed.) *The Olympics: A critical reader*, London: Routledge, 430–49.

Green, M. and Houlihan, B. (2005) *Elite Sport Development: Policy learning and political priorities*, London: Routledge.

Hargreaves, J. (1986) *Sport, Power and Culture: A social and historical analysis of popular sports in Britain*, Cambridge: Polity.

Hargreaves, J. (1994) *Sporting Females: Critical issues in the history and sociology of women's sport*, London: Routledge.

Hawkins, R. and Fuller, C. (1999) 'A prospective epidemiological study of injuries in four English professional football clubs', *British Journal of Sports Medicine*, 33: 196–203.

Hindson, A., Gidlow, B. and Peebles, C. (1994) 'The "trickle-down" effect of top level sport: Myth or reality? A case study of the Olympics', *Australian Leisure and Recreation*, 4(1): 16–24.

Hoberman, J. (1992) *Mortal Engines: The science of performance and the dehumanization of sport*, New York: Free Press.

Houlihan, B. and White, A. (2002) *The Politics of Sport Development: Development of sport or development through sport?*, London: Routledge.

Howe, P. D. (2004) *Sport, Professionalism and Pain: Ethnographies of injury and risk*, London: Routledge.

International Olympic Committee (2002) 'Olympic Charter', Lausanne, Switzerland: IOC.

Junge, A., Engbretsen, L. and Mountjoy, M. (2009) 'Sports injuries during the summer Olympic Games 2008', *American Journal of Sports Medicine*, 37(11): 2165–72.

Kennedy, E., Pussard, H. and Thornton, A. (2006) 'Leap for London? Investigating the affective power of the sport spectacle', *World Leisure*, 3: 6–21.

Kohl, H., Craig. C. and Lambert, E. (2012) 'The pandemic of physical inactivity: global action for public health', *The Lancet*, 380: 294–305.

Kotarba, J. (2001) 'Conceptualizing sports medicine as occupational health care: Illustrations from professional rodeo and wrestling', *Qualitative Health Research*, 11: 766–779.

LHC and LDA (London Health Commission and London Development Agency) (2004) *Rapid Health Impact Assessment of the Proposed London Olympic Games and their Legacy*, London: LDA.

LOCOG (London Organizing Committee of the Olympic and Paralympic Games) (2011) 'Olympic Games healthcare guide', London: LOCOG.

Lupton, D. (1995) *The Imperative of Health: Public health and the regulated body*, London: Sage.

Malcolm, D. (2006a) 'Unprofessional practice? The status and power of sports physicians', *Sociology of Sport Journal*, 23(4): 376–395.

Malcolm, D. (2006b) 'Sports medicine: A very peculiar practice? Doctors and physiotherapists in elite English Rugby Union', in S. Loland, B. Skirstad and I. Waddington (eds) *Pain and Injury in Sport: Social and ethical analysis*, London: Routledge, 165–81.

Malcolm, D. (2009) 'Medical uncertainty and clinician-athlete relations: The management of concussion injuries in Rugby Union', *Sociology of Sport Journal*, 26(2): 191–210.

Malcolm, D. and Scott, A. (2011) 'Professional relations in elite sport healthcare: Workplace responses to organizational change', *Social Science and Medicine*, 72: 513–20.

Malcolm, D. and Scott, A. (2013) 'Practical responses to confidentiality dilemmas in elite sport medicine', *British Journal of Sports Medicine*, doi:10.1136/bjsports-2013-092458.

Mangan, J. and Park, R. (eds) (1992) *From "Fair Sex" to Feminism*, London: Frank Cass.

Mansfield, L. and Rich, E. (2013) 'Public health pedagogy, border crossing and physical activity at every size', *Critical Public Health*. Online at: www.tandfonline.com (accessed 26 May 2013).

Mansfield, L., Weed, M. and Dowse, S. (2010) 'Re-thinking the role of values in Olympic/Paralympic legacy planning: Using the London 2012 games to get the nation moving', in R. Barney, M. Heine, K. Wamsley and G. MacDonald (eds) *Rethinking Matters Olympic: Investigations into the socio-cultural study of the modern Olympic movement*, London, Ontario: International Centre for Olympic Studies Publications, 412–26.

NEPHO (North East Public Health Observatory) (2006) *The Health Impact of the 2012 Games. A screening health impact assessment of the North East's draft vision for the London Olympic Games and Paralympic Games 2012*, Newcastle: NEPHO.

Nettleton, S. (2006) *The Sociology of Health and Illness*, Cambridge: Polity Press.

Paraschak, V. (2012) 'Public health, elite sport and "risky behaviors" at the Canada Winter Games', in D. Malcolm and P. Safai (eds) *The Social Organization of Sports Medicine: Critical socio-cultural perspectives*, New York: Routledge, 126–49.

Pollock, M., Gaesser, G., Butcher, J.-P., Després, K., Rod, B., Franklin, C. and Garber, C. (1998) 'ACSM position stand. Quantity and quality of exercise for developing and maintaining cardiorespiratory, muscular fitness, and flexibility in healthy adults', *Medicine and Science in Sport and Exercise*, 30(6): 975–91.

Safai, P. (2007) 'A critical analysis of the development of sport medicine in Canada, 1955–1980', *International Review for the Sociology of Sport*, 42: 321–41.

Satterthwaite, P. (1999) 'Risk factors for injuries and other health problems sustained in a marathon', *British Journal of Sports Medicine*, 33(1): 22–6.

Seagrave J. and Chatziefstahiou, D. (2008) 'Pierre de Coubertin's ideology of beauty from the perspective of the history of ideas', in R. Barney, M. Heine, K. Wamsley and G. MacDonald (eds) *Pathways: Critiques and discourse in Olympic research*, ICOS: UWO Ca, 31–44.

Shilling, C. (1993) *The Body and Social Theory*, London: Sage.

Smith, S. (2000) 'British nonelite road running and masculinity: A case of "running repairs"?', *Men and Masculinities*, 3(2): 187–208.

Theberge, N. (2007) '"It's not about health, it's about performance." Sport medicine, health and the culture of risk in Canadian sport', in J. Hargreaves and P. Vertinsky (eds) *Physical Culture, Power and the Body*, London: Routledge, 176–94.

Theberge, N. (2008) 'The integration of chiropractors into healthcare teams: A case study from sports medicine', *Sociology of Health and Illness*, 30: 19–34.

Tunstall Pedoe, D. (no date) 'London Marathon: what we know about the incidence of injury, illness and death in the London Marathon'. Online at: www.pponline.co.uk/encyc/london-marathon-what-we-know-about-the-incidence-of-injury-illness-and-death-in-the-london-marathon-881 (accessed 6 July 2013).

Turner, B. (2000) *The Body and Society*, 2nd edn, London: Sage.

Waddington, I. (1996) 'The development of sports medicine', *Sociology of Sport Journal*, 13: 176–96.

Waddington, I. (2000) *Sport, Health and Drugs: A critical sociological investigation*, London, E & FN Spon.

Waddington, I. and Roderick, M. (2002) 'The management of medical confidentiality in English professional football clubs: Some ethical problems and issues', *British Journal of Sports Medicine*, 36: 118–23.

Waddington, I., Roderick, M. and Naik, R. (2001) 'Methods of appointment and qualifications of club doctors and physiotherapists in English professional football: Some problems and issues', *British Journal of Sports Medicine*, 35: 48–53.

Waitt, G. (2003) 'Social impacts of the Sydney Olympics', *Annals of Tourism Research*, 30(1): 194–215.

Weed, M., Coren, E., Fiore, J., Mansfield, L., Chatziefstahiou, D., Wellard, I. and Dowse, S. (2009) *A Systematic Review of the Evidence Base for Delivering a Physical Activity and Health Legacy from the London 2012 Olympic and Paralympic Games*, London: Department of Health.

Weed, M., Mansfield, L. and Dowse, S. (2010) 'Active celebration: Using the 2012 Games to get the nation moving', London: Department of Health.

Weed, M., Mansfield, L., Wellard, I. and Dowse, S. (2011) *Evaluation of Change 4 Life sports clubs*, SPEAR, Canterbury Christ Church University and the Youth Sport Trust.

Weed, M., Dowse, S., Mansfield, L., Chatziefstahiou, D., Lovell, J. and Wellard, L. (2012) *A Systematic Review of the Evidence for the Potential of Live Sites to Generate Community and Public Health Outcomes*, SPEAR, Canterbury Christ Church University: NHS Eastern and Kent Coastal.

WHO (World Health Organization) (2012) 'Global recommendations on physical activity and health', WHO Press: Geneva, Switzerland.

Index

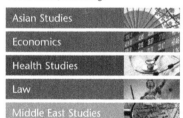

Lightning Source UK Ltd.
Milton Keynes UK
UKOW06n2051250516

274979UK00001B/95/P